LAW AND EQUAL OPPORTUNITY: A STUDY OF THE MASSACHUSETTS COMMISSION AGAINST DISCRIMINATION

A publication of the Joint Center for Urban Studies of the Massachusetts Institute of Technology and Harvard University

LAW AND EQUAL OPPORTUNITY

A STUDY OF THE
MASSACHUSETTS COMMISSION
AGAINST DISCRIMINATION

By LEON H. MAYHEW

Harvard University Press   Cambridge, Massachusetts   1968

TO TALCOTT PARSONS

PREFACE

In the spring of 1959, Chairman Mildred Mahoney of the Massachusetts Commission Against Discrimination visited Professor Gordon Allport's Harvard University seminar in group conflict and prejudice. She told the assembled students of the work of the Commission. As a member of the seminar, I listened with avid interest because I was developing an interest in the relations between law and sociology. I resolved at that time to undertake a sociological study of the Commission. In September 1961, with the helpful encouragement of Professor Allport and the kind permission of Chairman Mahoney, I began the work. It was financed by a grant from the Joint Center for Urban Studies of the Massachusetts Institute of Technology and Harvard University, whose aid and cooperation have been crucial at several junctures.

Almost all of the field work for this study was conducted between September 1961 and September 1962, although I returned to Boston for a few follow-up inquiries in August 1963.

The civil rights movement in the 60's presents a rapidly changing picture. There have been great changes since 1963, both in Massachusetts and in the nation. In this work I describe the formation and operation of a state commission against discrimination during the "classic era," that is, the years before the civil rights revolution quickened the pace of legal activity on the racial front. Nevertheless, I believe this study remains timely for several reasons.

The patterns of regulatory activity established by state civil rights commissions represent deeply intrenched strategies of adjustment to the problems of regulation. Even today they are hard to escape. We are becoming increasingly aware of the weaknesses of the classic strategies. Indeed, I would argue that the deficiencies of the standard approaches to the administration of civil rights statutes help to explain the current demands for more militant forms of social intervention. In this sense a description of the Commission in the early 60's illuminates the present.

At the same time it is more than a history for it attempts in a modest way to contribute to sociological theory. Throughout the investigation my work was guided by the idea that race relations law can only be understood in the light of the theory of institutions. There is a classic sociological literature on the relation of human institutions to social ideals. We have long recognized that activity intended to implement social values often comes to have a tragic character. Our intentions are subject to unexpected transformations and deformations as we strive to cope with the obstacles of the real social world. I have sought to make this book a contribution to our understanding of these institutional constraints on social action.

More than the usual expressions of gratitude are in order: This study would not have been possible without the unstinting cooperation of Mildred Mahoney, first Chairman of the MCAD. Many of the conclusions of this study imply that I do not agree with some of Mrs. Mahoney's ideas and policies. For the record, let it be understood that I have a profound respect and admiration for Mrs. Mahoney and for her ebullient enthusiasm, her boundless good will and ability to persuade and conciliate. In no sense can this study be considered a challenge to her good faith.

Several other people deserve special gratitude for their

contributions to this project. Above all, I acknowledge a debt of gratitude to Talcott Parsons, whose theoretical insights shaped the inquiry from beginning to end. Stanton Wheeler helped me to understand the methodological problems involved and encouraged me to ask the right questions. Robert C. Angell, Robert Carrol, Beverly Duncan, Otis Dudley Duncan, Amos Hawley, William Gamson, Richard Mann, Thomas Pettigrew, Albert Reiss, Jr., Albert Sachs, Robert Somers, and Henry Stetler gave important aid at one point or another. The weaknesses and limitations of the study stem from the author's obtuseness, not from any poor counsel from these teachers and colleagues.

I owe a special debt to Janet Mayhew, cryptographer extraordinary, who transcribed one entire draft of the manuscript from scribbled marks on yellow paper.

Of course, my many informants, who must remain nameless, made the study possible. It is not possible to make their identity clear in the course of the text. One guiding principle shaped the use of information gleaned in interviews. No hearsay evidence was accepted. No informant is cited as to something he had heard. Only events in which informants personally participated are chronicled in this work.

In a study of this type my own values should be explicit. I believe in equal opportunity and I support the attempt to implement the ideal through legislation. In fact, it is my firm hope that this study will make a modest contribution to the ultimate success of that endeavor.

LEON H. MAYHEW

Ann Arbor, Michigan
May 1967

CONTENTS

TABLES

LAW AND EQUAL OPPORTUNITY: A STUDY OF THE
MASSACHUSETTS COMMISSION AGAINST DISCRIMINATION

CHAPTER I. INTRODUCTION: A CASE STUDY IN

INSTITUTIONALIZATION

Negroes are awarded the law as a weapon in the caste struggle. Here we see in high relief how the Negroes in their fight for equality have their allies in the white man's own conscience. The white man can humiliate the Negro; he can thwart his ambitions; he can starve him; he can press him down into vice and crime; he can occasionally beat him and even kill him; but he does not have the moral stamina to make the Negro's subjugation legal and approved by society.—[Gunnar Myrdal]

The statute books of the Commonwealth of Massachusetts include a number of laws prohibiting racial discrimination in employment, housing, and education, and in access to places of public accommodation. These laws, which may be referred to as antidiscrimination statutes, are designed to insure equality of opportunity to minority groups that have been excluded from full participation in community life. This study is a sociological investigation of the role of antidiscrimination law in the Boston community in the period from 1959 to 1963.

Massachusetts is not alone in including antidiscrimination statutes among its public laws. In fact, virtually all Northern industrial states have passed some legislation designed to secure greater opportunity for members of minority groups. The Northern Negro has been provided with the protection of law. But, despite the wide array of legal prohibitions, discrimination, at least discrimination of the racial variety, remained and remains a fact of life in the urban North.

It comes as no surprise to a sociologist that the statute

books of a community do not constitute an adequate description of its social structure. Sociologists have always tried to discover the reality that lies behind the "official blueprint."[1]

The disparity between social reality and legal commands may be extreme. On July 1, 1954, the governor of Louisiana signed an act repealing two civil rights statutes. The statutes, originally passed by a Reconstruction legislature in 1870, forbade exclusion from "places of public accommodation and resort" by reason of race or color, on penalty of civil damages and loss of license to operate such an establishment. Louisiana's decision to repeal these laws appears to have been in retaliation to the Supreme Court's famous 1954 desegregation decision. We may assume that the gesture was entirely symbolic. Louisiana Negroes had been systematically excluded from numerous places of public accommodation for half a century.

Would repeal of the civil rights statutes of a Northern community be equally symbolic? Or do the many Northern laws truly produce equal opportunity for all?

It is interesting to point to divergencies between official morality and the real structure of society, but as a final goal of inquiry it is sterile. The crucial question is, how, or under what conditions, can official morality play a role in regulating the social process? In one sense law is always symbolic; laws are formal expressions of required, prohibited, or permitted courses of action. The question is, What are the functions of such symbolic expressions? Do they reflect a desire to pay "lip service" to some community ideal, or do they actually regulate activity?

There is one clear indication that the Northern antidiscrimination statutes are more regulatory than Louisiana's recently eliminated acts. Northern statutes are backed by specialized enforcement agencies, devoted to investigating and conciliating cases of alleged discrimina-

2

tion. Such agencies attempt to eliminate discrimination wherever it is discovered. An investigation of the role of equal opportunity laws in the life of the community necessarily includes examination of the activities of the legal agency responsible for implementation. In Massachusetts this agency has been designated the Massachusetts Commission Against Discrimination, or, more popularly, the MCAD. The question becomes, What part have the Massachusetts' laws against discrimination and the corresponding administrative agency played in regulating race relations in the Boston community?

The question, so phrased, seems somewhat vague. What does it mean to say that we want to know "what part" something "plays"? Would it not be more concrete and more useful to ask whether antidiscrimination legislation has reduced discrimination and increased opportunity? This is indeed a significant question, but it is also a very difficult question to answer. In fact, it is virtually impossible to answer the question in the context of the study of a single community. The law might appear to have reduced discrimination by a certain amount, but how do we know that discrimination would not have been reduced by the same amount, or even more, if the law had never been passed? A question of that type seems answerable only in the framework of a comparative study. Comparable communities with and without laws might be compared to isolate the effect of law from the effect of the various other factors that contribute to the reduction of discrimination. The various social forces that tend to break up patterns of racial exclusion are difficult to separate in a case study. Suppose we know that a particular firm has changed its racial policy as a result of an action brought through the offices of the MCAD. Do we then say that the law produced this change? Perhaps the firm was in short supply of labor and needed to begin to exploit the

3

Negro labor market. The action by the Commission was only the "last straw," so to speak, and a straw that may not have been necessary within a very short time. Perhaps the moral pressure generated by groups supporting civil rights was becoming too much to withstand. Legal factors, moral factors, and economic factors can combine in variable proportions and in complicated, interrelated ways. The bare fact of change is not enough to demonstrate that any particular proportion is attributable to legal causes.

In fact, changes in employment patterns may not even represent a decrease in conscious discrimination. Educational upgrading, changing modes of recruitment, changing neighborhood characteristics, changing labor needs, and changes in the organization of work can produce changes in the extent of Negro participation in the community even in the absence of any conscious decisions to cease discrimination.[2]

In sum, a complete solution to the problem of how much discrimination law can eliminate or how much opportunity law can create, will require a systematic comparative study of a large number of communities over extended time periods.[3]

If systematic comparative study is a prerequisite to determining how much discrimination has been eliminated by antidiscrimination legislation, how then, can intensive study of a particular commission in a single community during a given period of time be justified?

The justification is simple. There are many important questions that can be asked about these laws besides the rather quixotic query, What might have happened if the law had not been passed?

We need to know how commissions organize to implement the law. What policies do they choose from among what alternatives and what considerations dictate policy decisions? What are the relations between the commission and other agencies concerned with discrimination? How do the various segments of the community use the law? What practical problems arise in attempting to enforce the law or to conciliate cases under the law? How do these practical problems relate to the established structure of the community? What kinds of complaints are brought under the law? Who complains about whom? Is there a pattern in the process of conciliation under the law.

These questions have a sociological dimension. In fact, the questions can be combined into one grand query: What social organization does the law produce? The community's response to the law is made up of a complex set of responses by a variety of organizations and populations. Whatever the effect of the law, it is mediated by the social organization that comes to surround it. Hence, in order to understand the effect of the law, we must understand how the law operates on and within the surrounding social order.

Our purpose is the depiction of the social organization evoked by a law. The Massachusetts laws against discrimination have evoked a set of responses from the various constituent parts of the community; the segments responded to each other's responses, and in the process a systematic organization developed. These actions and reactions of groups and populations are the referent of the vague phrase, "the part that law plays in the regulation of race relations in Boston."

The social organization that surrounds the law is a product of both the content of the law and the organization of the spheres of social life that the law purports to regulate. Massachusetts law prohibits discrimination in both employment and housing. The two institutional spheres can be expected to produce varying responses to law as a consequence of the differences between their social organization. Thus, although the study of one commission in one community is necessarily a case study, a comparative dimension is introduced.

The comparative analysis of the difference between the operation of the law in employment and in housing cuts to the heart of sociology of law. We are allowed to observe two laws, similarly worded and identical in form, enforced by the same agency, but producing different effects as a consequence of the social differences in the spheres of social life to which they are applied.

The materials of this study are varied. The core of the investigation is based on an analysis of 118 cases of alleged discrimination brought to the attention of the MCAD during 1959 and 1960. These cases constitute virtually all of the cases brought before the Commission by Negro complainants alleging discrimination in either employment or housing by a respondent located in the Boston Metropolitan Area as defined by the United States Census Bureau. The law forbids disclosure of any information pertaining to a case that has not been fully closed by the Commission. Since cases may remain open for a rather long period, 1959 and 1960 are the most recent years for which almost all cases were closed at the time the data was gathered. In addition, about 60 additional cases were examined that did not because of their time or location qualify for inclusion in the case sample.

Interviews were conducted with Commission personnel, former Commission officials, complainants, respondents, business leaders, Negro leaders, and officers of community agencies and professional associations. A total of 105 persons were interviewed between 1960 and 1963.[4]

The author spent approximately a year in concentrated field investigation, visiting the offices of the MCAD, talking to the Commissioners and the other employees, gathering information from the files and in traveling around the Boston area interviewing persons whose position in the community had brought them into confrontation with antidiscrimination legislation.

The materials of this study distinguish it from previous investigations of similar problems. There is a substantial body of literature devoted to the study of antidiscrimination law.[5] Most such studies seem to have been animated by a desire to demonstrate (popular opinion notwithstanding) that law can change behavior and attitudes. Studies have shown that law can change practices; they have shown that legal agencies can cope with their critics and opponents and persuade businessmen to change their procedures.[6] Other studies have shown that after law or other administrative action has changed behavior patterns changes in attitudes and beliefs often follow.[7]

Unfortunately, most of the studies that deal directly with the specific role of law have had to rely primarily on the published reports of public commissions. These reports are, to a degree, self-justifying. Very few investigators have been able to delve beneath the surface of "official reality" to probe the day-to-day operations of antidiscrimination agencies.[8]

The present author was fortunate in being allowed to examine not only the spectacular successes that are touted in official publications but the daily frustrations and failures as well. The materials available to the author have permitted a more critical sociological study of the forces that facilitate, shape, and obstruct the legal implementation of social ideals.

The Theory of Institutionalization

Assessment of the influence of antidiscrimination laws involves us in one of the central problems in sociological theory—the role of ideas in action.

7

The notion that social ideals can be implemented, either by law or through any other process, is periodically under attack. There are several well-rooted traditions in sociological thought that deny to values, ideals, and norms the power to transform social reality. According to the proponents of this view norms and values do not govern behavior; to treat normative ideas as having moving power is to indulge in reification, circular reasoning, and simple naïveté. Actors do not *deduce* appropriate behavior from norms that are "out there." On the contrary, norms are built up by a process of *induction* as actors seek to describe their actual behavior. Regular patterns of behavior emerge in society as men seek to coordinate their activity and meet recurrent problems. Once such patterns are established men may seek to perpetuate them by making conformity obligatory, but the norms that emerge from this process are built up slowly through experience; they are fundamentally descriptions of how men have organized their social life.

The famous sociological pioneer, William Graham Sumner, subscribed to this "inductive" view of the normative order. In *Folkways,* Sumner describes the emergence of custom from man's ceaseless struggle to survive in the face of the conditions of life.[9] As men come to recognize that their customs are vital to the success of the group, folkways become associated with general ideas of group welfare; the resulting complexes of ideas and norms are termed *mores.* The mores, though they may be more general and philosophical than folkways, have the same historic roots in experience; they serve not to guide development but to summarize it.

In view of Sumner's fundamental ideas, it is not surprising that he heaped scorn upon those who would have us believe that idealistic reformers could pull their ideas out of a philosophical hat and make them work through the simple expedient of passing a law. Thus, Sumner is usually treated as one of the main sources of the pessimistic view of the capacity of the law to affect such deeply rooted social patterns as discrimination and inequality.

Sumner's views are not without force. It is true that idealists have often failed to provide a naturalistic account of how values affect society. They indulge in circular arguments. First they abstract a set of characterizing attributes from a concrete historical situation. Then they call these attributes a "spirit" or a set of values and attribute causal force to their own abstraction, treating it as an explanation of history.

The sociological ideas that animate the present study represent a middle ground. This study rests on the theory of *institutionalization,* a set of postulates that accepts the naturalistic account of the origin and function of normative ideas but, at the same time, gives to norms and values a capacity to shape social development. The theory does not treat values as actors that do things. It merely recognizes that as communities face collective problems, as they strive to achieve goals, and to coordinate community activity, they draw upon value traditions for guidance. In this way values come to be embodied in the regular social life of the community, that is, in the institutional order.

Thus, as a community faces problems of racial tension it seeks possible answers in its heritage of ethical ideas. If that heritage affects the collective attempt to seek an organized solution, we may speak of the institutionalization of values. If institutionalization is possible, then we may adopt a more optimistic attitude toward the role of law in race relations, for we may see the law as an element in an organized effort to seek a solution to a community problem through normative regulation.

Although the term "institutionalization" has been used by sociologists in several senses, there is a common core of meaning in the various uses. Usually, there is some reference to the phenomenon of regularization, that is, the establishment of a continuing and repeating pattern of activity. This usage of the term is consistent with the use of the term "institution" in ordinary English to refer to some "law, custom, usage, practice, organization, or other element" that is *established.*[10] Institutionalization is a process of establishment, a process whereby some norm that was fluid, undefined, honored in the breach, unknown or undeveloped, becomes regularly followed and a part of the structure of social life.

For those who believe that values shape institutions, the term takes on additional meaning. "Institutionalization" comes to refer to the process whereby abstract ethical principles, such as values, become transformed into institutions, that is, regular, normatively controlled activity, supported by social organization. Thus, in the present context, we ask how the ideal of equality of opportunity comes to be embodied in the norms governing the employment relation and in the norms governing the housing market. We ask how the community develops organization to enforce these norms.

Institutionalization and integration. The ideas about institutionalization used in this study stem in large measure from the sociology of Talcott Parsons. Parsons' earliest careful statements on institutionalization are found in his collaborative work, *Towards a General Theory of Action.* In that work, Parsons and Edward Shils define the term in several ways in different contexts but the various definitions are not contradictory; they may be combined into one summary definition.[11]

We may say that a value is institutionalized in a system of social factors when:

a) There are a set of complementary roles which derive from the value and define a set of obligations for actors;

10

b) There is substantial conformity to these roles;

c) Actors expect other actors to conform;

d) Deviance from role requirements is punished, and conformity is rewarded;

e) Actors are motivated to conform to the expectations of the role (internalization);

f) There is consensus on the value and its derivative roles.

According to Parsons and Shils, institutionalization is the primary source of integration in social systems.[12] Regularities in patterns of action permit actors to adjust their behavior to the predicted behavior of others. Conformity is more likely and prediction more accurate when the patterns are governed by norms that, in turn, are supported by sanctions. Values play an important part in supporting the whole system in that the congruence of social demands and accepted values makes conformity meaningful. Further, the consensual character of values promotes agreement about acceptable patterns of behavior.

The idea of institutionalization as used in this study is very similar to the concept outlined by Parsons and Shils. However, the ideas as originally set forth must be modified and expanded in several ways.

Group interests. In recent years Professor Parsons has expanded upon his earlier formulations of the concept of institutionalization. In *Towards a General Theory of Action* and in *The Social System* actors were usually seen as persons, and persons acting in roles were the units of the "social system" referred to in the definition of institutionalization. As his interest in the organization of economic systems developed, and as he struggled with the problem of depicting total societies, Parsons moved well beyond the early systematic paradigms describing a small number of actors in face-to-face interaction.

Discrimination cannot always be treated as the act of an individual. In many institutional spheres the most important actors are organized groups, and discrimination in those spheres is a consequence of the organization and interests of groups. In this connection Parsons' recent statements on institutionalization are very useful. Where earlier statements usually referred to actors and their need-dispositions, more recent definitions speak of "acting units" and their "interests." Interests are to groups what motives are to personalities. The crucial insight here is that group interests can play the same role in institutionalization as personal needs for, like motives, group goals are not innate; they are shaped by shared values:

> The basic consequence of the institutionalization of normative culture is to produce an area of the coincidence of normative obligation on the one hand, "interest" on the other, that is to say for acting units it becomes to their interest to do what, in terms of the normative order, they ought to do.[13]

The regulation of private action. Legislation prohibiting discrimination is often seen by lawmakers and administrators as an educational device. It is designed to reeducate economic groups, to make them recognize an interest in respecting their obligations under American values. However, American values also call for freedom of action. Economic groups are to be permitted to respond to economic sanctions in the light of their own interests.

Economic groups face sanctions other than the punishments of legal agencies. It would be a mistake to use the term "sanction" only to refer to deliberate attempts to reward or punish, for systems of sanctions may operate automatically and impersonally.

Classical economic theory describes such a system. When we buy brand X rather than brand Y, we are not necessarily attempting to sanction the makers of these brands according to whether we see their behavior as deviant. We are simply expressing a preference. Yet, from the point of view of the market our act was a sanction adjusting the behavior of manufacturers to the demands of consumers. To the manufacturer, the market is a sanction system and, in a larger sense, any system that rewards or punishes actors as a result of the conduct of other actors is a social-sanctioning system.

The prominence of automatic sanctioning systems has important implications for the institutionalization of values in American society. Since American values stress the right of units of the economy to pursue private goals within a set of broad limits of permissibility, our values permit the extensive utilization of self-regulating markets as means of allocating rewards. Individuals are permitted to determine their own economic conduct within the context of market forces on the premise that "free" markets maximize flexibility by permitting rapidly changing conditions to be quickly reflected in the pressures of supply and demand. Actors are *supposed* to respond to these forces in terms of their own self interest.

Herein lies a paradox of institutionalization. On the one hand the value system *calls for* self-interested, self-reliant action. On the other hand, the implementation of other values implies limitation on the right of the actor to choose his own goals. How can social values be institutionalized in a society that expects actors to follow the forces of the market? As we shall see later, some discrimination cannot be treated as purposeful violations of standards of equality. It occurs automatically as actors respond to impersonal pressures and forces. How, in the face of our regard for rational private action, are we to regulate such behavior?

In theory the paradox has two solutions. One solution starts with recognition of the fact that self-interest is a normative phenomenon. The norm permitting self-interested action does not say "act as you please." In the economic sphere it might be defined as an obligation to set and pursue productive goals, and the corresponding right to pursue goals is subject to the limitation that the goals be compatible with publicly recognized values.

The other solution to the paradox derives from the fact that the pursuit of private interests may *support* further implementation of values. It may be that actors, in pursuit of self-selected goals, will automatically conform to new ethical demands. In other words, value concerns may be translated into market forces. When one group of actors conduct themselves in accordance with the demands of value premises, their behavior becomes a condition for actors who are merely acting in self-interest. Thus, as Negroes come to see themselves as legitimate participants in the economic process and make themselves available for industrial roles, they become a resource, and resource allocators cannot, according to the Siamese-twin values of self-interest and efficiency, afford to ignore economic resources.

On the other hand, these solutions are mere theoretical possibilities and, in practice, the opposition of deeply intrenched and partially legitimate group interests is one of the main obstacles to the implementation of equal opportunity.

The implication of the foregoing analysis is that the theory of institutionalization must take account of interests other than individual willingness to abide by normative obligations. The study of institutionalization must include examination of automatic sanctioning systems which create group interests that support or hinder the implementation of values.

Conceptions of the world. Groups do not always react to their true interests. Groups' perceptions of their interests are often distorted by various ideological themes. The various threats that businessmen and real estate men associate with the inclusion of Negroes as employees and clients may or may not be realistic. A great deal of socio-logical research has been devoted to showing that they are not. Nevertheless, to the businessman they are real, and they affect his perceptions of his interests. Thus, ideologies about the relation between property values and race affect a property owner's views of his stake in residential segregation.

In recent statements Parsons has stressed the ideological component in institutionalization. Indeed, the cognitive element of the problem becomes quite evident when we recognize the significance of rational instrumental interests as they are shaped by automatic sanctioning systems. "Ideas concerning the conditions of operation of the system and the benefits and costs involved in the alterna-tives of success and failure" clearly affect actors' percep-tions of their interests.[14]

Jurisdiction. One more new element in the concept of institutionalization is particularly important in this study. In the context of face-to-face interaction, access to most types of violations is not problematical; in a large commu-nity access is a crucial problem. Some access to violation and to violators is a prerequisite to applying norms and punishing offenses. Parsons argues that the ultimate nega-tive sanction is physical force and, in consequence, institu-tional order requires the organized control of force in a territorial area.[15] Hence he comes to stress the impor-tance of the concept of territorial sovereignty as an element of institutionalization.

In the present study territorial sovereignty is not a var-iable; it can be taken for granted. However, given territorial sovereignty, the problem of access to violation remains. The patterns of violation and their location in the social structure may operate to prevent access to violations from being translated into actual jurisdiction. Thus, it is some-times said that if the laws against various types of sexual

15

practices between husbands and wives were strictly enforced, a large portion of the population would be imprisoned. One of the factors preventing mass incarceration is that the offenses in question are so located as not to come to the attention of law enforcement officials, either directly or through the complaints of incensed citizens. The system, though it in theory has jurisdiction over sexual practices, does not in fact assume jurisdiction. Jurisdiction or access to violation is a crucial precondition for the operation of any sanctioning system and many of the problems of implementation in antidiscrimination law derive from jurisdictional obstacles.

Ideal and real social systems. Parsons does not suppose that values are ever completely institutionalized. Institutionalization is a matter of degree; it exists to the extent that a set of conditions are met.[16] Since Parsons is constructing general theory, he adopts the strategy of developing a model of an ideally integrated social system rather than describing an actual on-going society. A useful model should suggest the relevant dimensions along which a concrete society can be measured. The model provides a basis for analytically separating the elements of institutional structure.

Since society is made up of a variety of organizations and groups with variable purposes and variable experiences, we do not expect uniformity in the actual patterns of institutionalization in the various sectors of society. For example, we would expect persons at different locations in the social structure to have variable perceptions of values and reality. Thus, actors may act and evaluate the actions of others according to different norms even though there is general agreement on the relevant social values at a more abstract level.

Accordingly, when we discuss institutionalization in a concrete society, we cannot simply refer to the integration

16

of values and interests. We must describe the *distribution* of relevant interests in the various sectors and spheres of the society and assess the extent to which they contribute to the support of values and to institutional order. Similarly, for the other components, distributions in the society, and the consequences of those distributions are the object of study.

The components of institutionalization. The four elements whose distribution must be described can be drawn from Parsons' original statement and his recent elaborations of the concept.

1) *Interpretation.* Institutionalization is, in part, a logical process. Ideas about the implications of abstract ideals for concrete behavior are the first component of institutionalization.

2) *Ideology.* There is a second ideal element in the process. Ideology shapes institutions because definitions of the social world affect actors' definitions of their interests and their perception of the community to which values are applied.[17]

3) *Interests.* The production of motivation to support the institutional order is a crucial element of institutionalization. However, the exclusively psychological connotation of the term "motivation" makes "interest" a better concept in this context.

The structure of interests depends, in large measure, on the structure of sanctions. The interests of actors and groups are shaped by the sanctions that are imposed on them for various courses of behavior. Thus, *the extent to which the structure of interests supports institutionalization is dependent on the capacity of the system to support values through imposing sanctions.*

4) *Jurisdiction.* Further analysis of the capacity of the system to impose sanctions reveals that the putative power of the system to structure interests so as to produce

17

compliance is not meaningful if the system has no access to violations or violators. The degree of access depends on the nature of violations and their distribution in the social structure.[18]

In sum, the theory of institutionalization is a theory of integration. It purports to explain how a group of actors comes to coordinate their conduct and resolve their conflicts. It starts with the assumption that groups have shared conceptions of a desirable state of social organization. These conceptions are called social values. According to the theory, integrative problems are solved by working out the normative implications of social values in the context of concrete social situations. A variety of interpretations may be suggested and the version of the value system one prefers reflects his position in the social system. But not all versions have equal capacity to coordinate activity and resolve conflict and to survive and spread their influence. This capacity depends on the degree of assent the interpretation can command and the extent to which it can be enforced or, in other words, on the conditions of institutionalization.

Successful institutionalization involves the development of a set of norms that are not only legitimate but are also effective in the face of the exigencies of hard social reality. The support of ideology, interests, and an appropriate structure of jurisdiction is necessary if a set of values and their corresponding norms are to regulate and coordinate social life.

Legal institutionalization. The foregoing discussion of institutionalization has proceeded without special reference to the potential role of law in the process. Institutionalization may involve the restructuring of interests through systematic application or threat of legal sanctions and the establishment of implementive organization with sets of legal powers.

A value is said to have legal *institutionalization* when:

a) the value is embodied in a legal norm, that is, one interpretation of the value is legally enforceable (legal interpretation);

b) there is legal machinery for obtaining interpretations of the legal norm in particular instances, that is, there is machinery for invoking sanctions against violations (legal organization);

c) the legal machinery is systematically invoked in cases of possible violations of the norm.

Systematic enforcement implies that the organization in control of legal machinery has:

a) knowledge of violations;

b) the power to remedy violations;

c) access to violations.

Organization and "metaphysical pathos." A complete study of the institutionalization of a law would give equal attention to the responses of all of the segments of the community whose behavior affects the establishment of the law's ideals. This study is primarily concerned with the responses of the legal agency which had been given responsibility for enforcement of the law.

The MCAD had been charged with the task of producing social change through implementing ideals. Some sociological writing and research on organization for social change is enveloped in pessimism and fatalism. It is alleged that organizational means inevitably subvert organizational ends; as organizations come to terms with the conditions of their own survival they compromise and weaken their ethical commitment.

Thus, in a classic sociological discussion, Weber describes the routinization of critical movements as the leaders of the second generation, ungifted with the charisma and furor of the original leader, come to depend on ordinary organizational techniques to insure discipline and solvency. Adapting to the requisites of routine administration means, in effect, coming to terms with the forces of everyday life.[19]

Roberto Michels, in expounding his "iron law of oligarchy," takes the pessimistic view that implementive organization destroys the very ideals that it is supposed to support.[20] Inevitably oligarchical leaders come to have an interest in maintaining the organization, and their action comes to be predicated upon those goals rather than the idealistic *raison d'être* of the movement.

Phillip Selznick describes the consequences of attempting to work through established organization in the Tennessee Valley Authority. In order to protect the stability of the organization, TVA utilized a technique known as cooptation. The power groups that threatened its existence were allowed representation within the organization but in consequence some of the goals of TVA were thwarted.[21]

Seymour M. Lipset examined the modifications introduced in a socialist program of social reform as a consequence of reliance on established bureaucrats to staff the administrative hierarchies. The staff of officials were unsympathetic to the projected reforms but their expertise made them indispensable. They were able effectively to prevent implementation of many of the policies established by the higher levels of government.[22]

A large body of modern research revolves around the deviance of organizational goals from organizational values as original purposes are forgotten and ethical purposes are subordinated. Over time emphasis shifts from external to internal goals and conservation of the organization, its procedures, and its structure becomes the goal of the group. According to this view, official policy will not be implemented if it threatens the stability of established organization.

Thomas Pettigrew and Ernest Campbell have noted the ineffectiveness of official declarations favoring racial tolerance in churches where ministers are judged according to their capacity as administrators. There is no support in the organization for the minister's prophetic role; hence in crisis situations policy is not implemented. [23]

One analysis suggests that the dilution of goals is particularly prominent when organizations are tied to "precarious" values. Burton Clark, in examining the implementation of an adult education program in California, showed that the low priority of adult education relative to child education gave the program marginal legitimacy and the practical goal of the organization became building a large enough enrollment to justify their existence. The attempt to build attendance led to emphasis on popular courses and educational frills rather than the development of a program designed to serve the educational needs of the community. [24]

Students of the administrative process have also noted the tendency of implementive organization to compromise in the face of organizational constraints. Observers have suggested that federal regulatory agencies have been captured by the interests they purport to regulate. Administrative agencies are said to have a life cycle. The original legislation generates an enthusiastic corps of initial administrators who gradually give in to the demands and pressures of industry and to the exigencies of routine administration.

Marver Bernstein, James Landis, Thurman Arnold, and Bernard Schwartz have discussed this tendency[25] and the factors promoting "industry orientation" in the administrative agencies. Agencies must recruit personnel who have gained expertise through experience in industry. Industry recruits personnel from the administrative staff of agencies, making civil servants sensitive to the power of regulatees to offer future rewards. Constant day-to-day contact with the regulated industry brings assimilation of ideologies and perspectives. Regulatory agencies come to feel a proprietary responsibility for the well-being of "their" industry vis-à-vis competitive industries. The support of industry is used as a political weapon in protecting the agency and the power of officials within the agency.

The latter source of "industry orientation" may entail simple attempts to curry favor in the hope of future support. However, students of administrative regulation have also noted the frequency with which cooptation is used as a political device.

Avery Leiserson in his classic work on administrative regulation takes the position that the provision of channels for the effective presentation of the interests of regulatees is a legitimate and necessary element of successful administration in a pluralistic society.[26] Allowing the representation of interests within the organization does more than provide political protection, it establishes channels for communicating vital interests and concerns to administrators, permitting them to adjust and mediate interests before conflict reaches the political level. Leiserson notes, however, that

> The objection to "democratizing the organization of authority" on the basis of a shared responsibility between administrators and group representatives, is that it may in practice become a means of reflecting the views solely of the organized sector of a single private interest. As long as this interest . . . can be identified with the concept of the welfare of the community, this problem is not serious. However, when the vested interest of the private organization becomes unrepresentative of the group . . . or opposes a planned program of community welfare and development, a question of public, if not of political importance is raised.[27]

The author goes on to say that it is precisely when conflicting groups *are* represented that the implementive functions of interest representation are threatened.

22

Assuming that the objective of public administration is to secure the routine acceptance of duly authorized administrative action, the dilemma obviously arises as to how such acceptance can be brought about when the policy making authority is itself internally divided between representatives of conflicting groups.[28]

In its extreme forms the theory that organizations abandon goals in favor of organizational stability and persistence is not a theory of institutionalization; it is a theory that claims institutionalization to be impossible. Organizations cannot implement values in the face of resistance from the established structure because the maintenance of the organization demands adjustment to the very forces that must be overcome.

All sociologists are not so pessimistic. Alvin Gouldner has derided the fatalism surrounding organization theory, describing it as a form of "metaphysical pathos" unsupported by theory or facts. According to Gouldner sociologists should pay equal attention to the social forces that generate continuing attacks upon organizational constraints.[29]

Peter Blau suggests that, under some conditions, bureaucratic organization intensifies concern for social reform. Blau does not deny the possibility of bureaucratic distortion of goals. He particularly stresses "ritualism," or the stress upon established procedures even at the cost of success in achieving goals. Following Merton he refers to this phenomenon as *goal displacement*.[30] Yet Blau found in one federal agency that goals were not only preserved, but as old problems were solved, officials turned with eagerness to new and equally idealistic tasks. Of course, the discovery of new goals contributed to the maintenance of the organization, but it should not be overlooked that in accepting new jurisdiction the agency accepted new challenges. Official acceptance of these challenges was supported by a progressive ideology within the bureauc-

23

LAW AND EQUAL OPPORTUNITY

racy and by confidence engendered by success in establishing the original law in the face of industry objection. Blau calls this process the "succession of goals."[31]

The views of the critics seem correct; there is no inevitable trend toward compromise. In fact, the quest for continued existence may impel the organization to become *more* radical over time. One of the most pressing sociological tasks is the delineation of the factors that favor the establishment of values and the factors that favor displacement of goals.

The present study indicates that some of the fatal attributes of organization *have* impeded the implementation of the law. At the same time the investigation also provides clues about the positive forces that maintain commitment and effectiveness.

Four conditions that favor achievement of ideal goals loom large in this study:

1) The strength of the values themselves is important for power struggles are not naked. When there is a firm commitment in the society to the abstract values that are being applied, the enforcement agency has considerable leverage over the power it must regulate. The fact that industry is wealthier than the administrative agency, or has more support in the legislature, does not mean that industry will prevail. The agency can counter with the leverage that comes from its symbolic representation of the values of the community.

2) The law itself gives the agency power. Courts are bound to interpret the law and the state is bound to enforce the interpretations of the court. Accordingly, passage of a reform law may radically alter the balance of power between groups who support extension of the values and groups who oppose.

3) Organization among the groups in the community who favor greater implementation of the ideal can provide

24

the agency with support vis-a-vis the pressures of regulatees who would use their power to compromise the purposes of the agency.

4) General social changes in the society at large may transform the structure of interests in the society. Implementive organization may be supported by emergent social forces that motivate regulatees to bow to social regulation. Thus, for example, in the case at hand increasing social demands for trained manpower have encouraged industry to adopt the policies demanded by the state.

Institutionalization and administrative agency. The four elements of institutionalization—interpretation, ideology, jurisdiction, and interests—are applicable to the administrative agency charged with enforcement of the law just as they are applicable to other segments of the community. The agency interprets the values and norms it is implementing as it formulates policy and applies the law in specific situations. The agency develops an *ideology* about the nature of the society in which it operates. It develops theories about its role in the community, the needs of the community, and the most efficient and effective means of accomplishing its tasks. The agency has a certain degree of effective *jurisdiction* or access to noncompliance.

Finally, the agency has a position in the structure of interests within the community. In applying the elements of institutionalization to administrative agencies, it is useful to speak of the agency's position in the structure of interests as its *power* position. The agency has an interest in implementing the law and, to this end, it is invested with power, or the capacity to reorganize the pattern of community interests by applying sanctions to violators. On the other hand, the agency also has an interest in maintaining and supporting its existence. Thus, its effective capacity to impose sanctions may either be compromised by political instability of reinforced by community support. The power of an agency may be defined as its capacity to achieve its goals by changing others' interests without threatening its own interest in continued existence.

The Institutionalization of Antidiscrimination Law

This study was guided throughout by the general concepts outlined above. The inquiry proceeded on the assumption that perceived racial differences create an integrative problem for the community. Some way of providing for the orderly participation of various groups in the life of the community must be worked out if social harmony is to be maintained. Several modus vivendi are conceivable. A rigid pattern of separate but equal activity could be developed together with a formalized code of etiquette governing unavoidable contact. Or the Negro could participate in the general life of the community at the lower end of the scale, and be taught to "know his place," and accept it. Both of these solutions have counterparts in history, but in Boston neither solution has been possible because neither corresponds to the social value placed on equal opportunity. Accordingly, some version of the ideal of nondiscrimination became the basis for mediating the relations between groups. Various interest groups in different sectors of the community have proposed a variety of versions of the ideal as workable and legitimate solutions.

The community, through its legal apparatus, has proposed one solution. The problem before us is, Have the patterns of values, ideologies, interests, and access permitted the institutionalization of the legal solution and, thereby, the integration of the community?

The first component of institutionalization seems particularly relevant in the case of nondiscrimination. Several variable definitions of discrimination were apparent from the first preliminary investigations. Research on the particular conception of discrimination embodied in the law and in the decisions of the Commission seemed a fruitful line of inquiry. The capacity of the administrative agency to establish an acceptable and practical definition of discrimination is a crucial determinant of its effectiveness. Is the definition rigorous enough to permit finding discrimination where its existence seems obvious to the Negro community? Does the Commission's definition imply a challenge to conceptions of discrimination current in business circles? How does the Commission mediate between the variable conceptions of discrimination prominent in the community?

A second interpretive problem concerns the Commission's interpretation of its powers under the law. The law is cast in general terms; it does not specify particular courses of action in detail. A number of alternative policies are permissable under the law. The Commission's conception of its mandate and its definition of discrimination may be expected to reflect both the realistic exigencies of administration and legal reasoning about the meaning of equal opportunity. Such working interpretations of the law have important consequences for administration.

One guiding hypothesis concerns the relation between ideology and interests. According to one theory the structure of interests should support the elimination of discrimination. It is adaptive for the social system to make the most efficient possible use of resources and, therefore, decisions based upon irrelevant qualities are uneconomic. One of the functions of a market system is that it translates inefficiencies into costs (or sanctions) to acting units. The acting unit that refuses to make rational decisions will be penalized by extra costs.

On the other hand, markets do not operate perfectly. Ideology may distort perceptions of costs so that econom-

27

ic decisions are not based on realistic assessments of benefits and costs. Racial ideologies can distort economic practices as, for example, when some housing accommodations are overused and others underused because owners keep nonwhites segregated in certain areas of the city on the supposition that nonwhite occupancy has a deleterious effect on property values. The available evidence indicates that property values rise as often as they fall on conversion to Negro occupancy.[32] Yet economic decision continues to be based on a false assumption. An employer may not utilize Negro labor because he thinks his white employees will resign or that Negroes cannot be trained to do the job. If his suppositions are not true, then racial ideology has distorted the economic process. Distorting ideologies can be self-perpetuating if no one tests them by experimental action. Law can restructure interests by changing perceptions of interests. If ideology is twisting purely instrumental decisions, law can force recognition of the real situation by forcing action that will make underlying interests more discernible.

There are authentic examples of this process. One illustration is provided by the integration of department store sales forces. One of the persistent problems in the department store business is the supply of sales personnel. Yet in the late forties most large city department stores excluded Negro employment on the assumption that customers would resent Negro sales personnel. Yet, when the prodding of the New York State Commission Against Discrimination produced integration of New York City department stores, no loss of business followed. False expectations were disproved and the potential labor market expanded.[33]

On the other hand, ideologies may be highly resistant to change and in some cases persons and groups may have authentic interests in resisting the law, if only out of a concern for maintaining autonomy and freedom from

28

controls. Thus, some segments of the community might make a concerted effort to resist the Commission.

The author was aware that the MCAD had come under considerable attack for its allegedly conservative policies. It was widely believed that Commission policy reflected the personality and philosophy of a weak and ineffective chairman. If the sociological framework of this study is valid, the ideology of the Commission should be found to correspond to its political position. Conservative enforcement reflects an attempt to protect the Commission from political attack, to insure continued existence and expanded jurisdiction.

Accordingly, a part of the investigation was devoted to delineating the power relations between the Commission and the industry it purported to regulate. If the interests of the regulatees in avoiding enforcement are strong and organized we would expect the power of the Commission to restructure interests to be correspondingly weak, since they would not be in a political position to utilize their legal power.

The concept of jurisdiction played a major role in guiding the inquiry. The main expectation was that the initiation of enforcement action by the Commission would be a more effective base for jurisdiction than the process of investigating complaints. Where jurisdiction is dependent on the initiation of complaints by aggrieved individuals, it is likely that the Commission will not acquire jurisdiction over a wide segment of the market. Constraints on the filing of complaints will produce a pattern in the distribution of complaints that does not correspond to the distribution of the violation. The limited perspective of the lone individual does not permit careful choice of targets for legal action. The individual's complaints will reflect his daily experience rather than general knowledge about the patterns of discrimination. Further, for some violations legal redress will seem to a complainant inappropriate or futile.

A final guiding principle is found in the very concept of institutionalization. The concept of institutionalization assumes that values and norms have effects on social structure; they are not mere generalizations that emerge as ways of describing patterns of interaction.

Hence, the operation of an antidiscrimination law is not to be seen as a naked power struggle between those who have interests in continuing discrimination and those who have interests in eliminating discrimination. In the first place, the interests of many who work for equal opportunity are ideal interests. They have little to gain economically, or politically; they are committed to the value. In the second place, those who work to secure passage and implementation of antidiscrimination laws have a very important lever working for them. They can be sure that even those who violate the ideal can be forced to bow to it in their public action. In consequence, the violator, constrained by moral pressure, is denied effective use of his power. An important part of the study is devoted to an examination of the moral and legal tools used by civil rights groups in attacking discrimination.

The Passing of the Classic Era

In large measure this study is a historical work; it is a study of the classic era of antidiscrimination law. The tools of protest are changing rapidly and the problems of the classic era help to explain this change. It has been noted that there are variable definitions of discrimination. The movement that led to the enactment of antidiscrimination statutes in various states, and finally, in 1964 and 1965 to national civil rights acts, was a movement based on one version of the American tradition of equal opportunity. This version might be termed the "color-blind" theory. It assumes that the solution to problems in discrimination lies in enforcing standards of equal treatment. By this standard race must be eliminated as a valid criterion for making decisions about human beings. In later chapters we will see that this theory is facing an emergent challenge. Indeed, our analysis of the classic era will clarify the inherent weakness of the classic approach and will illuminate the forces that are shaping new approaches and forcing new definitions.

We must face the possibility that the national civil rights acts were achieved only after their basic assumptions had become obsolete. Increasing recognition of the obstacles to equal participation and new and more vigorous demands for equal participation have created pressures which outreach the integrative capacity of traditional legal approaches.

CHAPTER II. DISCRIMINATION AND THE NEGRO

COMMUNITY

The Yankee conscience was divisible on the race issue.—[Malcolm Ross]

The Negro Population of Boston

In 1960 the Census Bureau enumerated 63,165 Negroes in Boston. Compared to the massive Negro concentrations in New York, Chicago, Detroit, St. Louis, and Washington, this number does not seem impressive. Yet, it is nearly a tenth of the population of the city and the proportion is steadily increasing. The famous "Black Metropolis" studied by St. Clair Drake and Horace Cayton during the thirties and forties was about the same proportion of the Chicago community.[1]

The roots of the Boston Negro community are deep in American history. Negro slaves were imported to Boston in 1638. By the beginning of the eighteenth century nearly 400 slaves were residing in Boston as well as a handful of free Negroes.[2]

During the eighteenth century Negro slavery disappeared in Massachusetts. By 1790 the first annual census listed no slaves in the Commonwealth. It is difficult to give a precise date to the demise of slavery for many slaves were manumitted voluntarily or by purchase. Several law suits declared slaves to be free by the common law of England and finally the courts held that the 1780 declaration of rights prohibited the enslavement of any person.[3]

The free Negro community continued to grow, increasing to 1,174 by 1800, to 2,000 by the Civil War, and to over 11,000 by the turn of the present century.

Before the Civil War the growth in the Negro community occurred primarily by natural increase. Since the Civil War, immigration has been a dominant source of growth, so that by 1910 only five percent of the Negro population of the city were native Bostonians, and two thirds were born in the South.[4]

Table 1. Negro population of Boston and Greater Boston, 1800 - 1960

Year	Boston		Greater Boston	
	Number	Percent of total	Number	Percent of total
1800	1,174[a]	4.7	–	–
1830	1,815[a]	3.0	–	–
1860	2,284[a]	5.7	–	–
1890	8,125[a]	1.8	12,832[a]	1.5
1910	13,564[a]	2.0	23,115[a]	1.7
1920	16,350	2.2	–	–
1930	20,574	2.6	33,820	1.5
1940	23,679	3.1	36,180	1.5
1950	40,157	5.0	51,568	2.2
1960	63,165	9.1	77,781	3.0

Source: The U. S. Decennial Census for the year named and John Daniels, *In Freedom's Birthplace* (Boston 1914).

[a] These figures are taken from Daniels, *In Freedom's Birthplace.*

For half a century, between about 1890 and 1940, Boston's Negroes constituted a fairly stable proportion of the population. The growth of the Negro population was matched by a proportional growth of the population of the city.

In contrast, the proportion of the population that was Negro tripled between 1940 and 1960. The rate of immigration picked up sharply during World War II and has remained high ever since. Between 1950 and 1960 the city

33

experienced a seventeen percent overall decline in population while the Negro population increased by fifty-seven percent. In consequence the percentage of Negroes in the city nearly doubled.

The migration to Boston, while substantial, does not match the tremendous influx to some other Northern cities, but the twin obstacles of insufficient preparation for urban life and antagonism in the white community faced the Negro in Boston just as they faced his cousins in Chicago and New York.

The attitudes of the white community have been significant. Bostonians played an important role in several movements intended to clarify and implement the American value tradition. New England was a central locus for the initial formulation and institutionalization of our value system. The Puritan ethic, "Yankee" values, and our first indigenous philosophical and literary movements all centered in and around the Boston area.

The abolitionist movement, an important development in the implementation of American value premises, flourished in Boston from about the third decade of the nineteenth century. In 1826 a group of Negroes organized as the General Coloured Association of Massachusetts began an antislavery campaign. The movement, originally Negro, had a profound impact on certain reform-minded white Bostonians, notably William Lloyd Garrison, who began publication of "The Liberator," most famous of the antislavery journals, on New Year's Day 1831.

The appearance of "The Liberator" marked the beginning of full-scale abolitionist agitation and Garrison became a central figure in the movement and, after the emancipation proclamation, in the new civil rights struggle. His New England Anti-Slavery Society was one of the main organizational bases for the movement. Frederick Douglass, the famous escaped slave and abolitionist orator, was "discovered" by the society and used as an effective agent in their propaganda campaigns. Other prominent abolitionists such as W. W. Brown, Wendell Phillips, Charles Sumner, Charles Remond, John Greenleaf Whittier, Theodore Parker, and William Ellery Channing also worked in Boston. Boston's role was not limited to the production of antislavery propaganda; before emancipation Boston was one of the principal stations on the underground railway.[4]

After the Civil War Boston became an important stronghold of Republican radicalism and civil rights agitation. Sumner, Phillips, and others continued to work in the movement that led to passage of the first national civil rights legislation, the postwar constitutional amendments, and the Civil Rights Act of 1875.

Boston's prominence in these movements might lead us to conclude that the tenets of the value creed were firmly institutionalized in the Hub. Indeed, to this day, popular conceptions of the status of the Boston Negro are influenced by her historic role. However, Boston's reputation, established by her famous liberals, is not entirely justified. From the beginning, abolitionist sentiment existed side by side with several varieties of institutionalized segregation and discrimination. In the words of Malcolm Ross, "The Yankee conscience was divisible on the race issue."[5]

In the earliest days Negroes were restricted to segregated pews or galleries in the very churches whose creeds generated the prevailing value tradition. Later, separate Negro churches were organized. Segregated housing emerged very early. Separate schools were not abolished until 1855, when passage of a state law forbidding racial distinctions in school attendance was secured by a Negro pressure group.[6]

Indeed, the doctrine of separate but equal was born in a Massachusetts court. In Sarah C. Roberts v. City of Boston, decided by the Massachusetts Supreme Court in 1849, the

Negro-School-Abolition Party sought to have separate schools for Negroes declared unconstitutional. The court declared that there was nothing unconstitutional about separate schools as long as they were equal. The case was cited and its reasoning borrowed in the famous Plessy v. Ferguson case of 1896.[7]

Massachusetts law and the courts of the Commonwealth have not always been solicitous of Negro rights. In fact, one of the earliest statutes concerning Negroes sought to reduce Negro immigration to the state. An act of 1788 provided that no African or Negro, other than citizens of Morocco or some state of the United States, could remain in the commonwealth over two months. A variety of similar measures was discussed and proposed over the next forty years.[8]

After the Civil War the discrimination facing Boston Negroes at theatres, restaurants, barber shops, and other public accommodations brought about passage of the public accommodations act of 1865. The act fared little better in Massachusetts courts than the federal Civil Rights Act in the courts of the United States. It regularly suffered judicial debilitation, necessitating periodic returns to the legislature for amendment for legal deficiencies.[9] Furthermore, despite the act, discrimination continued.

The most serious problems of discrimination have arisen in the areas of employment and housing. Discrimination in these spheres is fundamental in the sense that it supports and promotes discrimination in other sectors of life. Residential segregation creates isolation and job discrimination supports poverty, and the combination of isolation and poverty denies both the opportunity and the means for improvement.

Negro Employment in Boston

The Boston Negro, like other urban Negroes, has suffered

from the vicious circle of discrimination and lack of training since the first migrations to the Hub. Originally slaves and servants, then small farmers, Negro migrants to Boston have had little opportunity to learn urban roles. The Negro was prepared only for menial jobs at the bottom of the status ladder, and discrimination has operated to prevent access to positions where training could be achieved. Hence, Negro participation in the economic life of the community has been segregated and limited to certain sectors.

In the early nineteenth century almost all employed Negroes were household servants and laborers. Only a handful had trades, the most common of which was barber. At the turn of the century the proportion of Negro males engaged in menial occupations such as servant, waiter, porter, helper and laborer, was 61 percent, nearly five times greater than the proportion of whites engaged in similar work. Females were over-represented by two and a half times in menial occupations such as servant, laundress, and laborer.

John Daniels, an author who usually ascribes the Negro's position to innate inferiority, describes conditions at the beginning of the century in these terms:

Except in the case of the menial occupations in which Negroes are most numerously engaged, it is much harder for a Negro to get employment than it is for a white person. Even in the case of those menial occupations, moreover, it is difficult for a Negro to obtain work if the particular employer to whom he applies has not been accustomed to employing Negroes. As a rule this prejudice increases in strength as the grade of work ascends. Speaking very broadly, one may say that in low grade work a Negro finds it twice as hard to obtain employment; in work of intermediary grade, such as the trades and lesser clerical lines from ten to fifty times harder; and in work of high grade such as that of bank clerks, salaried officials of business houses, and the like, a hundred times harder than is the case with applicants of the other race; and that furthermore there are some occupations from which Negroes are practically shut out. With respect, secondly, to advancement after employment is once

37

secured, the Negro is likewise, though in lesser degree, the object of prejudice. In order to gain promotion he must do work which is not only equal in quality to that of white employees of the same sort, but better . . . The prospects of advancement diminish as the grade of work ascends, and after a certain point they sink to zero. [10]

With due reservation as to Daniels' ratios, the statement stands in 1967 as an accurate description of the problems facing Negroes in the economic sphere.

Nevertheless, insistence on the reality of current discrimination should not blind us to the substantial progress that was made in opening new spheres of opportunity between 1940 and 1960. Nor should we overlook the profound changes that have occurred in the occupational composition of the Negro community since 1940.

Negro occupational distribution can be compared with the white distribution by constructing indices of occupational representation. The ratio of the percentage of Negroes in a given occupational category to the percentage of whites in the same occupational category provides an index that gives the degree of over or under representation of Negroes in that category. Thus, an index of occupational representation equal to unity means that whites and Negroes are represented equally, an index of 2.0 indicates that there are twice as many Negroes as whites in the category and an index of 0.5 would mean that only half as many Negroes as whites are represented in the category.

The indices are particularly useful in viewing changes over time because the effect of changes in occupational structure are eliminated. Thus, the fraction of Negro women engaged in domestic service declined from about 55 percent in 1940 to only 14 percent in 1960, but this reflects a general reduction in domestic employment. During the same time period the fraction of white women doing domestic work declined from about 12 percent to between 3 and 4 percent. Even though the fraction of

Negroes in domestic service declined to a quarter of its former value, Negro women were still over-represented by four to one in the category.

Tables 2 through 5 show the general outlines of change quite clearly. Before World War II Negroes were well confined to traditional "Negro jobs." Among Negroes half of the male labor force and more than three-fourths of the female labor force were occupied in service roles. More than half of the women were in domestic service. About one fifth of the men were janitors and porters. Less than 15 percent of the men and less than 10 percent of the women were in white collar occupations. Within the small group of Negro professionals, only musicians, clergymen, nurses, and female teachers were represented in substantial numbers.

The war, with its consequent labor shortages, created great pressures for opening factory work to Negroes. Negro employment in the category "operative" rose substantially between 1940 and 1950, increasing from 12.7 percent to 22.5 percent of men, and from 11.7 percent to 31.5 percent of women. In consequence, Negro representation in male service occupations declined. On the other hand, female representation in service occupations did not decline; it actually increased. As factory opportunity increased and domestic help became priced out of the market, whites left domestic service at a faster rate than Negroes. Whites had first call at factory jobs and Negroes were still relatively excluded from clerical and sales capacities. This left a substantial number of Negro women in the declining domestic occupations.

The shift from service to factory work was the most pronounced change during the fifties. By 1960 Negro males were *over-represented* as operatives by 1.6 to 1 and 1.85 to 1 for males and females respectively. Before the war Negroes had been substantially *under-represented* in that category.

Table 2. Distribution (percent) of the employed labor force, white and Negro, for the Boston metropolitan area, 1940, 1950, 1960. Male.

Occupational group	1940 BMD[a]		1950 BSMA		1960 BSMSA		1960 BSMSA Corrected[b]	
	White	Negro	White	Negro	White	Negro	White	Negro
Professional, technical and kindred workers	8.4	5.0	11.2	4.2	15.0	6.2	16.0	7.2
Managers and proprietors	12.2	2.3	13.0	2.8	11.7	2.5	12.4	2.9
Clerical	20.0 }	7.1 }	9.1	6.1	9.2	7.5	9.8	8.7
Sales			9.1	1.7	8.6	1.6	9.2	1.8
Craftsmen, foremen, and kindred workers	19.4	8.9	21.6	12.7	20.1	12.9	21.4	14.9
Operatives	21.0	12.7	19.2	22.5	16.4	26.4	17.5	30.6
Service occupations	9.8	50.5	8.5	31.7	7.8	19.5	8.3	22.5
Laborers	7.2	12.9	6.6	16.7	5.0	9.7	5.3	11.2
Minor categories and occupation not reported	2.0	0.7	1.5	1.7	6.2	13.6	0	0
Coefficient of dissimilarity	0.46		0.37		0.34		0.33	

Source: U. S. Department of Commerce, Bureau of the Census, *Census of Population,* 1940, vol. II, pt. 3; 1950, vol. II, pt. 21; 1960, vol. I, pt. 23.

[a]The 1940 data are not entirely comparable with the data for 1950 and 1960. Data for the occupational composition of the labor force by race were not available for the Boston Metropolitan area in 1940.

[b]Corrected by a proportional allocation of those who did not report any occupation.

Table 3. Distribution (percent) of the employed labor force, white and Negro, for the Boston metropolitan area, 1940, 1950, 1960. Female.

Occupational group	1940 BMD[a]		1950 BSMA		1960 BSMSA		1960 BSMSA Corrected[b]	
	White	Negro	White	Negro	White	Negro	White	Negro
Professional, technical and kindred workers	14.5	4.2	14.3	5.3	14.5	7.5	15.6	9.0
Managers and proprietors	2.7	0.7	3.4	1.1	3.0	0.7	3.3	0.8
Clerical	36.9 }	4.5 }	36.5	9.4	36.4	14.4	39.3	17.2
Sales			8.1	2.1	7.5	1.8	8.1	2.1
Craftsmen, foremen, and kindred workers	1.3	0.6	1.8	0.9	1.3	0.9	1.4	1.1
Operatives	19.2	11.7	19.1	31.5	15.8	29.2	17.1	34.8
Domestic service	12.2	55.3	4.5	27.9	3.4	13.8	3.6	16.4
Other service	11.5	21.3	10.4	19.1	10.4	15.2	11.3	18.1
Laborers	0.5	0.6	0.6	1.7	0.3	0.4	0.3	0.5
Minor categories and occupation not reported	1.2	1.1	1.3	1.0	7.5	16.0	0	0
Coefficient of dissimilarity	0.53		0.46		0.37		0.37	

Source: U. S. Department of Commerce, Bureau of the Census, Census of Population, 1940, vol. II, pt. 3; 1950, vol. II, pt. 21; 1960, vol. I, pt. 23.

[a]The 1940 data are not entirely comparable with the data for 1950 and 1960. Data for the occupational composition of the labor force by race were not available for the Boston Metropolitan area in 1940.

[b]Corrected by a proportional allocation of those who did not report any occupation.

Table 4. Index[a] of occupational representation of Negroes relative to whites in the Boston metropolitan area, 1940, 1950, 1960. Male.

Occupation	1940 BMD	1950 BSMA	1960 BSMSA	1960 BSMSA Corrected[b]
Professional	0.59	0.27	0.42	0.45
Managers and proprietors	.19	.21	.22	.24
Clerical	.35	.67	.82	.89
Sales		.19	.18	.20
Craftsmen and foremen	.46	.59	.64	.70
Operatives	.60	1.17	1.61	1.74
Service	5.17	3.74	2.51	2.72
Labor	1.80	2.53	1.92	2.09

[a]Ratio of percentages of Negroes to whites in each category, from Tables 2 and 3. However, these indices cannot necessarily be reproduced accurately because they are based on computations in which the numerators and denominators were accurate to two decimal places; Tables 2 and 3 only give one decimal.

[b]Corrected by a proportional allocation of those who did not report any occupation.

The other changes were not as pronounced. In some spheres there was slow and steady progress and in other spheres there was no progress at all. In clerical and professional occupations Negroes were gradually catching up to whites. In the skilled trades progress was slow but steady. In the sales category there was virtually no change and Negroes were not able to make inroads into the managerial occupations.

Between 1940 and 1950 Negro males did not participate in the rapid expansion of professional and technical occupations. Negro professionals remained concentrated in music and the clergy. The rapid regaining of lost ground

Table 5. Index[a] of occupational representation of Negroes relative to whites in the Boston metropolitan area, 1940, 1950, 1960. Female.

Occupation	1940 BMD	1950 BSMA	1960 BSMSA	1960 BSMSA Corrected[b]
Professional	0.29	0.37	0.52	0.57
Managers and proprietors	.26	.32	.23	.25
Clerical	.12	.26	.40	.44
Sales		.26	.24	.26
Craft	.48	.52	.72	.79
Operatives	.61	1.65	1.85	2.03
Domestic service	4.54	6.16	4.11	4.53
Other service	1.85	1.83	1.46	1.61
Labor	1.06	2.86	1.37	1.53

[a]Ratio of percentages of Negroes to whites in each category, from Tables 2 and 3. However, these indices cannot necessarily be reproduced accurately because they are based on computations in which the numerators and denominators were accurate to two decimal places; Tables 2 and 3 only give one decimal.

[b]Corrected by a proportional allocation of those who did not report any occupation.

in the "professional, technical and kindred worker" category during the decade 1950 to 1960 is due in large measure to a substantial increase in the number of Negroes in occupations requiring important technical skills. For example, there was a five-fold increase in the number of Negro engineers, designers, and draftsmen from 41 in 1950 to 218 in 1960.[11]

The increase in Negro representation among female professionals was the result of regular increases in opportunity for Negro nurses, female school teachers, and social workers.

The manager and proprietor class had very little Negro

membership. Over half of the males who are so classified were proprietors of small businesses with a primarily Negro clientele. In 1960, only 422 male Negroes were classed as managers and proprietors and of those only 163 were salaried officials in private business.

There has been considerable demand for clerical employment in Boston because of the massive record keeping associated with the insurance industry. The larger bureaucratic companies have instituted extensive recruitment programs that have led to increases in Negro clerical employment, especially for females. However, many of the smaller firms and the clerical operations of other industries have not afforded very many opportunities to Negro clerical workers. The Negro was and is still underrepresented in this area. Similar processes have occurred in sales occupations. Wartime shortages and the passage of the law produced integration in some of the larger department stores and in some other sales occupations, but most sales jobs remained closed to Negroes. This was particularly true of the lucrative types of sales jobs open to men in manufacturing and wholesale trade.

The skilled trades have presented a varied range of opportunity for Negroes but they have also been a source of frustration. The increase of Negro representation in the "craftsmen and foremen" category was a product of increasing opportunities for mechanics, machinists, and repairmen. Ever since 1940 these categories have accounted for between one half and two thirds of the total. Negroes were also well represented in some metallurigical trades, constituting for example, 12 percent of the metal molders. On the other hand, Negroes have never been well represented among foremen, or in the construction, electrical,[12] or railroad trades.

The operative category also presented a mixed picture. In 1940 most male Negro operatives were concentrated among teamsters, laundry and dry cleaning equipment operators, and in the food, apparel, textile, and leather industries. By 1960 Negroes were still represented in those capacities but had also come to occupy many positions in the electrical and metallurgical industries. Negro women were also concentrated in laundries and in food, apparel, or textile manufacturing businesses but had moved into assembly work in the electrical equipment industry during the fifties.

Negro service workers have always been concentrated in the ranks of the janitors, porters, cooks, domestics, elevator operators, attendants, and charwomen, and underrepresented in the protective categories, policemen, firemen, guards, and watchmen.

Some clear areas of discrimination remained in 1960. The substantial gains made during the forties and fifties led some officials to minimize the problems of employment discrimination in 1960. They did not attempt to claim that employment discrimination does not exist. The official phrase was "pockets of discrimination remain."[13] Unfortunately these "pockets" contained a high proportion of the high-paying and high-status positions in the economy.

Civil rights leaders admitted that a broad range of opportunities has developed, but continued to complain about perennial problems in important sectors of employment. The author has validated many of the allegations of the civil rights leaders with both census information and interviews with business leaders. There are several spheres within which Negroes faced and still face considerable discrimination:

1) *Positions of line authority.* Negroes are seldom promoted to either blue-collar or white-collar positions of line authority except in departments that are primarily Negro. Thus, various managerial and executive positions in production supervision and even low-level leadership jobs within plants are not ordinarily given to Negroes.

The difficulties facing Negroes in advancing through executive hierarchies have militated against the participation of Negro men in the extensive banking and insurance industries in Boston. Positions were available at the entry level, that is, relatively low-level clerical positions, but such opportunities tend to be unattractive if there is little chance for future advancement.

2) *Sales positions.* Some Negro females were able to find jobs as sales girls, but major opportunities for sales careers were still closed to Negro men in 1960. Remunerative positions in industrial and wholesale sales were not ordinarily open to Negroes. The restriction operated even in sales to the Negro community. At the time the field work for this study was completed only two Negroes were employed as route salesmen for companies supplying the Roxbury area stores with consumer goods. Most of the small shops in the Roxbury area and all of the large chains were still owned and operated by whites. One could walk for a block in Roxbury and not see a single Caucasian until one stepped into a business establishment.

There were Negro insurance men and Negro real estate men but these businesses were also dominated by whites, even in the Negro districts.

3) *Certain skilled crafts.* Several factors operated to minimize Negro employment in skilled crafts. Crafts which are controlled by unions are often hard to enter. In some cases, the union did not actively discriminate against Negroes but favored the relatives and friends of persons who already worked in the craft. Where unions control entry into the craft and allocate craftsmen to jobs, as in the case, for example, in many segments of the construction industry, Negroes can face difficulties even where business is operating without discrimination.

One of the barriers preventing entrance into crafts was the difficulty of entering apprentice training programs. The census classified only four Boston Negroes as apprentices in 1940. By 1960 the number for the entire Boston metropolitan area was still only twenty-two. Discrimination against a person with important industrial skills was rare, especially when those skills are in short supply; the difficulty is in acquiring the skills. Admission to apprenticeship is usually either controlled by unions, many of which impose selective barriers, or is a reward for good performance on the job, in which case the Negro faces the constraints that always apply to the upgrading or promotion of Negroes.

4) *Position in small firms.* Many small firms develop an ingroup feeling. There is a great deal of emphasis on working together. The small firm is not dependent on bureaucratic procedures for developing and administering a labor force. Administration is on a personal, face-to-face basis, and personal preferences play a large role in personnel decisions. Many small firms operate on a familistic or quasi-familistic basis, excluding not only Negroes, but all who do not meet whatever idiosyncratic standards might be imposed.

5) *Certain nonsales positions involving contact with the public.* Certain types of repairs and installations involve entering people's homes. This has been one of the factors producing exclusion of Negroes from jobs in the public utilities industry, and minimizing Negro employment as electricians, plumbers, and similar occupations.

Various kinds of business occupations besides sales require extensive participation in social relationships and dealings with other businessmen.

6) *Other barriers.* In addition to the special barriers imposed on the positions and roles described above, there are a number of other types of discrimination which are prevalent in occupations and firms in which Negroes find employment more readily. For example, firms often limit the number of Negroes they hire in certain departments

47

or capacities out of fear that the job or department may become defined as "Negro," thus scaring away potential white applicants. In some cases firms limit Negro employment to light-skinned "attractive" Negroes whom they think will be more acceptable to other employees or customers.

The various dimensions of business treatment of Negroes will be more fully treated in Chapter III. The present discussion can be summarized in a few simple statements. By 1960 the Negro *had* broken through the skill barrier. Negroes who had acquired important technical skills were usually afforded the opportunity to use them. The Negro had not broken through the human-relations barrier. Jobs that required human-relations skills rather than technical skills have remained closed to Negroes until very recently. A white person untrained in technical skills may be able to exploit his personality; a Negro without a technical skill is doomed to service or laboring occupations.

The limitation of high- and medium-status employment for Negroes to technical positions in combination with the various barriers to technical education and training for Negroes, have produced a Negro population with relatively low economic status.

The relative economic position of whites and Negroes is placed in dramatic contrast by comparing the median incomes of the two groups. In 1959 median Negro income per person was less than three quarters of median white income per person. Median Negro income per person increased between 1949 and 1959, but the increase was only barely enough to keep pace with the increases in white income. The ratio of Negro to white median income was virtually constant during the period, changing from 0.724 in 1949 to 0.720 in 1959. Among males the ratio of median Negro income to median white income actually *declined* from 0.719 in 1949 to 0.662 in 1959. The figures for the total population remained constant because the relative loss among males was compensated by a gain among females.

Female employment was concentrated at the lower end of the occupational scale for both whites and Negroes. Negro women were more concentrated in factory work and white women in clerical occupations, but the rates of pay in the two spheres were comparable. Hence, income comparisons between women do not show the same striking differences as comparisons among males. The relative exclusion of Negro males from the more remunerative occupations brought about a relative decline in Negro male income.

The relative economic deprivation of the Negro community has continued despite a considerable improvement in the relative educational status of the races. Between 1950 and 1960 the median number of school years completed by nonwhites increased by one full year from 9.5 to 10.5. During the same period the mean number of school years completed for the whole population increased by only three tenths of a year from 11.8 to 12.1. By 1960 the ratio of school years completed among nonwhites to school years completed for the whole population stood at 0.868. In 1950 it had been only 0.805.[14]

The comparisons between white and Negro income and education are presented in tabular form in Table 6.

Negro Housing in Boston

Almost from the beginning the Negro community has been residentially segregated, at least in the de facto sense. In the earliest days most of the Negro population was permanently attached to white households as slaves or servants. As the free population grew, it settled in a common area, and this pattern of segregation has contin-

Table 6. Median annual income (dollars) and median education (school years completed) by Negroes and whites in the Boston metropolitan area, 1950 and 1960

Category	White	Negro	Negro/White	Total population	Nonwhite	Nonwhite/total
			Income[a]			
Persons 1950	2191	1587	0.724	–	–	–
Persons 1960	2291	2369	0.720	–	–	–
Males 1950	2796	2011	0.719	–	–	–
Males 1960	4737	3136	0.662	4657	3027	0.650
Females 1950	1423	1199	0.843	–	–	–
Females 1960	1836	1765	0.961	1804	1741	0.961
Families 1960	–	–	–	6687	4447	0.665
Families and unrelated persons 1960	–	–	–	5537	3232	0.584
			Education[b]			
1950	–	–	–	11.8	9.5	0.805
1960	–	–	–	12.1	10.5	0.868

Source: U.S. Department of Commerce, Bureau of the Census, Census of Population, 1950, vol. II, pt. 21; 1960, vol. I, pt. 23.

[a]Median income in dollars among the population fourteen and older with income.

[b]Median school years completed among the population twenty-five years of age and older.

ued though the area of Negro residency has changed location several times. Originally pockets of Negroes lived in various portions of the North End and middle sections of the city. Then, in about 1800, the Negro population began to move to the West End. By the Civil War virtually all Boston Negroes were congregated in a compact section of the West End on the northwesterly slope of Beacon Hill from Jay Street to several blocks below Cambridge Street. Well-to-do Negroes led a migration to the South End in the last decade of the nineteenth century and gradually the West End became a Jewish area. Then, as the South End deteriorated, the movement to Roxbury began. By 1910, the area enclosed by Northhampton, Ruggles, Washington and Tremont streets was the principal area of Negro concentration. By contrast, in Cambridge the Negro area has never changed; it has always been located along the Charles River in the Cambridgeport area.

Roxbury has been the main Negro residential neighborhood since the turn of the century. The general movement has been southward toward North Dorchester and Negroes have now moved into the fringes of North Dorchester itself.

The extension of the boundaries of areas open to Negroes has not occurred on a block by block basis. No single area of the city has ever been devoted entirely to Negro occupancy. In 1960 Roxbury was 57 percent white and only 43 percent non-white.[15] There were only two census tracts that are more than 90 percent Negro and fifteen tracts were more than half Negro.[16]

Since some whites live in the area of Negro concentration it is not entirely accurate to term this area a "ghetto." On the other hand it was a ghetto in the sense that Negroes were limited to its confines. Ninety-eight percent of the city's Negroes live in the three adjoining neighborhoods of

51

the South End, Roxbury, and North Dorchester plus small adjoining sections of Jamaica Plain and the Back Bay.

Eighty percent of the Negro population is concentrated in 20 adjoining tracts among the city's 156 tracts:[17] In the words of one commentator: ". . . it is safe to surmise that the only reason Boston doesn't have a Harlem or a South Chicago is that we don't have enough Negroes yet to completely fill this belt."[18]

A similar situation prevails in the suburbs. Ninety-eight percent of all Negroes living in Boston suburbs are in eight inner cities and within those cities, Negroes are concentrated in a few census tracts.[19]

The "color tax." That the supply of housing open to Negroes was limited can be demonstrated by comparing the rents that were paid by whites and Negroes for comparable housing.

Of the rental housing units occupied by whites in the city of Boston, 13.4 percent were substandard, either because they lacked plumbing, or were dilapidated or deteriorating. In contrast, 25.6 percent of the rental units occupied by Negroes were substandard.[20]

Negro families paid higher rents for substandard housing than whites. The median gross monthly rental (including utilities and fuel), paid by Negroes for substandard units was $65. Median gross monthly rent for whites in similar units was only $59. Median contract monthly rent for substandard units was $35 for whites and $44 for Negroes (in substandard units.) More than 16 percent of the substandard rental units occupied by Negroes cost more than $80 per month.[21]

Yet, a national study shows that in 1965 substandard Negro housing was in *worse* condition than substandard white housing. The rental units in the worst state of repair are designated as dilapidated. Of the substandard units occupied by Negroes 37.7 percent were dilapidated while only 17.7 percent of the white substandard units were in this condition.[22]

The greater price to Negro occupants cannot be attributed to the relatively large size of the family on the theory that large families require large apartments. Negro families *are* larger but they did not find larger apartments in consequence. Median number of rooms per dwelling unit was 4.5 for Negroes in Boston and 4.6 for all dwellings.

The relative exclusion of Negroes from low price housing can be shown by examining the non-white occupancy of accommodations in various price ranges. In general the lower the rental the larger the proportion occupied by non-whites. However, this tendency was reversed at rentals of less than $40, indicating the exclusion of Negroes from the least expensive housing in various parts of the city.

The relatively high rent which Negroes had to pay for relatively poor accommodations is sometimes referred to as a "color tax." The color tax can be a considerable burden to the economically depressed Negro. It forces the Negro to pay a large proportion of his small income for housing, of poor quality.

Negroes as homeowners. Negroes were under-represented as home owners and the homes that they own tend to be substandard. Table 7 shows the representation of non-whites as home owners in 1950 and 1960 for the city of Boston and for the SMSA.

Eighty-eight percent of white owner occupied units in the city were sound and included all plumbing, but only 59 percent of the nonwhite owner occupied units met that standard.

Economic pressures in housing and employment are considerable. Discrimination can be expensive. When manpower resources are not utilized, output is curtailed. The social cost of inefficient use of human resources may be transmitted to the businessman in the form of reduced

Table 7. Index[a] of home ownership of nonwhites in the City of Boston
and the Bostom Metropolitan Area in 1950 and 1960

Year	City of Boston	Metropolitan Area
1950	0.54	0.42
1960	0.57	0.41

Source: Data computed from Commonwealth of Massachusetts, Brief for Petitioner, Commission Against Discrimination v. A. J. Colangelo et al., Supreme Judicial Court for the Commonwealth, January sitting 1962, p. 99.

[a]Ratio of percentage of nonwhites who are homeowners to percentage of nonwhites in total population.

profits. For example, the general scarcity of manpower in wartime accentuated this problem and in consequence we saw wartime increases in the use of Negro manpower.

On the other hand, wartime conditions did not produce breakdown of racial barriers in the housing market. There is no indication of any appreciable decrease in residential segregation between 1940 and 1950. One index of segregation stood at 86.3 in 1940, 80.1 in 1950, and 83.9 in 1960.[23]

The restriction of Negroes to well-defined areas was clear in 1940 and remains clear today. Economic pressures have operated to expand the boundaries of the ghetto but have not produced a general trend in the direction of open occupancy. Discrimination in housing has a set of associated social costs. A captive market reduces incentive to maintain housing structures in good condition. In the absence of open occupancy, urban renewal attempts tend to fail. Residential segregation produces de facto segregation in schools. As in the case of employment, the social costs of discrimination are the costs of misallocation of resources. But, in contrast to the labor market, these social costs are not communicated to important decision-makers in the private sector. In the first place the recipients of the "color tax" actually gain by the situation, and in the second place, the factor of prejudice affects perceived demand for housing in integrated areas.

Thus, the patterns of Negro housing appear to reflect the prejudices of the community rather than its values.

CHAPTER III. DISCRIMINATION: VALUES, NORMS,

AND SOCIAL STRUCTURE

We don't discriminate against Negroes; the tenants do.—[A Boston landlord]

Normative Conceptions of Equal Opportunity

Malcolm Ross' reference to the "divisibility of the New England conscience" illustrates a common proclivity among social analysts; discrimination is frequently represented as a simple case of deviance. Men cut themselves off from their value premises in order to indulge their prejudices. According to one version of this theory, there is a split between the ideals to which Americans pay lip service and their "real" feelings of prejudice. Thus, Bernard Rosenberg and Penney Chapin interviewed business officials to ferret out the prejudice, ambivalence, and stereotyping that lay beneath their surface disclaimers of discriminating behavior.[1]

Discrimination is described as if it were a product of inconsistent attitudes within the individual and this same psychological inconsistency is also seen as the germ of a possible solution to the problem. Progress in implementing equal opportunity will come about as men try to avoid becoming impaled on the horns of the American dilemma.[2]

There is an element of validity in this conceptualization. The normative tradition *is* a powerful force for improvement of the Negroes' status and discrimination *can* produce psychological tension in the individual. The importance of prejudice, both manifest and latent, should not be minimized.

56

On the other hand, exclusive focus on the consequences of prejudice may obscure the structural elements in the production and maintenance of discrimination. In recent years sociologists have stressed the inadequacy of the concept of prejudice and insisted on greater attention to the institutional framework within which race relations occur.[3] According to this view "attitudes are subordinated to and mobilized by definitions of the situation supplied by organizations."[4] It follows that if analysis is limited to attitudes toward Negroes and equality the analyst will overlook the institutional settings, the norms, and the organizations that shape the expression and inhibition of attitudes.

Full appreciation of the structure of discrimination requires analysis of at least two sets of factors besides personal attitudes. The sociologist must study the normative patterns and social structures that define and perpetuate discrimination.

In the first place several structural features serve to perpetuate unequal participation in society. Inequalities in some institutional spheres are reproduced in others. An unprejudiced person can apply standards in a completely universalistic and equitable manner and still exclude Negroes. Thus, to take a clear and current example, school administrators can operate segregated schools simply by assigning pupils to schools in their neighborhoods; residential segregation produces de facto school segregation without any intentional exclusion and with strict adherence to standards of selection. Analogues to de facto school segregation exist throughout society. In the last analysis the tendency to endogamy within racial groups is an ultimate source of unequal participation in the larger society because the ramifications of kinship patterns are reproduced in larger social structures. Furthermore, variable child-rearing practices in various groups produce persons who are either more or less equipped to cope with the competitive forces in modern society.

A second important dimension, one that is often overlooked, derives from the distinction between values and norms. Consensus as to the desirability of a society that affords equal opportunity is consensus at the value level and does not imply consensus at the normative level. Persons who agree that equality of opportunity is desirable may not agree as to what binding obligations are implied.

The community is made up of a number of actors in various types of roles. Action in social roles is regulated by norms that define the binding obligations incumbent on the occupants of various types of roles. Agreement on community values may leave considerable room for argument as to the content of these norms. Accordingly, we find divergent *interpretations* of the meaning of values in particular contexts existing side by side with value consensus at a more abstract level.

The two dimensions of discrimination that have just been introduced, the structural and the normative, are closely related. The particular definitions of equal opportunity that come to be institutionalized affect the degree of structural discrimination. The connection between the structural and the normative factors in discrimination is crucial because the ultimate capacity of law to restructure the participation of Negroes in the community is dependent on the capacity of law to effect the institutionalization of norms that deter structural as well as intentional discrimination. The eradication of the prejudiced attitudes that lead to intentional exclusion of Negroes attacks only one element of the problem because social forces maintain established structures despite changes in the attitudes of individuals.

Let us consider the normative dimension first.

There is a high level of agreement at the value level. Few members of the New England community would disagree on principle with the concept of equal opportunity. Even Carleton Putnam, the foremost Yankee apologist for segregation, avows his support of the principle of equal opportunity.[5] The most extreme position (and this is Putnam's position) is that equal opportunity is desirable, but in the case of Negroes equal opportunity cannot be implemented and we should not try. Innate racial inferiority is cited as an insurmountable barrier. The cancellation of equal opportunity for exceptional Negroes is justified by an appeal to administrative difficulties and other dangers. This is, of course, a limiting case of acceptance of equal opportunity. Many New Englanders accept the ideal in a less limited form. They are willing to make the link between equal opportunity and discrimination.[6]

One approach to nondiscrimination can be called the "fair-share" approach. The fair-share concept is prevalent among Negroes and is institutionalized in the demands made by some militant Negro organizations. Whenever a group makes a demand that the proportion of Negro employment in a given firm or industry approximate the proportion of Negroes in the community, or the proportion of Negro customers, or some similar standard, the fair-share standard is implied. Levels of skill and motivation in the Negro community, application patterns, the recency of Negro entry into the field, or vacancy rates are not treated as legitimate excuses. According to this type of thinking, discrimination exists until the Negro has his fair share.

Until recently the fair-share notion had not received vigorous institutional expression in the Boston community, but it is a pervasive habit of thought. The author asked one intelligent civil rights leader whether there was employment discrimination in Boston.

Q. Is there racial discrimination in Boston firms?
A. There certainly is.
Q. How would I go about proving that discrimination exists?
A. You just go down to the ___ building; you won't see many black faces.

The "faces" approach is really a weak version of the fair-share standard; there is no explicit quota set, only a demand to "see more faces." The question will inevitably arise, How many faces is enough? and it is clear that ultimately some standard of fairness is assumed.

In Boston even such conservative organizations as the Urban League are beginning to lean toward this approach. It is not enough for firms to sit back and take applicants as they come, treating them equally without regard to race; there is a positive responsibility to take active steps to improve the quantity and quality of Negro employment.

The legal definition of discrimination does not allow for reference to quotas and percentages. According to the legal approach, nondiscrimination consists in the universalistic treatment of all persons according to legitimate standards of qualification. In fact, it could be argued that active attempts to increase the number of Negro employees would be illegal since they would involve unequal treatment. Thus, in New York the State Commission Against Discrimination refused to enforce a quota agreement between the brewery industry and the Urban League.[7]

All the civil rights commissions have rejected the fair-share approach in most contexts. Some laws specifically protect the right to impose legitimate qualifying standards. The Massachusetts commissioners have been unanimously opposed to the fair-share standard, maintaining that non-discrimination is a matter of equal treatment not of percentages.

Businessmen, particularly employers, tend to stress the economic irrationality of discrimination, and in so doing tend to assimilate the value of equal opportunity to business ideology. Businessmen believe in the open society and in the equilibrium between reward and merit that is possible in an open society. They believe that the balance between reward and merit is a crucial factor in the efficient allocation of resources.

60

They also believe in the "cost" principle. Economic rationality means obtaining maximum output at minimum cost; accordingly, if discrimination is expensive, it should be eliminated. Thus, business tends to be responsive to the economic pressures that undermine discrimination. The personnel manager is interested in recruiting a labor force of maximum quality; to turn down qualified Negroes is self-defeating.

On the other hand, the personnel manager is interested in recruiting a labor force of maximum quality *at minimum cost*. Thus, if the ordinary channels of supply which suffice to satisfy the firm's manpower needs do not produce Negro applicants, the personnel manager does not feel any responsibility for taking the trouble to seek them. If patterns of Negro exclusion in other spheres of society are reproduced in his plant, that is no concern of his. If it is cheaper to hire trained personnel, then trained personnel will be hired. The firm accepts no obligation to provide training to groups who have not been able to secure equal training.

Business thinking reflects the American theme of individual responsibility. Equal opportunity is accepted as a value. It is seen as a complementary part of economic rationality. There is an obligation to apply standards universalistically. However, there is no responsibility to seek to implement equal opportunity as a collective goal of the society. One must obey the mandates of efficient allocation of resources insofar as the exigencies of the market come to bear on the firm; one need not correct deficiencies in the larger structure of the society. Ultimate responsibility rests with the individual (and in this case the individual Negro) to overcome obstacles, prepare himself, and seek available opportunities. The whole intellectual edifice is supported by a "cream will rise to the top" ideology.

In the process of assimilating the equal opportunity value to the economic rationality value, the businessman has come to define discrimination and good business as mutually exclusive terms. Discrimination is not good business, *but by the same token that which is not good business cannot be discrimination.* In this regard the business interpretation runs counter to the legal interpretation.

The standard of nondiscrimination institutionalized in industry and business is similar to the legal standard. Nondiscrimination is the fair application of standards. There is, however, a significant difference in the businessman's thinking. For some businessmen, race itself *is* a qualifying standard for many kinds of jobs and openings. Every position should go to him who can fill it best and to refuse to admit a Negro to a position that he can fill better than any other available applicant, just because he is a Negro, is discrimination, and it is reprehensible. But according to much business thinking, there are many positions that a Negro, by virtue of his race, cannot fill. If clients would object or refuse to buy, or if tenants would move out, then, in some sense, the applicant is not qualified. In short, if prejudice distorts market forces, one responds to the market, and thus to prejudice, not to an ideal conception of a "perfect market." This approach to the problem can be called the "racial-qualifications" approach.

The "racial-qualifications" definition was clearly in effect in at least thirteen of the twenty-seven Boston firms visited by the author in 1962. Representatives of thirteen firms *admitted* that certain types of positions were unavailable to Negroes. Sales positions, supervisory positions, and positions requiring contact with the public were most frequently mentioned. The other firms insisted that there were no bars of any kind to employment in any capacity, though some may have been merely expressing an official line. In view of the fact that these firms are among the most liberal in the area, it seems safe to assume that the "racial-qualifications" conception is widespread.

Nineteen personnel managers answered hypothetical questions designed to probe their conceptions of the meaning of discrimination.[8]

    Q. A company uses Negroes in its factory but it doesn't have Negro salesmen because of customer objection. Is this firm discriminating? Yes—6 No—13

    Q. A company insists that its managers be white because this job includes attending meetings at private clubs and in private homes. Is this company discriminating? Yes—11 No—8

The comments of informants who answered "No" to these questions are illuminating:

No, because again it becomes part of the qualifications for the job. We use French salesmen in Lowell because that's what kind of people they meet. Companies shouldn't have to hamper growth and profit to accommodate people's feelings.

No, that's a basic requirement of the job. It wouldn't be discrimination any more than if a degree in electrical engineering were required.

No, not if it is part of the practical operation of making a profit. . . Not if it keeps the company afloat.

No, that's just good business. It's a requisite of doing business.

Some real estate operators and property owners seem less interested in avoiding the stigma of discrimination. Profit and discrimination are not always defined as mutually exclusive.

It's discrimination. I do it. I do it to protect my investment.

Nevertheless, analogous reasoning does appear among realtors. Discrimination is arbitrary and unreasonable action unsupported by rational business considerations.

I haven't anything against Negroes, but if it jeopardizes the value of your property it can't be discrimination.

People are confusing the term "discrimination" with loss of income. I mean they aren't against Negroes but against losing money: it isn't discrimination, it's economics.

To me it isn't discrimination if I can't do it from a money angle because of other tenants.

We don't care where the money comes from. We want to keep the building full, so why should we care? We don't discriminate against Negroes, the tenants do.

The MCAD rejected the racial-qualifications approach. Although it admitted the possibility that for some jobs race might be a legitimate qualification, and established a procedure whereby exemptions could be granted, the Commission did not in practice grant such exemptions, and rejected a priori arguments that Negroes cannot perform certain jobs. They demanded that the Negro first be tried. Then if it turns out that he cannot fill the position, he can be dismissed. For example, a salesman might not be able to sell and his race may account for his failure, but he can be dismissed anyway.

In practice this type of question did not arise frequently, but the mental set of the commissioners was quite clear.

Q. What if a public accounting firm refused to hire a Negro accountant because the firm's clients objected to allowing Negroes to work and gather data in their offices?

A. No, that would subvert the purposes of the law, which is to stop just that kind of situation.[9]

In sum, antidiscrimination commissions in general, and the officials of the MCAD in particular, have taken the position that discrimination is a matter of unequal treatment, that the fair-share and racial-qualifications standards are not legally enforceable.

The Emergence of New Interpretations

One of the central assumptions of the theory of institutionalization is that interpretations of values serve to integrate the community. When established interpretations fail to satisfy, pressing social demands will become modified and new normative conceptions, with more integrative power, will emerge. Accordingly, it is important to examine the pressures that have come to bear on various conceptions of equal opportunity.

According to one version of the equal opportunity ideal,

Negroes must earn the right to enter the life of the community by developing the traits valued by the American tradition. At one time the mainstream of Negro protest conformed to this conception. It received classic expression in Booker T. Washington's famous "American Standard Speech:"

This country demands that every race measure itself by the American standard. By it a race must rise or fall, succeed or fail, and in the last analysis mere sentiment counts but little.

During the next half century or more my race must continue passing through the severe American crucible. We are to be tested by our perseverance, our power to endure wrong, to withstand temptations, to acquire and use skill; our ability to compete, to succeed in commerce, to disregard the superficial for the real, the appearance for the substance, to be great and yet small, learned and yet simple, high and yet the servant of all. This, this is the passport to all that is best in the life of our Republic, and the Negro must possess it or be debarred.[10]

The "American-standard" conception expressed the assimilationist ideal. As any minority group is acculturated it is to be accepted as part of the community, but acceptance may be delayed pending acculturation. In the meantime, because of the unacceptability of many members of the group, race remains a qualification for some positions and roles. Thus, there is a close affinity between the American-standard notion and the racial-qualification approach.

The American-standard idea, though it may have facilitated white acceptance of early Negro progress, did not bring the same degree of social acceptance as was granted to newly acculturated Caucasian immigrant groups. It became clear that the version of equal opportunity that had permitted the gradual assimilation of white ethnic groups would not serve the same integrative ends for the Negro.

The racial-qualification concept is highly unstable, even in the case of white ethnic groups, and there has been a predictable movement away from it. The upwardly mobile, middle-class elements of an unassimilated ethnic group refuse to be judged on a group basis, nor need they be so evaluated for they can very effectively mobilize the individualistic strain in American values on behalf of a demand for equal treatment. Leaders in the Negro middle class thought that the equal-treatment idea was a viable technique for increasing their participation in economic and social life. Equal treatment should afford opportunity to the able and educated Negro, despite the general cultural deprivation of his race.

The equal-treatment movement reached its culmination in the successful demand for Fair Employment Practice Commissions during the forties and fifties. Aided by wartime manpower shortages, the Negro made important advances during the World War II era. It was natural to attribute part of this progress to the success of the FEPC movement, and thus equal treatment under law became the central focus of Negro hopes. The demand for equal treatment could be successfully legitimized in terms of the American value system and the American legal tradition. Witness the success of the National Association for the Advancement of Colored People (NAACP) in education cases before the Supreme Court during the late forties and early fifties, culminating in an apparently complete triumph in the 1954 desegregation decision. Furthermore, it appeared that the demand for equal treatment was not only legitimate but effective, for many racial barriers seemed to have fallen under its power. Negro leaders put considerable faith in the potency of "color-blind" attitudes.

The delay and defeat of Southern school integration under the Court's order began to dampen enthusiasm. Intrenched Southern opposition to equal treatment played a role in defeating faith in the ordinary legal process. These factors are commonly cited as partial explanations for the new

Negro militancy,[11] but important as these problems were, especially in the South, the most important source of strain on the old modus vivendi had a different origin. Liberal optimism about equal treatment had not reckoned with the structural elements of the problem.

The demand for equal treatment led to considerable business acceptance of the obligation to be color blind. One factor that supported acceptance of this obligation was the discovery on the part of business that a change in attitude and policy in the upper echelons does not usually upset the status quo. A color-blind management can let the established social structure do the work of discrimination, leaving clear consciences. Color blindness does lead to some change, for some individuals can and will take advantage of an offer of equal opportunity. But change will be gradual because mere color blindness permits many of the forces of the status quo to continue operation. *Structural* or *passive* discrimination remains.

Structural discrimination has several sources which can be grouped in four categories:

1) *Differential recruitment.* All of the firms interviewed had, at one time or another, used standard bureaucratic techniques for generating a supply of labor and skills. Such techniques include newspaper advertising, the use of professional agencies, and systematic canvassing of educational institutions. However, these techniques are used only when the natural flow of labor is insufficient. To some extent labor forces reproduce themselves. Present workers inform their relatives, friends, and neighbors of opportunities. Personnel managers ask employers to suggest possible recruits. All of the firms interviewed relied to a greater or lesser extent on networks of primary-group affiliation as channels of information and recruitment.[12] It is a cheap and efficient method. Even when these techniques do not provide a sufficient body of qualified applicants, the second

line of recruitment may involve particularistic elements. Thus, one personnel manager actively recruited at a group of middle-class high schools in white areas at which he had personal connections with counselors. In general, reliance on such particularistic connections permits the discriminatory tendencies inherent in personal social networks to operate even within supposedly bureaucratic and universalistic organizations.

In addition to the structural sources of differential recruitment, there is a psychological source. Many Negroes wish to avoid the humiliation and embarrassment of discrimination and firms and neighborhoods that already contain Negroes seem to provide less risky opportunities.

2) *Decentralization.* In some cases, nondiscrimination is well institutionalized among personnel officials but the central personnel office has little power in making specific decisions.

Many personnel offices are simply central clearing houses. The central office recruits and processes a supply of possible applicants who are then sent to the various departments and divisions for further assessment and final decisions. Discrimination at this level can negate the universalistic attitudes of professional personnel men. In some firms hiring is entirely decentralized; there are no personnel specialists imbued with the theory of impartiality.

Decentralization is even more prominent in the up-grading process. Candidates for promotion must be evaluated on the job by their immediate superiors. Even unprejudiced superiors tend to sponsor applicants who belong to informal cliques. Thus, patterns of "ethnic sponsorship" develop that effectively exclude Negroes from advancement.[13]

When personnel decisions are delegated down the line, very subtle types of prejudices and preferences operate to favor members of particular ethnic groups and informal groups organized along ethnic lines and, consequently, to exclude Negroes.

Because of the effect of differential recruitment and decentralization, bureaucratization is sometimes a precondition for the implementation of programs of equal opportunity. Case studies of the efforts of the New York State Commission Against Discrimination illustrate the role of bureaucratic procedures. For example, the elimination of discrimination in a union hiring hall required elimination of the informal features of the "shape up," and the development of a regularized and controlled "first come—first served" system.[14]

The importance of bureaucratization is also illustrated in the author's studies of eight insurance firms. Personnel managers were interviewed at four large (1700-6000 employees) and four small (50-375 employees) insurance companies in Boston and Hartford. All of the smaller firms had personnel officers who were committed to the idea of nondiscrimination. None of these officers had the power to actually hire or promote candidates, though in some cases by catering to the desires of department heads, personnel men had been able to avoid having their candidates turned down. The small firms' recruitment techniques did not produce many Negro applicants. Only one of the firms had Negro employees, and that firm had only four. Personnel directors were happy with this situation because they anticipated difficulties with other departments if Negro applicants were to emerge.

Among the larger firms, employees were recruited directly in local high schools, according to very formalized and bureaucratic procedures. None of these firms had ever *tried* to recruit Negroes on a systematic basis, yet all employed Negroes in substantial numbers. None had less than 4 percent Negroes; one had nearly 7 percent.

Decentralization can have similar effects in housing. Top-level apartment owners can maintain a clear conscience while superintendents and other employees exclude Negroes.

For example, one large property owner maintained a firm commitment to open occupancy. Negroes lived in some of his buildings in predominately white areas. When asked whether any of his assistants might discriminate, this man responded:

I have a branch office. She's instructed that she must rent to Negroes. Janitors have been instructed too, but instruction doesn't make the difference. She's going to get herself in trouble with the law. I probably have superintendents that do this too.

In both housing and employment there seems to be a view that discrimination and particularism at lower levels is not the fault of management. Systematic campaigns to bureaucratize the allocation process in order to avoid discrimination were not to be found.

3) *Quasi-ascriptive standards.* Even when companies are fully bureaucratized and their recruitment procedures produce Negro applicants, Negro candidates may be at a competitive disadvantage. Some legitimate standards of qualification tend to work against Negroes. If Negroes have been excluded from a certain job category in the past, then the demand for experienced or trained applicants automatically excludes Negroes in the future. Similar considerations apply to such qualifying standards as seniority, location of residence, quality of schools attended, and income.

In some cases qualifying standards bear subtle relations to race, in which case they border on the illegal. Thus, the demand for "acceptability to the public," "acceptability to fellow workers," of "attractiveness," may require judgments that are likely to be influenced by racial factors.

4) *Cultural differences.* The historic isolation of Negro society from the mainstream of American development has permitted the maintenance of cultural variations within the Negro group. Characteristic patterns of child rearing, family organization, and peer socialization produce distinctive types of personality and motivation. The total life ex-

perience of living in a subordinate role may have determinate effects on Negro personality. In consequence, many Negroes may fail to develop the motivation and the personality traits that are valued in the larger society.[15]

Cultural deprivation in the home would not be as serious if it were not reinforced by de facto segregation in schools. The Negro child enters a vicious cycle involving insufficient preparation for insufficient training, a cycle which tends to perpetuate the exclusion of Negroes from full participation in the community.

In sum, exclusion from some areas of life inevitably produces exclusion from others, for institutional spheres are not totally separate; they are linked by a vast network of interdependencies.

Sociologists have called attention to the increasing bureaucratization of society. There has been an increase in the number and influence of organizations and institutions within which rational choice on the basis of technical criteria is supposed to prevail. However, even within bureaucratic structures and processes, networks of informal relationships exist. The nexus of solidary relationships is an underlying foundation of the total social order and its patterns are repeated within society's more bureaucratic organizations. In fact, two features of bureaucratic organization *facilitate* the transmission of patterns of discrimination. First, the emphases on efficiency and minimum cost support the use of established social patterns as channels of recruitment and communication. Second, the insistence on qualification according to universalistic criteria ensures that persons whose training is deficient by virtue of exclusion from some sectors of society will also be cut off from participation in other areas.

In consequence, whenever decision makers are oriented to economic rationality in the short run, they will be blind to the long-run social cost of the underdevelopment of stores of human resources. Such costs are only communicated by serious disturbances in the patterns of everyday life. When severe labor shortages or other disturbances threaten, the rational potential of bureaucratic organization can be released. Bureaucracy is tied to particularistic organization only by the exigencies of convenience, not by any normative valuation of particularism for its own sake. Direct action can cut through the ascriptive barriers that ordinarily operate within large-scale organization.

It is not surprising that Negro leaders should come to demand that bureaucratic power be put to use in direct attack upon patterns of unequal participation. As the limitations of policies of equal treatment have become clear, Negro leaders have come to demand affirmative action. Recognition of the insufficiency of the "color-blindness" approach did not await sociological analysis of the mechanisms of structural discrimination; the relative deprivation of the Negro group has been a sufficient stimulus.

The Negro upper-middle class can afford to remain content with equal treatment. Educated, and acculturated to middle-class standards, the middle-class Negro can accept equal treatment as a relatively effective guarantee of equal rewards. For the mass of Negroes, more active programs of equalization are required. As the demands of Negroes at lower levels in the social hierarchy achieve more effective political expression, pressures for a reinterpretation of the value of equal opportunity mount and the "fair-share" approach comes to be embodied in the concrete demands of organizations.

The demand for a fair share meets strenuous opposition at first for it does not seem to correspond to the value of equal opportunity; it even appears to involve discrimination against whites. The businessmen interviewed by the author in 1962 were unanimous in their rejection of any "quota" approach to nondiscrimination. None felt any moral responsibility to take active steps to combat structural discrimination. Only three had ever actively sought additional Negro participation. Two of these firms had sought Negro sales personnel for work in outlets in Negro areas and the other, a large government contractor, had been impelled by the federal government's compliance program.

The establishment of a quota is an obvious way of insuring the elimination of structural discrimination. However, a bald quota is difficult to legitimize, especially if discrimination against white workers is implied or threatened. The advocates of quotas are likely to assume an equivocal and apologetic tone:

No one in responsible leadership advocates firing whites to hire Negroes. Whitney Young of the Urban League . . . points out that his group does not demand the firing of any white persons or the use of racial quotas . . . Given the discriminatory job market of years past and the fact that Negroes have lacked opportunity and incentive to train for jobs from which they were excluded, there is a need for affirmative action to involve them in currently all white employment . . .

A rough rule of thumb in terms of numbers or percentages can help determine when the affirmative approach no longer will be needed.[16]

The demand for a quota is defined as a temporary expedient and affirmative action is taken to be repayment for past wrongs. Couched in this language, the demand for a fair share can be related to the traditional equal-opportunity value. We will see in a later chapter how well the proponents of a fair share have succeeded in placing their demands on a moral platform.

In sum, antidiscrimination statutes took shape at a time when the equal-opportunity concept was in ascendance. In Massachusetts, both the statute and its official administrative interpretation have stressed equal treatment, but there are indications that the strict equal-treatment interpretation may not effectively mediate social conflict in the community. The emergent demand for substantive equality, supported by both an aroused Negro working class and frustrating experiences with color blindness, could make the legal approach obsolete. Thus when we come to examine the actual administrative process it will be important to note whether the MCAD was ever able, in its informal negotiations, to make effective demands for more affirmative action.

CHAPTER IV. THE STATUTES

It works because we are asking for what everyone pays lip service to. The legislature isn't actually convinced about the bills.—[A civil rights lobbyist]

Passage of the Employment Law

The passage of a law proscribing discrimination is the end product of one phase in the institutionalization of equal opportunity. This section outlines the history of the original passage of the Massachusetts Fair Employment Practices Bill in 1946 and the Fair Housing Bill in 1959. From this outline will emerge a picture of the role of established and emergent interests in permitting or stimulating the legal institutionalization of an ideal. The account will also show the crucial importance of the existence of the ideal itself.

Massachusetts first enacted fair practices provisions governing certain kinds of state-supported employment in 1920. These provisions were supplemented in 1941, but in both cases the acts were bare policy statements without accompanying enforcement procedures. The core of the civil rights statutes under discussion is the administrative procedure that permits a realistic possibility of enforcement. This section chronicles the events leading up to the establishment of the FEPC in 1946 and the subsequent extensions of its jurisdiction.

The Massachusetts Fair Employment Practices Commission was created on the heels of the demise of the original federal FEPC after World War II.

The war had provided auspicious conditions for pressing Negro demands. The demand for manpower was great and so was the need for high morale in all segments of the population. Further, there was an intensification of the need to present outwardly clean hands for propaganda purposes. Perhaps the gap between the ideals that Negroes are being asked to fight for and the reality of Negro deprivation heightened Negro discontent and this, in turn, made it easier for Negro leaders to mobilize mass protest.

Other emergent social changes helped to create a sounder social base for effective organization for protest. The Negro had been moving to the North, had been becoming better educated, and had become a voter in two-party elections.

Negro discontent reached a fever pitch at the start of the decade of the forties. The beginnings of the defense effort had started to pull the nation from a decade of economic depression. But progress was considerably slower for the Negro worker. The depression had been especially hard on the urban Negro labor force. Unemployment and relief rates were two and ten times as great as comparable rates in the white labor force.[1]

As the Caucasian work force approached full employment, the Negro work force, excluded in large measure from the defense industry that was sparking the economic upswing, lagged behind. This produced a classic case of "relative deprivation." The prime Negro demand of the early forties was for broad inclusion in all defense industries.

Negroes and white liberals mobilized for the fight; the NAACP, the Urban League, the National Negro Congress, and diverse labor, professional, and religious groups participated in a variety of activities designed to communicate and dramatize their demands. Petitions, mass meetings, and propaganda battles were the order of the day. The support of white liberals was solicited and obtained. At first the response of the government was one of indifference, but public pressure plus a dramatic symbolization of Negro protest finally produced a direct government response. Spurred by a threatened "March on Washington," President Roosevelt created on June 25, 1941, the first Federal Committee on Fair Employment. The committee was given the power to receive and investigate complaints, to take appropriate action to redress valid grievances, and to recommend further action to the President and other branches of government.[2]

The subsequent history of this committee consists of a series of attempts to implement and strengthen this order in the face of powerful and stormy political attempts to eliminate or hamper its operations. The political opposition was ultimately successful. In 1944 Senator Russell of Georgia was able to secure congressional acceptance of a measure designed to bring the financing of the committee under the direct control of Congress and the next year the committee's appropriations were reduced by more than half. Further, an amendment to the appropriations bill specified that the money was for the purposes of terminating the functions of the committee.[3] President Truman continued the committee by executive order, but at the same time stripped it of its power to issue corrective orders, thus reducing it to a mere fact-finding body. The stage was set for its complete demise and on May 3, 1945, all active operations ceased.

Supporters of civil rights could see the incipient destruction of the committee and began a drive to establish a permanent FEPC with legislative backing but the movement was unsuccessful, and the civil rights forces turned their attention to the states.

The Movement in Massachusetts

Massachusetts did not escape the malaise and discontent that gripped the American Negro at the outset of the defense boom of the early forties. There, as elsewhere, the Negro did not feel that he was sharing in the general recovery. Depression conditions lingered in the Negro community and Negro leaders sought relief from the racial barriers that seemed to be responsible.

Governor Saltonstall responded by establishing a Commission on the Employment Problems of Negroes. The commission studied the distribution of the Negro population, the occupational and industrial distribution of Negro workers, the extent of Negro employment and unemployment, employer attitudes, the Negroes' relations with organized labor, and the role of the United States Employment Service. The commission concluded that the Negro was economically disadvantaged and faced racial barriers in employment. In 1942 its members passed on to the governor a set of recommendations for strengthening existing legislation against discrimination in state employment, public works, public utilities, and licensed employment agencies, and for bringing to the governor's office and other state offices a greater recognition of problems of equal opportunity.[4]

These recommendations fell short of calling for the legal prohibition of discrimination in private employment. However, the report constituted official recognition of the problem, and some of the recommendations recognized the need for some sort of efficient *enforcement procedure* if civil rights laws were to make a significant contribution to solving problems of Negro employment. The labors of the commission did not produce any immediate results.

In 1943 a nationwide outburst of riots and violence gripped the country, producing in their wake numerous committees designed to investigate the causes of racial tension and to mediate racial conflict. Boston's most dramatic outburst of intergroup tension was a disturbing wave of anti-Semitic vandalism. As in the case of a number of sister communities, the response was the establishment of a special committee, the Massachusetts Committee on Racial and Religious Understanding, created by Governor Salton-stall in 1943.[5]

This committee was the direct ancestor of the MCAD. Its function was to carry out investigations of discriminatory situations and to sponsor and assist educational programs designed to combat discrimination. Once formed, the committee supported passage of a Fair Employment Practice Act.[6]

The legislature, prodded by the FEPC movement which had turned its attention to the states, gave full consideration to a permanent FEPC law in 1945. The New England Division of the American Jewish Congress introduced a bill similar to the Ives-Quinn Bill which was being considered in New York. The AJC was able to secure support from a variety of sources. Indeed, the supporters of the legislation succeeded in shaping such a powerful image of the moral sense of the community that some political analysts thought the bill was sure of passage.[7]

The legislature's Committee on State Administration sent the bill to the House Ways and Means Committee where it suffered a blow from which it never recovered. On June 9 the committee recommended rejection and substituted a measure calling for a special legislative commission to study antidiscrimination legislation.[8]

The matter was considered on the floor of the House on June 20. In a session described as the "wildest of the current session" the House approved the idea of a special commission of inquiry by a roll call vote of 117 to 103. The Ways and Means Committee of the Senate swept aside the House recommendation and recommended consideration of the original legislation, but the motion was killed on the Senate floor by a 17-to-17 tie vote, with Senate President Arthur Coolidge casting the decisive vote.[9]

Political techniques. The story of the successful effort of the following year deserves presentation in some detail.

79

The techniques used in securing passage of antidiscrimination legislation reveal the interplay between written statutes, unwritten values, and organized interests.

The political methods of the unsuccessful 1945 campaign were not ill-conceived. The winning effort in 1946 was based on the same principles.

A veteran civil rights lobbyist outlined the principle to the author in succinct and frank terms:

> It [our method] works because we are asking for what everyone pays lip service to. The legislature isn't actually convinced about the bills.

The technique involves a paradoxical principle: the value system can be used as a tool to secure legislation designed to create compliance with values, even though the attitudes or the behavior of the community deviate from value ideals. The activities of the civil rights lobbyists are designed to make maximum use of the compulsive power of abstract values.

These activities can be divided into two categories:

1) *Programs designed to reinforce and interpret the values.* Such programs must create an image of value consensus and community support for the lobbyist's interpretation of the values. This is the technique used at public hearings. One musters support from as many sections of the community as possible and sends witness after witness to the stand to testify as to the moral necessity of immediate action. Preferably, the witnesses have a structural position that permits them to speak for a large segment of the community or for an important organization that has the function of a moral caretaker.

2) *Programs designed to put decision makers into a position where they must either act on behalf of the legislation or create an appearance of public disavowal of the values that have been established by the programs described above.* For example, a legislator may be confronted by a delegation

purporting to represent the moral sense of the community, and told that he must take a stand. Such a technique is not irresistible, but it puts the decision maker on the moral defensive and prevents him from handling the matter behind the scenes where pressures from powerful interests can win the day.

Let us turn to an account of the 1946 campaign and see these techniques at work.

In the fall of 1945, Governor Tobin, with the support, (in fact the prodding) of Republican Lt. Governor Bradford, created a Committee to Study and Recommend Fair Employment Practice Legislation. Former Mayor Frederick W. Mansfield was appointed chairman. The group was to study existing legislation and other proposals and work out a satisfactory statute for Massachusetts. But the act that they wrote was strikingly similar to the Ives-Quinn Bill in New York, and to the legislation proposed by the American Jewish Congress the year before. Boston lawyer Charles P. Curtis was a member of the committee and is sometimes alleged to have written the bill, but most observers give credit to the AJC. Whatever role Mr. Curtis played, the term "copied" would be more accurate, for most of its various provisions were quite directly copied from the New York legislation and the unsuccessful Massachusetts bill of the preceding year, though some of its provisions were somewhat stronger than those of the New York act.

The study committee unanimously backed the proposed statute and Governor Tobin introduced it into the legislature.

The fight for passage was engineered by Henry Silverman, executive director of the New England Division of the American Jewish Congress, in an ad hoc role as chairman of the steering committee of the Committee for a Massachusetts FEPC.[10]

The proponents of the bill adopted a strategy involving

what they termed a "people's lobby." Developing a people's lobby involves enlisting the support of a wide variety of groups and organizing local committees for support of particular pieces of legislation. The year before, the push had come from Boston alone. This time, committees were formed in thirty other communities. Religious groups, labor, veterans, minority groups, civic, business, and political organizations were involved in the campaign. A complete list of all the groups would be quite long. At one point Mr. Silverman assembled representatives of 160 different organizations in one room. Suffice it to say that the American Jewish Congress, the NAACP, the League of Women Voters, the CIO, the YWCA, the Democratic party, and the American Legion were among those represented. Father John Sexton, representative of Richard Cardinal (then Archbishop) Cushing and editor of the diocesan newspaper, *The Pilot,* served on the central committee and many Protestant and Jewish leaders were represented.

Throughout the campaign legislators were invited to meet with the FEPC Committee and explain their views. If they opposed passage, attempts were made to persuade them to change. In each case the committee demanded public commitment.

The first task was to obtain a favorable report from the Committee on State Administration. This committee held a public hearing on February 6, 1946, in Gardner Auditorium at the State House. Supporters of the bill packed the galleries with seven hundred spectators, who watched fifty persons testify in favor of the bill. Senator Saltonstall, busy fighting for federal FEPC in Washington, sent a telegram of support. Mayor Mansfield of the drafting committee reported that he had held eight public hearings on the subject and had heard over two hundred witnesses testify in favor of the legislation as against only one witness who had been opposed.

Henry Turner, chairman of the New York Commission, commented on his experiences, pointing to the success of conciliatory efforts and the infrequent use of the law's compulsive powers. High Boston officials of the Episcopal, Methodist, Unitarian, Congregational, Baptist, and Presbyterian churches spoke in favor of the ordinance as did representatives of the Massachusetts Council of Churches and the Greater Boston Ministerial Alliance.

Labor was represented by the Massachusetts Federation of Labor, the state CIO and several locals. Of course, minority group representatives also spoke in favor of the bill.[11]

February 18 was set aside for the testimony of opponents. Only one witness made an appearance. Jarvis Hunt, former president of the Massachusetts Senate, spoke as legislative agent of the Associated Industries of Massachusetts.[12] Mr. Hunt thought that the law would be a burden on business. He claimed that the employers of New York and New Jersey had found it intolerable and had had to stoop to under-the-counter dealing in jobs. Newspaper advertising had to be given up in favor of private reference systems. According to Mr. Hunt, the best legal minds in the Commonwealth had challenged the constitutionality of the proposed law.

The witness felt that Massachusetts was free of bias; he knew of no cases of discrimination. He complained that the governor had stacked the cards against the opposition by appointing a committee to decide what kind of legislation to pass rather than to determine whether legislation was needed. This had made the opponents feel that opposition was useless, and that, he alleged, was the reason why more of the many opponents of the bill had not come to speak against it.

Mr. Hunt was not correct in this judgment. More people did not come to speak against the bill because the proponents had taken the moral offensive. To speak against the

83

bill was to take on the combined religious and civic organization of the community. The position of the Associated Industries seemed hopeless, not because of the type of committee the governor had appointed, but because the Committee for a Massachusetts FEPC had created the appearance of an inexorable tide of organized public opinion. They had created the organizational symbols of the moral support of the community. Passage of some sort of act seemed inevitable to most observers,[13] but that did not mean the opponents had given up, as Mr. Hunt suggested. It merely seemed safer to work behind the scenes to force obstructive legislative maneuvers or eviscerating amendments, than to publicly oppose a bill of impeccable moral intentions.

The upshot of the public hearing was a unanimously favorable committee report. Even the two members of the Committee on State Administration who had opposed the 1945 bill went along this time. Support seemed to be mushrooming. The avowed support of leaders of both political parties and the unanimous committee recommendation heartened the pro-civil rights faction and analysts began to regard passage as a certainty.

Business became concerned. The Boston Chamber of Commerce conducted a poll of their membership and found that passage of the bill was opposed by a nine-to-one margin. Having discovered the degree of business opposition, they decided to work against passage. Warnings concerning the effects of the proposed laws on business practices were widely circulated. For example, the rules promulgated by the New York Commission were used as a weapon. The success of the New York law had been used as a debating point in Massachusetts. When the Chamber looked into the New York situation, they discovered that the commission had been very strict in enforcing a ban on any kind of pre-employment inquiry that might betray the race, religion, or national ancestry of the applicant. Even the question, "where were you between 1914 and 1918," was officially forbidden. The Chamber circulated New York's published rules as an example of how far a commission would go in interfering with everyday business practices.

Despite their efforts and the efforts of the Associated Massachusetts Industries, a vocal and organized opposition, comparable in breadth and energy to the Committee for a Massachusetts FEPC, did not develop. Businessmen confined themselves to behind-the-scenes maneuvers. They did not try to organize a massive grass-roots effort.

The public temper regarding open expressions of anti-minority-group feeling had been made quite clear by an event in March. In the course of debate on a proposal to teach racial tolerance in the public schools, Representative Charles H. Taylor is reported to have remarked, "This is just an attempt to whitewash the nigger." "What?" demanded a colleague. "I said 'whitewash the nigger, with two G's."[14] Minority groups set up a public clamor demanding Representative Taylor's immediate impeachment; his home was picketed and in less than a week he had been forced to an abject apology. "No offense was intended" he claimed. According to Taylor, in the district of Pennsylvania where he was raised, Negroes call each other "nigger" without rancor. He announced that he had "nothing but good will toward my Negro brother."

The lesson seemed plain. It would not be safe to oppose the forthcoming legislation by direct appeals to prejudice.

The next problem for the Committee for a Massachusetts FEPC was to move the bill out of the House Ways and Means Committee. On May 6, Ways and Means sat down to discuss the bill. In the words of one reporter:

What started out to be a leisurely discussion of the merits of the bill rapidly transformed into a one-hour bedlam on the fourth floor of the State House yesterday with 300 white, yellow and Negro citizens confronting legislative chiefs with a demand that the measure be brought out from the Committee at once.[15]

85

The shouting crowd demanded that Senate President Coolidge, Representative Roy Smith, Chairman of the Ways and Means Committee, and House Speaker Frederick B. Willis state their views. Then the group demanded that all members of the Ways and Means Committee come in and state their views. President Coolidge thought this a highly irregular procedure. He alleged that the legislative leaders thought that they were only being asked to come into the room to hear the views of several distinguished citizens who had helped to draft the bill. It was, said President Coolidge, as improper to ask a presiding officer his views as to ask a a judge how he felt about a case under consideration.

The *Boston Herald* reported that *all* legislators agreed that the demonstration had done no service to the cause. It was thought that the measure might pass eight-to-seven and a supposed lineup was reported. In reading the newspaper analysis of the day, we get the impression of a very close fight, suddenly jeopardized, perhaps fatally, by the massive attempt to influence the legislators.

Despite all the legislators' agreement that the supporters' tactics had not aided their cause, the Ways and Means Committee passed the measure to the floor with a favorable report, not by a vote of eight to seven, but *without dissent.* In fact, the vote in executive session *had* been eight to seven, but none of the seven opposers were willing to have their dissent recorded.

The floor battle began in the House on May 8. In a four-and-one-half-hour debate before packed galleries, Representative Robert Connolly led the opposition with dogged determination. Several members registered their opposition to the extensive lobbying efforts of the supporters of the bill.

Agitation from the outside is trying to drive us to do something we don't want to do.[16]

We saw an expression of mob rule led by a man who wants to get on the public payroll, wants to get his nose in the trough, wants one of these three jobs on the proposed commission which would administer this law.[17]

The comments of one representative who had voted against the bill the previous year indicates both a clear understanding of the tactics of the Committee for a Massachusetts FEPC, and a felt inability to escape them:

This legislature is on the spot, and rather than putting us in the position of saying that we are in favor of discrimination, we ought to pass some sort of bill here today.[18]

Representative Connolly was well aware of his opponents' tactics and attempted to counter them with an unprecedented motion that the house rules be suspended to permit Australian ballot on the issue rather than the usual roll call:

I have so moved because I believe that the secret ballot would give a true expression of the sentiment of this house and an accurate expression of public opinion . . . We have been subjected to pressure groups and I think that by voting secretly we will vote as we think.[19]

In other words, the only way to escape the pressure of mobilized public morality is to escape public visibility so that the forces of the established structure can operate in their usual fashion.

The motion was declared in order but was defeated after the floor leaders of both parties had argued against it.

A second strategy of the opponents involved bringing other value traditions to play on the issue. Massachusetts had never before established a quasi-judicial administrative agency, and administrative procedure eliminates some traditional rules of evidence, some traditional legal rights such as trial by jury, and the rigid structural separation of prosecution and judgment. In fact, the legality of the measure under the state constitution could be attacked. Questions of private property were also raised. The opponents could thus muster reasonable arguments to the effect that although discrimination is reprehensible, it should not be battled at the expense of traditional legal protections. The satisfactory experience of federal administrative agencies, operating under similar provisions and subject to similar judicial controls, helped to counter this argument. A substitute measure to simply declare discrimination a crime punishable according to ordinary procedures, thus defeating the easy administrative remedy that lay at the heart of the legislation, was defeated.

One tactic for demonstrating adherence to the principle of nondiscrimination and at the same time attempting to defeat an effective statute is to propose a substitute measure with weaker provisions, but the Committee for a Massachusetts FEPC had made it clear that only a vote for the measure *as written* was a vote against discrimination. Various weaker substitutes were defeated in early tests of strength.

Debate continued on May 14. The legislature spent nearly the whole day attacking and defending the techniques of the minority-group leaders who were pressing passage of the bill. A full gallery kept the pressure up. One representative attacked the gallery in these words:

It is discriminating for you to expect the Massachusetts legislature to pass an unjust, unworkable, discriminating act just as you have written it.[20]

Another legislator complained,

. . . unless you vote for House bill 1704, the CIO will get you.

Representative Connolly called attention to the ethnic origins of the bill.

I'm interested in who filed this bill . . . Last week the galleries were filled with Negroes but was this bill originated by Negroes? No, it was filed by Jewish people because the Negroes wouldn't have the ten cents carfare to come up here and file the bill. Somebody put up the money.[21]

Connolly received a gubernatorial rebuke for his intemperate language. His attempt to turn the pressure tactics against the backers of the bill by pointing to the extent of Jewish support was unsuccessful. After beating down half a dozen amendments and substitute bills, the act passed the final test in the House. By a vote of 164 to 59 the House voted not to refer the bill to the next session, whereupon the bill was engrossed by voice vote.

The substitute bill that came the closest to passing on the final day was a measure which would have allowed appeal to a court on questions of fact and trial of those facts by a jury, thus restricting the commission's role to investigation only. This measure failed 128 to 96.

With the exception of Mr. Connolly's vituperative outbursts, the opposition's tactics, their motions and their amendments were designed to escape the dilemma created by the Committee for a Massachusetts FEPC. Their actions professed great sympathy for the *goals* of the act but argued that the *means* were not appropriate. As one legislator expressed it:

I will vote against this bill because it will retard the cause of racial tolerance just as prohibition retarded the cause of temperance.[23]

Passage in the House set the stage for a repeat performance in the Senate. On May 15, even before the bill came to a first reading, the senators of both parties had caucused outside the Senate chamber. The decision of the caucus was to send the bill to the state Supreme Court for an opinion on its constitutionality. The idea of requesting an advisory opinion from the Supreme Court had been suggested to the senators by the Massachusetts Associated Industries.

When Silverman's forces got wind of this development, they swung into action. Any delay was to be avoided and consideration by the Supreme Court would be risky. A telegram campaign was begun and an ad hoc group began a twenty-four-hour State House vigil. On May 17, the Senate galleries were packed for the beginning of consideration of the bill. The Senate, *in open session,* could not carry out its caucus decision. After two hours of debate a motion to send the bill to the Supreme Court for answer to sixteen questions of constitutionality failed in a very close vote, seventeen to fifteen. Fourteen of nineteen Republicans supported the motion and twelve of thirteen Democrats opposed it. This was the closest to a party-line vote that had yet occurred and the supporters prevailed only because they were able to hold on to five Republican senators.

On May 20 the Senate, to gallery applause, again refused to send the bill to the Supreme Court by the same seventeen-to-fifteen vote. The bill was then sent to the Senate Ways and Means Committee where it appeared that the chairman would delay the bill by not allowing it out of committee. The chairman was immediately asked to pay another visit to the people's lobby and the bill was reported out of committee less than fifteen minutes after it had been referred to them. The report was favorable and there was only one dissenting vote. The bill came out of committee so unexpectedly that it went through three readings on the Senate floor and was engrossed by voice vote before anyone remembered to ask for a roll call. A roll call was duly requested and the measure was passed twenty-two to eleven, twelve of twelve Democrats and ten of twenty-one Republicans favoring passage.

On May 20 a motion was introduced in the House to defeat the bill by striking its enacting clause. The motion lost 134 to 157. The move only delayed the final signing of the act, which came two days later on May 23.

Thus, despite numerous defensive and dilatory strategies, an unwilling legislature passed the Fair Employment Practices Bill. It passed because the people's lobby mobilized the symbols of public consensus at every strategic juncture. Every hearing, every motion to table, every motion to substitute, every referral to committee, and every other parliamentary device encountered the public scrutiny of the peo-

ple's lobby. Every morally feasible objection to the law
was successfully defined as tantamount to rejection of the
expressed ideals of the community.

Passage of the Housing Law

The various housing laws passed without floor fights and
without formal public opposition. Several factors account
for the relative ease with which the housing laws were secured. The years between the immediate postwar era and
the late fifties had seen several developments that strengthened the public conscience on racial matters. The famous
1954 Supreme Court school desegregation case, and the
consequent struggles over its implementation, had focused
national attention on civil rights. Concern for civil rights
was further strengthened with the development of a more
vital Negro movement in the South, beginning with the
Montgomery bus boycott in 1957. The Northern mass me-
dia and public expression of Northern opinion was almost
universally favorable to desegregation. Public values were
more clearly expressed than ever before. Further Negro migration to Massachusetts, and a more effectively organized
Negro community, gave the Negro a more realistic capacity
to operate as an influential element in the body politic.

Civil rights advocates were able to work with a legislature
controlled by Democrats, whose various committee chair-
men and other parliamentary powers were willing to bring
moderate legislation to a vote without embarrassing public
displays of moral pressure. The unfailing success of civil
rights bills had made the legislators believe that whatever
the supporters of such legislation could move to the floor
of the legislature, they could push to passage. There is no
point in publicly opposing such legislation in a losing cause.

The fact that the housing laws were secured through more
direct access to the parliamentary machinery and without

91

vocal opposition does not mean that the principles of successful operation had changed. Strategy was still founded on the creation of a moral atmosphere which would make it difficult for opponents to operate effectively.

The first private housing bill was passed in 1959. It was drafted by the American Jewish Congress with the support of the Jewish Community Council and the NAACP. The equivalent of the Committee for a Massachusetts FEPC for this campaign was an organization known as the Massachusetts Committee for Fair Housing Practices Legislation. Again, the American Jewish Congress took a central role in the fight. The proponents of the legislation were able to have the legislation introduced jointly by the Speaker of the House and the Minority Leader. In the Senate, the legislation was introduced by the Majority Leader. The legislation went to public hearing before the House Legislative Committee on Mercantile Affairs where witness after witness, representing a wide variety of civic, religious, and minority groups paraded before the committee to testify to the evils of housing discrimination, the extent of discriminatory practice, and the need for remedial legislation. No organization spoke in opposition. A representative of the Home Rental Association (a branch of the Greater Boston Realty Board) was in attendance, but did not speak. One witness said that the hearing was so dramatic that he would have looked ridiculous if he had tried to oppose.[24]

The bill was moved along quickly. It passed the House and the Senate by acclamation and was signed by the governor on April 22. One active supporter of the bill gave this account of the passage of the bill:

We always avoid a floor fight. We never file a bill without getting a commitment from the men who run the state house, the President of the Senate, the Speaker of the House and the Majority Leader. Why will they favor our bills? I don't know. Senator Powers says how far he is willing to go and that's how we write it. That's half of it in a Democratically controlled legislature. If you can find a leader in the legislature, the opponents don't have the guts to fight it.

The futility of bypassing the established channels is demonstrated in the failure of a NAACP-backed bill sponsored by Representative Cella which would have prohibited all housing discrimination. It was defeated easily by standing vote.

The importance of routing civil rights bills through established political channels is further illustrated by the history of the later passage of the injunction amendment in 1961. The Commission had been hampered by the fact that housing cases became moot during protracted periods of negotiation and conciliation. A respondent could simply rent or sell the property to someone else while the case was still pending, thus denying the complainant realistic relief. An interlocutory remedy seemed in order and the American Jewish Congress drafted a bill that would permit the Commission to apply in Superior Court for an injunction to prevent the respondent from renting or selling property pending settlement of the case. In addition to providing interlocutory relief, the amendment created a powerful economic sanction to prevent dilatory tactics. The Massachusetts Rental Association was opposed to the bill. They did not believe that they could prevent passage of the bill but thought they could bargain for a bill they could "live with." On the other side, the AJC was not sure that they could pass the bill in the face of opposition from the Rental Association. The Rental Association drafted amendments to the bill calling for limitation of the number of units that could be held open to one unit and requiring three days' notice prior to the injunction hearing. The AJC accepted the amendments and took the bill to the leading figures in the legislature where it passed without opposition.[25]

The key role that the AJC has come to play in civil rights legislation has its obverse side. The channels of communication that it has built up in the course of numerous successful campaigns can be used not only to secure passage of additional legislation, but to block passage of civil rights acts that it does not favor. A bill was proposed in 1961 that would have prohibited discrimination by persons engaged in business with the Commonwealth. The bill would have authorized a compliance-reporting program similar to the one developed by the President's Committee on Equal Employment Opportunity. Compliance reporting can have beneficial effects, but the Committee on Law and Social Action of the American Jewish Congress objected to certain features of the bill. The "right people" in the legislature were contacted and the bill was killed.

The Opposition of Real Estate Interests. Considerable speculation and rumor surrounds the role of the real estate group in opposing the housing legislation. Some think that the housing interests were dissuaded from opposing the bill by the atmosphere created at the public hearing. They believe that the housing lobby did not feel that it could safely oppose the bill publicly and that the best course was to try to defeat the legislation by supporting, behind the scenes, a test of its constitutionality.

The official position of the Massachusetts Home Rental Association is that it did not oppose passage because its membership was evenly split on the issue. Hence their role has been one of insuring that all legislation passed includes maximum legal guarantees.[26] Most liberals in the Boston community are convinced that, despite its public protestation of neutrality, the association worked behind the scenes to defeat and subvert the act. There is some truth in both versions.

When the measure was about to come up for consideration, the board of directors of the association discussed possible opposition. Of the twenty-two members of the board, only one was willing to wage a public fight. Some Jewish members were particularly opposed. They did not see how they could reasonably oppose an act prohibiting discrimination against minority groups. In fact, some gentile realtors attribute the failure of the real estate interests to fight the bill entirely to the opposition of Jewish interests.

The decision of the board was that the law could be opposed, but not by the association as such. No letterheads or other references to the association could be used in raising funds. An officer of the association, whom we will call Mr. A, established the Massachusetts Owner's Fund. No important figures would lend their names to the group, but Mr. A continued his work. The association was polled as to its views on the law and as to whether it would contribute to finance a court test. The response was small, but among those answering, the overwhelming majority opposed the law. Mr. A discovered, however, that it was difficult to obtain funds in support of the opinions expressed in the poll. Mr. A contributed most of the money himself. The Massachusetts Owner's Fund financed the unsuccessful court test of the law, but the case had been lost in court before enough had been collected to pay the attorney. Mr. A was opposing the law on idealistic grounds. He believed that the right to use property as the owner sees fit was being eroded. He does not personally discriminate; his files contain letters thanking him for renting apartments to Negroes in his own primarily white buildings. He does not believe that property values were at stake in the case. He was very chagrined to discover that prejudice rather than idealism motivated the support of others who came to his aid.

The supporters of the housing legislation clearly overestimated the degree of unity and strength of opposition to the bill among the realtors and owners of real property. The legislation did not threaten the material and ideal interests of property owners in a uniform and powerful way. Very few real estate operators were willing to make a substantial investment of money or time and none were interested enough to risk their reputations in public opposition.

The experience of other communities shows that where

realtors are willing to make the necessary investment, measures of this type can be defeated. There is a large reservoir of grass-roots anti-Negro feeling in the housing market that can be mobilized in opposition to the value tradition.

The foregoing account suggests that civil rights struggles are won by the organizational prowess of minority groups, but surely organizational capacity cannot be denied the opposition. Successful resistance is possible if the opposition will take the necessary steps. It cannot be argued that Massachusetts realtors did not *know* that counter organization might be successful. They were aware that Rhode Island realtors were engaged in a successful grass-roots campaign to defeat a housing law, even as they were permitting the passage of similar legislation in Massachusetts. In fact, the organizer of the Rhode Island campaign spoke to the Massachusetts industry, offering his services for a similar effort in the Commonwealth.[27]

The problem remains as to why those interested in defeating the legislation did not take the necessary organizational steps to prevent passage. Two factors are involved here:

1) *Organizations that are opposed to the legislation place opposition low on the list of organizational priorities.*

Businessmen and business organizations had many problems in the post-World War II era. The National Association of Manufacturers and its local counterparts could have placed a great many resources behind opposition to the various state FEPC movements. However, the crucial legislative aims of these organizations were repeal of price control and legislation to curb labor. These were more important dollars-and-cents issues. Similarly, during the 1959 housing law movement, the prime goal of the Massachusetts real estate industry was tax reform, in the shape of lower property taxes and greater use of other forms of revenue.[28] Further, a bill to reestablish rent control posed a serious threat.[29] Mr. A's unsuccessful attempts to raise money for a court test indicate that, though feelings might have been strong on this issue, it was not worth very much monetary investment.

2) *Organizations that oppose the legislation face conflicts of interest within the group.*

All the members of the organization do not oppose the law. In the case of employment laws, some employers already hire Negroes, consider nondiscrimination to be morally and economically correct and welcome the support of law as a means of strengthening their position with respect to other employees, clients, and customers. Thus, for example, Carlton P. Fuller, executive vice-president of the Polaroid Corporation, testified in favor of the original FEPC bill.[30]

In the case of housing, the vocal protests of a Jewish minority with a psychological investment in the symbols of nondiscrimination were instrumental in preventing the most likely pressure group from taking a determined stand.

Constitutionality. The same factors that impeded effective opposition to passage also restricted legal attacks on the legislation after it was in the statute books.

During the debates on the first successful FEPC bill, it was freely predicted that the law would not survive a test of constitutionality. Some assumed that business would be able to kill the bill in court:

If this becomes law the legislature will look ridiculous when some employer with money takes the FEPC law to court and has it ruled unconstitutional.[31]

The expected court test of the employment law never came. The law as administered by the Commission did not threaten any employer's vital interests enough to justify the expense of litigation.

Adjudication of constitutionality, when it did come, revolved around a housing case. Fourteen years passed before

97

antidiscrimination legislation met a constitutional challenge. In 1960, A. J. Colangelo, owner of Glen Meadow apartments, refused to comply with an order of the Commission to cease denying accommodation to Maurice Fowler, a Negro contract negotiator for the United States Air Force.[32] The Commission submitted a petition to Superior Court begging enforcement of the order. Colangelo, financed by the small group of realtors and apartment house owners mentioned above, challenged the constitutionality of the law. He alleged that the action of the Commission was a taking of his property without compensation, and an invasion of his right of liberty to contract. In addition, a second respondent, John Nahigian, rental agent for Colangelo, alleged that the law infringed upon his freedom of association.

Attorneys for the Commission claimed that the law served a legitimate public purpose, that the means utilized by the statute were reasonable, and that the classifications it established were reasonable. In a split decision the Court upheld the act, ruling that the legislature's motives in passing the statute must be presumed valid, and that the act was within the police power of the state.

The legal attack, a decade and a half in coming, was poorly financed and has not been repeated. The law, and the activities of the Commission under the law, have not been subject to a direct organized attack.

The passage of antidiscrimination statutes is one element in the institutionalization of equal opportunity. Through legislation, one interpretation of the value tradition is given official normative expression and specified kinds of deviance become subject to official sanctions. Legislation may not immediately remake the society but it can provide both an enforceable interpretation of the value tradition and administrative machinery for the enforcement process. Legislation puts the organized power of the community at the service of those elements in the community with an interest in implementing equal opportunity.

It was the groups who received access to legal power that brought about passage of the law. Legislation is not a simple emanation from the value system. It is a product of an organized effort by groups with ideal and material interests in the equalization of opportunity. The success of the movement had a number of structural sources. The "liberal" groups were able to prevail because the opposition was not able to organize effectively. Lack of organization, in turn, was not a mere consequence of carelessness or sloth; it had a structural basis. The natural organizational sources of opposition are the groups whose activities will be regulated. These groups were not united in intense opposition. Many members either gave the issue a low priority or supported passage.

In short, the ideal had already achieved some measure of institutionalization. Some of the targets of the law already had psychological commitments to, or interests in, equal opportunity.

To say that legal institutionalization depends on an appropriate organization of interests in the community is not to say that the value tradition was not involved. The movement was not a mere power struggle. Much of the latent power of the opposition was enclosed in a moral muzzle. The civil rights lobby did not prevail simply because it was organized; it prevailed because it was organized to express and enhance community values. The value tradition gave the movement justification and a leverage on the status quo. The movement used the value tradition to prevent the forces of the status quo from achieving political expression.

It is important to recognize that packed galleries do not, by themselves, produce desired legislation. Just two months before FEPC carried, an unruly crowd of five hundred veterans jammed into a hearing to demand passage of a bill to provide a nine-hundred-dollar bonus to all veterans, to be financed by a state lottery. Their efforts were unsuccessful, but the full galleries at FEPC hearings and debates did not represent mere political pressure; they symbolized the voice of moral obligation. The legislator might have his own opinions on the moral dimensions of the issue, but the FEPC lobby forced him to compare his views with those of the community's specialists on religious and civic morality.

The same principle used in attracting support within the legislature also operates in building pressure outside the legislature. The individual minister, civic leader, or official may be uncertain or lukewarm on the legislation, but unable to find a satisfactory way of refusing to participate in the movement. In fact, it was alleged on the floor of the legislature that the governor and the lt. governor did not really want to see the bill passed.

The movement mushrooms on the same principle that supports Southern segregation. Only certain sentiments are expressible. The Southern moderate and the Northern racist are prevented from introducing their views into discussion. As a result they come, for lack of social support, to underestimate the degree of public support for their position.

In the case of the housing law, real estate leaders incorrectly assessed the possibilities of successful opposition. Despite their knowledge of the Rhode Island experience, they dreaded the power of moral opinion. Yet, proponents of the law knew that an organized campaign similar to the Rhode Island realtors fight would defeat the bill. Civil rights leaders were following the Rhode Island campaign at the same time they pushed passage of the Massachusetts law. They thought that the Massachusetts realtors did not know about the Rhode Island campaign and were apprehensive that the opposition would learn of the possibility for building grass-roots support.

That real estate interests knew of this possibility, but

were afraid to act upon their knowledge, is eloquent testimony to the compelling force of the symbols of community support for social values.

It would not be accurate to state that the supporters of the bill won because they discovered an effective rhetoric. The roots of their success lay deeper than mere rhetoric. Almost any cause, including bonuses for veterans, can be provided superficial garb from the value tradition at a merely rhetorical level, but the organizational devices of the civil rights movement effectively symbolized a deeply-rooted and compelling strain on the American ethic.

The Provisions of the Statutes

Further exposition of the activities of the MCAD and the problems of enforcement will require a prior description of the main outlines of the provisions of the written laws which established the right to equal treatment and created procedures for the protection of victims of unequal treatment.

The statute as finally approved on May 23, 1946, was entitled "An Act Providing For a Fair Employment Practice Law and Establishing a Commission to be known as the Massachusetts Fair Employment Practice Commission, and Defining its Powers and Duties."[33]

Section 1 established the right to work without discrimination in these words:

The right to work without discrimination because of race, color, religious creed, national origin or ancestry is hereby declared to be a right and privilege of the inhabitants of the commonwealth.

Sections 2 through 4 created the administrative agency and gave it the appellation "Massachusetts Fair Employment Practice Commission." The act called for a three-member commission, the members to be called commissioners and to serve for terms of three years. (The number

101

of commissioners was increased to four in 1963.) One of the commissioners was to serve as chairman and to receive a salary of $5,000 per year and the other two members were to receive salaries of $4,000 per year. (These salaries have since been raised to $9,500 and $6,000 respectively.) The commissioners are appointed by the governor, subject to the advice and consent of the governor's council.

There are two basic types of commission organization in the field of civil rights. They can be called the "strong commission" and the "strong executive secretary" forms. When the commissioners are paid substantial salaries they tend to be few in number and to take responsibility for the day-to-day administration of the commission. Relatively large renumeration implies full-time duty. In other states a larger number of commissioners are reimbursed only for expenses, or are paid a per diem for the days they are active.[34] In these states, responsibility for day-to-day administration tends to be lodged in a full-time professional executive secretary, and the commissioners devote the majority of their time to other pursuits, limiting their active participation to setting major policies and to sitting in judgment at formal hearings.

In this respect the Massachusetts Commission has an in-between status. It is somewhat ambiguous as to whether the commissioners are full-time or not. The mode payment is not per diem for days actually engaged in Commission business, but the salary paid is not large. In practice, Chairman Mahoney treated her position as a full-time job and the other members of the Commission have often been appointed from the ranks of persons occupying other full-time occupational roles in the community. The result has been to give Massachusetts the "strong commission" rather than the "strong executive secretary" for the organization, with one of the commissioners, the chairman, carrying the major burden of administration.

Both forms of organization have advantages. Full-time commissioners are sometimes race relations specialists with a special commitment to equal opportunity. Such commissions may institute vigorous and aggressive enforcement policies. On the other hand, if part-time commissioners take a more neutral stance, limiting their role to arbitrating cases, then the administrative staff can legitimately undertake a militant enforcement program without laying the commission open to the charge that prosecution and judgment are combined in one person.

Coverage. Section 4 of the law establishes Section 151 B of the General Laws of Massachusetts, which define unlawful discrimination and define and delimit the powers of the Commission.

No state has tried to outlaw all discrimination in blanket terms. The various state laws against discrimination all specify the types of discrimination and the types of organizations over which the law has jurisdiction.[35] The limitations on coverage have various sources. In the first place they reflect a conviction that some spheres of life are private and not subject to legal regulation. The legal regulation of discrimination begins in areas where interpersonal relations are relatively public, impersonal, and secular.

The first antidiscrimination statute covered only employment and exempted some types of employing organizations. Employers who employ fewer than six persons, and nonprofit social, fraternal, charitable, educational, and religious organizations are excluded. Any organization established for profit, labor organizations, employment agencies, and all of the branches of the government of the Commonwealth are included. Members of the family of an employer and his domestic servants are excluded from the coverage of the law. It is clear that the intent is to cover only relatively large, bureaucratic organizations and to exclude the small family firm and other relatively communal associations.

103

Definition of discrimination. Discrimination is not defined in great detail. The types of discrimination that are Specifically declared to be unlawful employment practices are these:

1) The use of race, color,[36] religious creed, national origin, or ancestry as a criterion for:

a) barring from employment, refusing to employ, discharging from employment, or discriminating in the compensation, terms, conditions, and privileges of employment by any employer or any agent of an employer.

b) excluding from full membership, expelling from membership or other discriminating by any labor organization.

2) Printing or circulating any statement or publication which expresses any limiting or discriminating policies with respect to race, color, etc.

3) Making any pre-employment inquiry as to race, color, etc., or using application forms requesting such information.

4) Discriminating against any person because he has opposed any unfair employment practices in any way, including the filing of a complaint under the act.

5) Aiding, abetting, inciting, compelling, or coercing unfair employment practices.

Throughout the list of unfair employment practices, there is a qualifying provision to the effect that such practices shall be illegal "unless based upon a bona fide occupational qualification." The inference is that there might be some types of jobs that require members of particular ethnic groups. The Commission has ruled that employers may make requests that a bona fide occupational qualification exemption be established.[37] Such requests are to be accompanied by "sufficient evidence" to substantiate the claim.

Pre-employment inquiry. The prohibitions on pre-employment inquiries have led to considerable discussion and to attempts to clarify exactly what kinds of inquiries can be made and what kinds of inquiries are illegal. The Commission has made several official rulings in this regard. It has been declared lawful to require an applicant to write or print his name on an employment application, to inquire into the maiden name of a married woman, to inquire as to whether an applicant has ever been indicted or convicted of a crime, and to inquire into an applicant's place of residence. It is also lawful to inform an applicant that a job requires work on Saturday, to inquire as to citizenship or intention with respect to citizenship, and to inquire as to whether an applicant has ever been interned or arrested as an enemy alien. Nothing in the act forbids inquiry into an applicant's academic, vocational, or professional education, his work experience, or his character. One may ask for the location of places of business of relatives in the United States, or other persons who might be informed in case of accident. One may inquire into military experience. Organizational memberships may be requested except those which indicate by name or character the religion, race, or national origin of their members.

On the other hand, it is unlawful to make inquiry into the original name of a person who has changed his name, the birth place of an applicant's parents, spouse or other close relatives, an applicant's church, parish, or pastor, or the religious holidays he observes. It is illegal to inquire into an applicant's color or to require that an applicant furnish a photograph. Inquiry as to how an applicant obtained his citizenship or the citizenship of his relatives is deemed unlawful, as is inquiry into the location outside of the United States of relatives' places of business, or inquiry as to the location of any particular relative. The maiden name of one's wife or mother, the person's foreign military experience, and his whereabouts during World War I, have been declared not subject to pre-employment inquiry. A prospective employer may not inquire into an applicant's membership in organizations whose name or character indicate the ethnic composition of its members.

This variety of prohibitions and permissions represents an attempt to permit all of those kinds of pre-employment inquiry that are essential to determine an applicant's qualifications and to establish ways of keeping in touch with him, without at the same time permitting inquiries that seem to be designed to determine an applicant's ethnic identity. It is clear from the examples quoted above that the line between a bona fide administrative requirement and a discriminatory practice is difficult to draw.

Employers feel that there is a similar difficulty in drawing the line between a bona fide occupational qualification and a discriminatory qualification. The Commission has been more careful and detailed in defining conditions under which race or color might constitute a bona fide occupational qualification. In general it can be said that state commissions against discrimination have not been liberal in granting occupational exemptions. Grounds such as the desires of co-workers and the preferences of customers that would defeat the intent of the law, have not been accepted as legitimate qualifications.[38] The MCAD has not been an exception to the rule of strictness in establishing bona fide exemptions. For example, they have refused to establish exemptions where restaurants have claimed an interest in maintaining a certain decor and alleged that it was necessary to limit hiring to given ethnic groups in order to maintain that decor.

It should be noted that, according to the Commission, nothing in the pre-employment inquiry prohibitions prevents a firm from keeping records of the ethnic backgrounds of their employees. Although the statute reads that "it shall be an unlawful employment practice . . . to use any form of application for employment or to make any inquiry *or record in connection with employment* which expresses either directly or indirectly any limitation, specification or discrimination as to race, color, religious creed, national origin, or ancestry. . ."[39] The Commission has interpreted this provision to refer only to pre-employment practices.

Inquiries, answers to which would directly or indirectly disclose a person's race, color, religious creed, national origin, age or ancestry, are designated as unlawful practices when such inquiries are made PRIOR to employment unless based upon a bona fide occupational qualification. No restriction is placed on inquiries made AFTER employment provided the information is not used for purposes of discrimination.[40]

The powers of the Commission. The original statute gave the Commission a number of functions, powers, and duties:

The Commission is directed to maintain its central office in Boston and is empowered to maintain other offices if it deems them necessary. It is empowered to hold meetings, to appoint and compensate personnel, obtain and utilize the services of other executive departments and agencies, and to adopt an official seal.

The Commission is given the authority "to adopt, promulgate, amend and rescind rules and regulations suitable to carry out the provisions of this chapter and the policies and practice of the Commission in connection there within."[41]

The Commission is further empowered to create such advisory agencies and local or statewide councils as would aid them in their work through study of the problems of discrimination in general or discrimination in specific instances. Such councils are supposed to "foster good will, cooperation, and conciliation among the groups and elements of the population of the commonwealth . . ."[42] and to make recommendations to the Commission on matters of policy, procedure, and public education.

Thus, there is in the wording of the law considerable emphasis on the importance of the educational approach to intergroup relations. This is not only apparent in the provisions allowing for community councils, but is reemphasized in the next section which gives the Commission the power to "issue such publications and such results of investigations and research as in its judgment will tend to promote good will and minimize or eliminate discrimination . . ."[43]

The heart of the Commission's legal power to correct existing unfair practices is established by Articles 6 and 7 of Section 3 of the act:

(The Commission shall have the following functions, powers and duties.)

6. To receive, investigate and pass upon complaints alleging discrimination in employment because of race, color, religious creed, national origin, or ancestry.

7. To hold hearings, subpoena witnesses, compel their attendance, administer oaths, take the testimony of any person under oath, and in connection therewith to require the production for examination of any books or papers relating to any matter under investigation or in question before the commission. The commission may make rules to the issuance of subpoenas by individual commissioners.

The nature of the process of receiving, investigating, and "passing upon" complaints alleging discrimination is further spelled out in Section 5 of the law.

Complaints may come from several sources. A person who considers himself aggrieved by an unlawful employment practice may "make, sign, and file" a verified complaint in writing, or he may do so through his attorney. The attorney general of the Commonwealth may also file a complaint. The Commission itself, "whenever it has reason to believe that any person has been or is engaging in an unlawful employment practice" may issue a complaint. Finally, an employer whose employees are resisting the law may file.

After a complaint from any of these sources has been filed, the chairman of the Commission is to designate one commissioner as investigating commissioner. After the appointed commissioner (with the assistance of the Commission staff) has completed his investigation, he makes a determination as to whether "probable cause exists for crediting the allegations of the complaint." Upon a finding of probable cause the investigating commissioner is instructed to "endeavor to eliminate the unlawful employment practice complained of by conference, conciliation, and persuasion." If conciliatory attempts fail, or if "circumstances so warrant," he may issue a written notice requiring the respondent to answer the charge at a hearing before the other two commissioners. The proceedings at these hearings are to be informal in nature. The strict rules of evidence observed in courts of law do not obtain and much of the legal paraphernalia of answers, legal representation, and transcription are optional at the request of the parties to a dispute. The previous attempts at conciliation are specifically excluded from presentation at the hearing. If upon "all the evidence" the Commission decides that the respondent has in fact engaged in unlawful practices, it is instructed to state its findings of fact and issue a cease-and-desist order. The Commission is empowered to take various kinds of affirmative action including the ordering of hiring, reinstatement, upgrading, payment of back pay, restoration to membership in a labor organization, and reporting to the Commission of the manner of compliance. The statute specifically states that affirmative action is not limited to the particular types of orders mentioned in the statute; other orders which . . . "in the judgment of the Commission, will effectuate the purposes of this chapter" are legitimate.

Another provision of Section 5 deserves special mention. The Commission is directed to refrain from disclosing what has occurred in the course of conciliation attempts until after the case has been disposed of. Nondisclosure provisions of this type are common in antidiscrimination legislation and are apparently designed to allow conciliation to take place in an atmosphere undisturbed by public pressure.[44] However, in some states nondisclosure provisions have been used as a tool to protect commissions from outside investigators or organizations that may be critical of commission policies.

Section 6 delineates the relations between the Commission and the court system. It provides that the Commission may use the Superior Court of the Commonwealth to obtain a court order for the enforcement of its edicts. The court may issue temporary relief and restraining orders pursuant to the findings of the Commission. It may order all or part of the Commission's order enforced, or it may modify or set aside the Commission's orders. If the court does enforce the Commission's orders, it has full power to issue injunctions and to punish for contempt.

The Section also provides procedures for judicial review. It should be pointed out, however, that a dissatisfied complainant does not have the right to judicial review if the investigating commissioner refuses to make a finding of probable cause, or refuses to take his case to hearing; the provision refers only to orders subsequent to Commission hearings.

The court procedures give a certain advantage to the Commission vis-à-vis the respondent. This is common in the area of administrative law, where a right to trial *de novo* would tend to nullify the purpose of the legislation, which is to make rights subject to administrative remedy. Thus, no objection which was not urged before the Commission may be urged before the court, and the findings of the Commission as to facts are considered conclusive if supported by "sufficient evidence on the record as a whole." Return to the Commission for rehearing can only be directed on showing reasonable grounds for failure to adduce relevant evidence at the original hearing. These provisions prevent respondents from treating the actions of the Commission lightly on the assumption that one need merely wait for his day in court, where he is not obliged to render account to

110

a professional race-relations specialist. They give, in short, the power of original jurisdiction to the intergroup-relations specialist.

In fact, the law as a whole may be said to be designed to give the Commission considerable power, and in this regard, Massachusetts has a more potent statute than many states, an act that enables the Commission to proceed in a relatively militant fashion.

It is true that the act stresses education, persuasion, and conciliation. Enforcement through legal compulsion is to follow attempts at moral or rational suasion. All of the acts have this design.[45] Nevertheless, at the formal level, the legislative grant of power to the Massachusetts Commission is extensive.

In the first place, many commissions cannot initiate complaints, but must wait for complaints to be filed by aggrieved individuals, or for action by the attorney general or industrial commissioner;[46] not all commissions have the power to subpoena books and records, and some commissions are explicitly limited in their authority to issue affirmative orders.[47]

The statute provides for up to one years' imprisonment, or fines up to five hundred dollars, for willful resistance or interference with the Commission or its orders.[48]

In sum, the wording of the Massachusetts statute, though it certainly emphasizes conciliation and persuasion, allows the Commission a great deal of power and latitude in deciding for itself what action is appropriate. An investigating commissioner may order a hearing prior to actual failure of conciliation. Flexibility and ingenuity is allowed in determining the provisions of affirmative orders. The provisions for research together with the Commission's power to initiate complaints would seem to permit independent and active efforts to eliminate discrimination.[49]

The expansion of jurisdiction. Massachusetts passed its

111

first statute aimed directly at housing discrimination in 1948 when the laws governing housing projects were revised to forbid discrimination because of race, color, creed, or religion in any public housing project.[50]

In 1950 responsibility for the administration of this statute was given to the Commission. At the same time segregation as well as. discrimination was outlawed in public housing projects and the Commission's name was changed from the Massachusetts Fair Employment Practices Commission to the Massachusetts Commission Against Discrimination, a name that reflected its broadened responsibilities.[51]

Massachusetts had forbidden discrimination in places of public accommodation since 1865. The right to equal access to accommodations applied to racial discrimination only and was enforceable only by an ordinary civil suit. Such suits had been extremely rare. In 1950 religious discrimination in public accommodations was declared unlawful and the MCAD was given jurisdiction over the revised statute.[52]

This study is not primarily concerned with discrimination in places of public accommodation, resort, and amusement, but the jurisdiction of the Commission over this unlawful practice became an important feature of the powers of the Commission to regulate housing discrimination in 1959 when Attorney General McCormack ruled that real estate brokers were places of public accommodation and must make their services available without discrimination.[53]

The responsibility for administration of laws forbidding discrimination by educational institutions was transferred to the MCAD in 1956.[54] The education law was originally passed in 1949 and enforced by the state board of education.[55] The act requires that "students, otherwise qualified, be admitted to educational institutions without regard to race, color, religion, creed or national origin . . ." (Religious schools are exempted from the religion clause of the act.)

112

The powers provided by this act could play an important role in the regulation of discrimination in employment, since secretarial, business, vocational, and trade schools are specifically included as coming under the jurisdiction of the act.[56]

The coverage of the housing law was extended in 1957 to include, in addition to public housing projects, certain categories of "publicly assisted" housing.[57] Publicly assisted housing is housing that has a tax exemption or some other form of public subsidy, or is financed by a loan guaranteed or insured by the federal government. The major coverage of the act extended only to multiple dwellings housing three or more families exclusive of the owner, to housing that is part of a parcel of ten or more units located on contiguous land, or to rooming houses with more than four tenants.

The acts forbidden were: refusing to rent or lease housing accommodations because of race, creed, color, or national origin; discriminating in the terms of conditions or the furnishing of facilities; and inquiring into or recording the ethnic origins of applicants.

Again we see an unwillingness to start with a blanket prohibition of all kinds of housing discrimination. The approach is a cautious one; first only public housing was included, then coverage was extended to publicly assisted housing, provided that it was part of a rather large complex of housing facilities owned by a single landlord or business. Relatively intimate owner-occupied premises are exempt, as well as the private homes of individuals. The law originally addresses itself to an attempt to regulate bureaucratic structures rather than individuals.

The first attempt to regulate purely private housing came two years later in 1959, when the antidiscrimination statute was amended to proscribe discrimination in rental or sale within any "contiguously located housing" or "multiple dwelling."[58]

The definition of "contiguous location" is similar to that given in the 1957 act:

Contiguously located housing means 1) housing which is offered for sale, lease or rental by a person who owns or at any time has owned, or who otherwise controls or at any time has controlled, the sale of ten or more housing accommodations located on land that is contiguous, (exclusive of public streets), and which housing is located on such land, or 2) housing which is offered for sale, lease or rental and which at any time was one of ten or more lots of a tract whose plan has been submitted to a planning board as required by THE SUBDIVISION CONTROL LAW. . .[59]

The definition of multiple housing was unchanged from the 1957 act and the same practices are declared unlawful, that is, refusing access, discriminating in terms or conditions, and making inquiries about race, creed or national origin. This was the extent of the types of housing covered during the time period when the field work of this investigation was underway.

On July 1, 1963, the coverage of the law was extended to include all housing made generally available to the public for sale, lease, or rental, by any means of public offerings except for two-family, owner-occupied structures,[60] giving the Massachusetts housing law nearly as broad a coverage as any of the other states that regulate discrimination in housing.[61]

Several amendments to the housing act have provided additional enforcement tools or have extended coverage in some way. The acts governing realtors were mentioned above.

Realtors were further placed under the jurisdiction of the Commission by a 1961 act that prohibited licensed real estate brokers and other agents from discrimination in the sale and rental of property covered by the law.[62] The original statute had referred only to owners, lessees, sublessees, and managing agents, and other persons having possession or the right to make leases or rentals. The new act made it impossible for owners to use realtors or office employees as screens for discrimination. The same act made refusing to negotiate with respect to sale of property an unlawful act, if done because of the race, creed, or national origin of the other party. This feature of the amendment prevents an owner or realtor from interposing the technical defense that he did not refuse to sell or rent, since he had never actually negotiated with the complainant. An act of 1960 declared it unlawful "to discriminate against any person in the granting of any mortgage loan, including but not limited to the interest rate, terms, or duration of such mortgage loan."[63] The act covers only those in the business of granting mortgage loans.

The law was strengthened in an important way in 1961. In housing, the problem of preventing a pending case from becoming moot can become a serious one. A respondent can rent or sell the disputed housing accommodation to a third party during the conciliation process. Chapter 570 of the Acts of 1961 gave the investigating commissioner the power to ask a superior court to grant an injunction preventing the respondent from making the accommodation unavailable. An injunction or restraining order can be requested at any time, once a finding of probable cause has been made, but it can only be done after a hearing which must be announced three days in advance. The amendment authorizes the court to grant "appropriate injunctive relief," including orders or decrees restraining and enjoining him from "selling, renting, or otherwise making unavailable to the complainant any housing accommodation with respect to which the complaint is made, pending the final determination of proceedings under the chapter."[64] The chapter does not, however, specifically limit injunctive interlocutary relief to housing cases.

The various laws covering discrimination in housing are all couched in the form of amendments to the original employment act. Chapter 151 B simply came to include more and more unlawful practices, but the procedures for remedy have not changed. Accordingly, the procedure for litigating housing complaints is no different from the procedures involved in employment. A sworn complaint is assigned to an investigatory commission for investigation, conciliation and, if necessary, appropriate corrective orders. Presumably, the establishment of councils, the publication of research and all of the other paraphernalia of education are in order.

The foregoing recital of the various features of the law is not intended as a mere encyclopedic listing of its provisions. It serves to establish several sociologically relevant characteristics of the law:

1) *The statutes are cast in general terms; they involve large elements of indeterminacy.* The statutes, of necessity, do not provide detailed definitions of what situations are to be considered discriminatory and what are not, nor do they provide for detailed regulation of the practices and procedures of the Commission. Many provisions do not direct the Commission to do anything, they merely empower it to take certain kinds of action if it seems appropriate. Some provisions invite the Commission to develop or invent its own policies, to make its own regulations and interpretations.

The indeterminacy of statutory provisions does not imply an abdication of legislative responsibility. It reflects the inescapable fact that experience is richer than words, and too varied to be anticipated in advance. The legislation sets the general policy of the state and the administrative agency is expected to tailor its implementation of the policy to the exigencies of situations as they arise.

Except for the subject of pre-employment inquiries, the Commission has not been vocal in producing official interpretations of the law. The systematic enforcement activities initiated by the MCAD have been almost entirely limited to the eradication of the symbols of discrimination. All overt reference to race and all hints of race have been systematically expurged from advertisement and forms. The involved rules regarding pre-employment inquiry emerged in this context. Similar rules on the substantial matters of discrimination have not been formulated. Issues have been resolved implicitly on a complaint-by-complaint basis. One of the functions of this study is to infer the legal interpretations that are implicit in the kinds of actions that the Commission has taken.

2) *The statutes place upon the Commission a dual responsibility: the Commission is both instructed to educate and empowered to enforce.* The wording of the law stresses the Commission's responsibility for community education. This is apparent in the provisions for community councils, the emphasis on the use of conciliation and persuasion, and the statutory encouragement of educational research.

On the other hand, the Commission is not limited to persuasive or educational methods. It is empowered to mobilize the compulsive power of the state behind the eradication of discrimination. The appropriate blend of the agency's educational and enforcement activities is not prescribed by law; it is left to the best judgment of the Commission.

3) *The enforcement powers of the Commission are extensive.* It is true that violation of the code of fair employment practices may not be treated as a criminal offense in the same sense that armed robbery is a criminal offense. The statute does require some prior conciliatory attempt, and punishment comes not for violating the law as such, but for willful resistance of an order of the Commission. In contrast, the armed robber is not given a right to continue his activities until caught and then to avoid punishment by merely ceasing and desisting from further larceny once apprehended. But the conciliatory features of the antidiscrim-

117

ination statutes must not be allowed to obscure the breadth and scope of its enforcement provisions. The Commission has extensive powers to conduct research that would ferret out discrimination, issue complaints against apparent offenders, and issue a wide variety of both negative and affirmative orders to insure elimination of illegal practices.

4) *The law limits the activities of the Commission.* The powers of the Commission are broad, but they are not unlimited. It may not act in the absence of evidence and may not issue orders without first attempting conciliation. It is subject to all of the constitutional limitations on the power of administrative agencies. The Commission can only enforce rights that are established by the statute against persons whom the statute covers. Its orders are subject to judicial review, which insures compliance with both statutory limitations and the limitations of the Western legal tradition.

Legal authority is power subject to legal definition and restriction. Legally induced change is change that is brought about by invoking the power of the state to enforce explicitly stated norms through established procedures. It is to be distinguished from the mere forceful imposition of change by the government. A government that is not bound by law can use whatever techniques appear to be either necessary or efficient. Force can be directed at strategic targets and transmitted by any effective vehicle, be it persuasion, legal action, intimidation or terror.

The limitations that law imposes on the exercise of power imply a limitation on the possibilities of legally induced change. The explicit character of legal, enforceable norms and the procedural rules governing the application of legal sanctions may, from one point of view, be described as protections or guarantees, but from another point of view they can be termed loopholes. Loopholes are not necessarily indications of poorly drafted legislation. Some degree of "loophole" is built into the legal approach to social control. Legal protections both guarantee the maintenance of rights and provide the time, the privacy, and the exceptions to the rules that make evasion possible.

5) *Nothing in the law prevents the application of bona fide standards.* Contrary to some popular impressions, the law does not require that one hire or sell, or rent to someone because he is a member of a minority group. It only forbids *discriminating against* such persons. This has important practical consequences; it means that a great deal of investigation and argument concerns the establishment of qualifications. It also leaves open the possibility that arguments about qualifications can be used as a screen for discrimination.

6) *The housing and the employment law are similar in form.* The definitions of discrimination are similar and the provisions for remedy are identical. The same Commission enforces both laws. This means that whatever differences we find in the administrative activities of the Commission and in the response of the community to the different laws cannot be attributed to the wording of the statute. Differences must be attributed to variations in the social organization and character of the institutions of the law regulates.

These points can be shown to have considerable sociological significance. Further chapters will show that the same generality and indeterminacy that permit the Commission to tailor its activities to the complex and changing exigencies of efficient enforcement also permit the adaptation of policy and practice to the constraints that arise from the Commission's political and social position within the community. The balance between educational and enforcement activity also depends on the social forces to which the Commission is subject. Finally, the extent to which the Commission makes use of its extensive enforcement powers depends on the support it receives from the elements of the community interested in eliminating discrimination.

CHAPTER V. THE POLICIES AND PRACTICES OF THE COMMISSION

The Commission has not conceived of the Fair Employment Practice Law as an instrument of compulsion.—[MCAD *Annual Report,* 1948]

Education and Enforcement

The generality of the law leaves great latitude to the leadership of the Commission Against Discrimination in setting policy, interpreting the provisions of the law and making implementive decisions.

The over-all guiding policy of the Commission was very stable during Mildred Mahoney's six terms as chairman of the Commission. Appointed in 1946 as the first chairman, Mrs. Mahoney was an outspoken advocate and practitioner of a policy of education, persuasion, and moderation.

The general features of Commission policy were clearly stated in the *Annual Report* for 1948:

From the beginning, this Commission has recognized that the elimination of discriminatory employment practices based upon individual and group prejudices could be accomplished most effectively by reason *instead of force.* It has endeavored to deal fairly in every instance with complainants and respondents. It has appealed to the intelligence and sense of justice of employers and workers alike in each attempt to break down the barriers of racial and religious intolerance.

In short, the Commission has not conceived of the Fair Employment Practice Law as an instrument of compulsion. Rather, it has regarded the statute as presenting an opportunity to wipe out the ignorance and doubts and fears which men have of other men who are different with respect to color, religion or national origin. Thus, in its whole work, it has attempted to substitute understanding for intolerance.

To a degree, a policy of persuasion is required by the statute. The law does require conciliative attempts prior to the application of legal sanctions. The law requires moderation in some contexts and several sections refer to "community understanding." But the moderation of the Commission goes beyond the requirements of the statute and is based on nonlegal as well as legal considerations. The policy reflects the belief of Chairman Mahoney and others that the persuasive moderate approach is the most practical technique in intergroup relations. That Chairman Mahoney placed a very high value on the body of good will that has been built up over the years with Massachusetts' employers is evident in many of her statements and her actions. In part, these views are based on the theory that the cooperation of respondents is necessary if long-run gains are to be secured. To antagonize a businessman is to provoke ill will that can affect his willingness to listen to the Commission's arguments in the immediate case and his permanent attitudes toward minority-group employment.

Establishing the Commission. It is clear that the considerations which motivate the policy of moderation go beyond the element of mere tact. Mrs. Mahoney wished not only to gain the good will of individual respondents but to gain the support of business as an organized interest in the community. She indicated that on the advisory councils she tried for big industrialists. She acknowledged that often people thought that ministers and minority group leaders would be most helpful, but she thought industrialists could give more help. Her concern was always with the power structure of the community.[1]

Commission officials would not say that their policies were generated by fear of the power of the business community to render the Commission ineffective. They usually stated the case positively; they said it was useful to have the cooperation of the business community. One commissioner alleged that the Commission could easily initiate more active and militant policies without fear of reprisal from the organized centers of community power. It is significant that in the course of the very interview where that view was expressed, the informant mentioned two incidents when sanctions had been directed toward the Commission. Once a commissioner was not reappointed because he pressed a case too hard against one of Massachusetts' largest industrial firms, and, on another occasion, the legislature discussed removing the Commission's enforcement powers if a projected public hearing were to cause the respondent to take his business to another state. The author's investigations do not completely support either of these allegations but they were nonetheless important in the mind of the commissioner.

Actual attempts to punish the Commission have been virtually nonexistent; even threats are very rare. Nevertheless, the Commission's policies can be seen as motivated by a desire to avoid negative sanctions from the group whose activities they purported to regulate. The leadership of the Commission admitted very freely that it believed it necessary to act in such a way as to secure the cooperation of the "power structure of the community," meaning organized business interests. The members further claimed that the Commission could not operate effectively without securing cooperation. Though the Commission tended to phrase the problem in positive terms, it was saying, in effect, that the business community was in a position to impose a negative sanction on the Commission. Hence, it felt that its policies must be designed to avoid such sanctions. The only argument concerns the nature of the sanctions. Commission leaders stressed the withholding of cooperation and minimized the more dire threats of disestablishment, loss of enforcement powers, loss of legislative appropriations, and failure of reappointment.

It is generally recognized that the latter possibilities were more realistic threats in the early years of the law, when memory of the close struggle for passage was fresher and all the fledgling commissioners were eager to avoid the fate of the federal FEPC. Self-protection was a more important motive at the time the initial policies of moderation were set.

We must remember that the state fair employment practices commissions were created very shortly after the failure of the federal committee. The early state commissioners could not have failed to take notice of the federal experience and to draw upon its lessons. These experiences have been well documented.[2] Numerous incidents and fiascos testify to the dangers of over-reaching the limits of effective social power: a member of the federal committee who was considered too militant failed to be reappointed; the railroad industry refused in writing to follow the formal orders of the committee and despite committee appeals to the President, the matter was allowed to die; the Commission was proven to have no effective power in the face of determined opposition by firms making crucial contributions to the war effort.

Despite heroic attempts to emphasize conciliation, tact, impartiality, patience and moderation, despite every effort to avoid the issuance of compulsive orders and the appearance of militancy, and a "do-gooder" attitude on political and social radicalism, the federal FEPC was ultimately destroyed by its enemies. A coalition of business interests and Southern political interests were not impressed with the committee's moderation.

To some extent the attitude of the early commissions might have been unduly conservative. After all they were located in Northern states. They were aware that they would not face the combination of business suspicion *and* Southern intransigence. Further, the state acts were not emergency measures tied to the war effort, which had lost

123

LAW AND EQUAL OPPORTUNITY

its compelling power with the end of hostilities. On the other hand, the attitude of wariness was based in part on recognition of an important sociological principle. It is one thing to muster enough social support to produce a law calling for innovation; it is quite another to mobilize the requisite organizational support to produce compliance with the law. In fact, as the Norwegian sociologist Torstein Eckhoff has pointed out, the existence of a law on the statute books of a state may represent a compromise between those who are in favor of the purposes of the law and those who are willing to see a law in the books as long as it is not enforced.[3]

There is considerable evidence that such a compromise was established at the inception of the Massachusetts Commission. Caught in the full public glitter of the morally powerful campaign waged by the civil rights forces, the business community was forced to make its moves behind the scenes. The organized symbolic expression of the value tradition made public opposition inappropriate and forced business interests to rely on the considerable social power that derives from their strategic structural location in the community.

The Associated Industries of Massachusetts dropped its initial opposition to the law, but the willingness of industry to cease active opposition to the law was clearly a consequence of compromise. One lobbyist for industry described the compromise in these terms:

We weren't able to beat it in '46. There was too much grass roots pressure. But because of our opposition they put in some good commissioners. They haven't given us any trouble.

The interviewer asked, "Do you think your opposition had anything to do with getting conservative commissioners?"

Yes, Governor Tobin said to us, "We have to pass this law. Everyone is committed to it. I know you boys are pretty upset about this, but I'll appoint some good people to the commission." And he did. [Proceeds to name and compliment the various commissioners.]

124

Another industry lobbyist explained industry change of heart with direct reference to the process of cooptation.

> We were afraid of the law. It gave anybody the right to claim he had been discriminated and on that basis a business could get a lot of bad publicity. Legislation is basically one group in the community grabbing the power of the government to use for its own purposes. Minority groups could use the law to make trouble for people and bad publicity. That's a hefty thing. In the abstract, it's frightening.
>
> What happened, once they got that Goddamned thing through. . . . [profuse apologies for so referring to the law and re-affirmations of his commitment to it]. . . .They were darned careful to create an agency with a lot of employer advisors on it. As a result a Negro's got to bring a good case, not because they don't believe in it but because they got some good advice.
>
> It looked like a naked power grab, but when it actually got going not a hell of a lot was really done about it.
>
> It's a pretty hard thing to prove discrimination when there are so many job qualifications.

Thus, at the time of original passage of the law, the Commission's position was marginal. Commissioners were appointed and sworn in on August 26, 1946, but permanent funds and authorization for employment of a staff were not forthcoming. The Commission had to obtain special permission to pay the first executive secretary by voucher. It was given authorization to engage field representatives only as temporary employees. The services of a public relations expert also required preparation of a special voucher.

The Commission was not immediately given office space and equipment. At first, the private offices of one of the commissioners were used as temporary headquarters. After three months the Commission moved to other temporary headquarters but had some difficulty in obtaining furnishings. One field representative has a vivid memory of conducting his first conference with a respondent while seated upon orange crates.[4]

The Commission's first annual report in 1946 was in part

125

a plea for the necessary funds and personnel to carry out its legislative mandate.

Not only did the Commission lack easy access to funds but it had only been in existence a few months when its very existence was threatened by a new fight in the legislature.

It appears evident that the Chairman's remarkable capacity to conciliate and to avoid recrimination contributed to the establishment of the Commission as a permanent feature of Massachusetts government during those first uncertain days. In 1963 the position of the Commission was more secure, but the vestiges of the early period of uncertainty remained in the presence of a form of cooptation.

Cooptation of the research program. To say that Commission policy had stressed education, persuasion, and conciliation is not to say that its activities have been limited to the arbitration of individual cases brought to its attention by aggrieved complainants. A variety of active educational programs have been instituted. The leadership of the Commission believed that these programs were a central component of their activities.

The structure of one phase of the Commission's educational work is of crucial importance because of its consequences for the enforcement process. In the preceding chapter, reference was made to the statutory provisions empowering the Commission to establish councils to study problems of discrimination and to make policy recommendations. Presumably the Commission's power to initiate programs of research could be used as a basis for developing information about (and evidence of) discrimination which would, in turn, facilitate a program of Commission-initiated enforcement activities. Such programs could be designed to supplement the complainant-centered enforcement program with systematic enforcement efforts in particular strategic industries, occupations, and localities.

126

The Commission established a set of community councils and used them extensively in programs of research and education throughout the Commonwealth, but these activities were strictly limited to educational efforts and attempts to generate good will.

Chairman Mahoney tried to utilize the councils as a means of involving business leadership in the concerns of the law. The presence of respected leaders on the councils can serve to symbolize business acceptance of the goals of the legislation. The symbol provided by business participation in Commission activities can be used as a lever on hesitant members of the business community. Finally, the good offices of business representatives can be used as a means of securing information about racial distributions and business practices, and as a means of disseminating information about the law and its purposes.

Reasoning along these lines, the Commission gave heavy representation to business interests on community councils. The Greater Boston Council has had as its chairman, the vice president of Filene's department store[5], the president of the Bay State Milling Company, the vice president of the Liberty Mutual Life Insurance Company, and the chairman of the board of Gillette Company. High officials from the John Hancock Mutual Life Insurance Company, New England Telephone and Telegraph, Dewey and Almy Chemical Company, the Eastern Massachusetts Street Railway, Marsh McLennan, Inc., Gilchrest's Department Store, Stop and Shop Inc., and the Raytheon Manufacturing Company are or have been members of the council. Liquor distributors, employment agencies, law firms, funeral parlors, and business clubs have also been represented.

Because of discrimination in labor unions, the cooperation of representatives of various unions has been considered important and representatives of the CIO, the AFL, the Printing Trades Union, the building and construction trades,

127

and other local unions have served on the council.

The organizational affiliations of the twenty-two members of the Greater Boston Council at the time this study began were as follows: business, twelve; labor, eight; government, one; university placement service, one. In contrast, no militant Negro pressure organization was represented, nor any other minority group or civil rights association except for the Civil Rights Committee of the Massachusetts AFL-CIO.

The business and labor representatives of industry have not always been chosen from the ranks of economic sectors that have provided employment opportunities for Negroes. Employment in the public utilities industry has been minimal. The construction industry has afforded little opportunity for Negro employment. Negroes have been very sensitive to the lack of Negro employment in the occupational category "route salesman" and liquor companies in particular have been under attack on this score. A great deal of money is spent by the negro community for liquor, yet at the time of this study not a single route belonged to a Negro. A Negro pressure organization made an *unsuccessful* attempt to secure a liquor sales position during the field work phase of the present study.

In short, no attempt was made to recruit militant or even intensely sympathetic businessmen for the Greater Boston Council. Rather, people were chosen to represent structural positions in the society, in the belief that this would facilitate the Commission's work. Choosing a business representative did not necessarily lead to the integration of the representative's industry or his firm. It only committed the firm to cooperation in research and educational projects and symbolized business acceptance of the main outlines of the legislation.

Community councils have initiated and supported a wide variety of educational and investigative programs. Some projects of the Boston Council have been: a survey of the high school training and the subsequent employment of high school training and the subsequent employment of Negro High School students conducted through the auspices of school guidance counselors (1952-53); a survey of apprentice training opportunities in metal trades and building trades (1953-55); study of employment policies of hospitals and nursing homes (1956); surveys of employment and upgrading in banks, public utilities and insurance companies (1956); study of placement in the printing trade (1958); study of programs in high schools with large Negro enrollments (1958); surveys of employment in industrial firms (1959); and meetings with minority group and social agency leaders to discuss the results of surveys and recommend appropriate action.[6]

Surveys were generally conducted by the staff on the Commission. Some were done by mail; some were done in person by visits to places of business. Questions were asked concerning the familiarity of the firm with the provisions of the law, the number of employees in the plant, employee turnover, sources of employment, racial distribution of employees, racial distribution of applicants, incidents involving discrimination, and the operation of apprenticeship and on-the-job training programs. Educational materials were given to the employer and his application forms were checked for conformity to the law.

The purpose of the program was considered to be attained if "a representative of the Commission has talked over with the representative of the company matters of importance to both; questions have been answered; Commission material has been left and some degree of mutual acquaintance and understanding has been established."[7]

There is no doubt that the councils have had a measure of success in securing aid in the sponsorship of studies and in helping to educate the industry to its responsibilities under the law. In the words of one annual report:

"The Commission is very proud of its eight advisory councils which assist it in educational work. The councils are made up of distinguished citizens well known for their civic interests. They translate the Commission to their respective communities and they keep the MCAD aware of what is going on in their areas. If tensions begin to develop or misunderstandings arise they are alert to report them in order that constructive action may be taken to prevent serious trouble. In this role they have been singularly successful."[8]

The author of the above passage made an effective choice of words in the phrase "they translate the Commission to their respective communities." In using industry leaders as communicators, the Commission subjected its message to translation into terms that industry would appreciate. At the same time, the translation may have involved selectivity and distortion, and is not likely to be stated in ways that run counter to established ways of thinking. For example, the tendency of business to define nondiscrimination as willingness to hire Negroes *in capacities for which they are well suited* will probably not be effectively combatted, since industry communicators will use their own sets of definitions.

Similarly, the reverse process of communication was subject to distortion. Industrialists and union leaders had a tendency to report their version of the situation. There was a constant pressure in the direction of acceptance and adoption by the Commission of the viewpoints, ideologies, explanations, and excuses of the groups they purported to regulate.

Research on employment policies, opportunity structure, and racial distribution is very valuable to the Commission. As communication channels the councils are useful. However, council work has never been a basis for systematic campaigns of eradication, using the enforcement powers of the law. In many cases, patterns of unequal opportunity were discovered, but the only action taken was dissemination of information about the law, discussions with minority-group leaders about the problems involved or the creation of new lines of communication between minority groups, government officials, and industry leaders. The neglect of systematic enforcement was the price paid for cooptation of the groups regulated by the law.

Cooptation. Cooptation, as defined by Philip Selznick, refers to "the process of absorbing new elements into the leadership or policy-determining structure of an organization as a means of averting threats to its stability or existence."[9]

According to Selznick, cooptation occurs when the legitimacy of a governing agency is questioned, when it is useful to rely in part on self-regulation of the groups subject to an agency's jurisdiction, and in response to pressures from centers of power in the community. "Cooptation reflects a state of tension between formal authority and social power." The importance of cooptation lies in its possible impact on the organization and goals of the coopting group. Cooptation may have its price in the "blunting of social purpose."

One consequence of cooptation was particularly relevant to the relation between the Commission and the groups whose activities they regulated.

Cooptation results in some constriction of the field of choice available to the organization or leadership in question. The character of the coopted elements will necessarily shape the modes of action available to the group which has won adaptation at the price of commitment to outside elements.[10]

The cooptation of industry by the Commission may not fit Selznick's definition perfectly. The actual threat to the existence or stability of the MCAD had become minimal and it was not the primary motive for cooptation. The legitimacy of the MCAD was not really in question and there is no evidence to suggest that the councils were industry self-regulating bodies, though they may have been intended to serve that function. The power of industry groups has not led to specific demands on the Commission. The function of the cooptation of industry has been to establish channels of communication and to facilitate educational work and research. In other words, cooptation has simply been a technique of administration. Nevertheless, the consequences were similar to those proposed by Selznick.

In choosing cooptation as a technique of administration the Commission cut itself off from other possible techniques. It could not make use of the findings of council-sponsored research projects in any way that would compromise continuing cooperation. Industry-dominated community councils were not interested in initiating and sponsoring programs designed to facilitate systematic use of the Commission's broad enforcement powers. Accordingly, the mode of council organization chosen by the Commission supported a policy that tied the enforcement process to proceedings initiated by private complaints.

Cooptation is a very difficult concept to measure. It would be quite hard to precisely determine the degree to which the incorporation of potential enemies of the Commission placed them under its influence and to weigh this against the degree to which the inclusion of opponents has influenced the Commission or inhibited its freedom of action.

On the other hand, there is no evidence to suggest that participation in community councils has led to greater employment of Negroes within the firms represented. At the same time there is a great deal of evidence, as we shall see in succeeding chapters, showing that reliance on complaints from aggrieved individuals is a weak enforcement tool.

Cooptation as political protection. If the Commission is to be judged by its degree of success in avoiding ill-will among employers, then the Commission has been successful indeed.

A 1952 mail survey conducted by the Commission produced 136 returned questionnaires. Former respondents and others who had official dealings with the Commission were asked to evaluate its work. Favorable responses outnumbered unfavorable responses by more than six to one among all respondents and by more than ten to one among employers who had actually had complaints lodged against them.[11]

The interviews conducted by the author in 1962 failed to produce a significant body of criticism of the Commission among former respondents in Commission cases.[12]

The "success" of the commissioners in dealing with employers on a conciliatory basis without recourse to the formal processes of law is demonstrated by the fact that no employment case had ever been to court, and that before the housing statute became law, only three cases out of more than 1600 went to formal hearing.[13]

The ability of the commissioners to handle complaints informally and to avoid complaints from respondents was evidently a factor used by politicians in assessing the value of their work. The attitude of the members of the political hierarchy was "the less heard the better." This attitude is well illustrated by some of the incidents that accompanied the confirmation of Chairman Mahoney's fifth reappointment in 1960. One member of the Governor's council, prodded by several civil rights groups, objected to the appointment on the grounds that the Commission had not been sufficiently militant. The response of Mrs. Mahoney's supporters was that her capability as chairman of the Commission was amply demonstrated by her success in avoiding trouble.[14] The standards for political evaluation did not revolve around the Commission's success in eliminating discrimination; the standard was success in handling cases without kickback.

Mrs. Mahoney's success in achieving confirmation also illustrates one of the political functions of cooptation. The members of the local councils wrote letters to the Governor's Council urging confirmation, thus protecting her from certain political enemies who were behind the ouster move.

Criticism of the Commission. The conservative policies of the early Commission paralleled the similar policies of cognate agencies in other states. Conservative policies, though they may contribute to preventing criticism from regulatees, lead to criticism by the groups that have secured passage of the laws and to organized demands for more aggressive enforcement policies. For example, Morroe Berger describes the formation of the Committee to Support the Ives-Quinn Bill which exerted pressure for more militant implementation of the New York Statute.[15]

A similar movement developed in Massachusetts in 1953 with the creation of the Blue Ribbon Committee of the Jewish Community Council and the American Jewish Congress. This committee reflected a growing belief within the liberal community that the policies of the law were not being implemented. After extensive study, the committee issued a very critical report and urged a number of reforms. They suggested a systematic follow-up program to study the long-run effects of litigation. They insisted that the MCAD take more action on its own initiative. Closer relations with employment agencies, especially the Massachusetts State Employment Service, were also recommended. The committee complained that the MCAD did not make sufficient use of their powers to force respondents to take affirmative action. The use of publicity as a compulsive device was urged.[16]

The MCAD attempted to implement a few of these suggestions, but the more radical of the demands went unheeded because it was believed that a great deal of investment in the good will of employers was at stake. To the end, Chairman Mahoney was unwilling to jeopardize her fund of good will. In consequence, criticism mounted steadily, reaching a high point in the 1960's with demands for her replacement as chairman of the Commission. An unsuccessful attempt to unseat Chairman Mahoney was made during the period under investigation and finally on December 4, 1964, Mrs. Mahoney stepped down amidst considerable public turmoil regarding the appropriate function of the Commission.

The civil rights leaders interviewed by the author in 1962,

in a unanimous chorus of criticism, alleged that the Commission was slow, passive, ineffective in the legislature, unnecessarily secretive, and that respondents were coddled.

By the time that the housing act was legislated in 1959, civil rights proponents were thoroughly disgruntled with Commission policies. The high degree of organized pressure for militant enforcement has prevented the Commission from successfully coopting the housing industry.

The failure of cooptation in housing. Given the Commission's success in coopting opposition from industry, it is not surprising that a similar tactic was attempted after passage of the housing law. Mrs. Mahoney had worked hard to build good will in the housing industry. She had met with numerous groups of realtors and property owners, culminating in a Conference on Housing, held at the Boston College Law School in April of 1960.[17] After her initial meeting with the Massachusetts Association of Real Estate Boards, Mrs. Mahoney expressed confidence that the housing industry would approach the law in the same "cooperative and friendly spirit" as had been evoked among employers. Her expectations were not realized. Relations with the housing industry did not parallel the early development of relations with employers.

Two factors appear to be responsible.

First, the Commission was not able to operate as moderately in the housing field. The commissioners were under the constant surveillance of organized civil rights groups who have exerted pressure for active and vigorous policies. Civil rights groups forced confrontations between the legal agency and those who represent the core of resistance to housing desegregation.

Second, the housing industry viewed the law as a serious threat and refused to become coopted. Housing respondents tended to view the filing of a complaint as the first skirmish in a legal battle and were not willing to negotiate in a

135

"human relations" framework. They came to "informal" conferences with legal counsel and were more likely, if pressed, to demand a formal hearing.[18]

The old techniques for assuaging the anxieties of the opposition did not work. Despite the general expressions of good will obtained at the Conference of Housing, Chairman Mahoney did not come to regard the good will of the housing industry as a viable or obtainable resource.

This is clearly reflected in the composition of the first Advisory Council of Housing, which, unlike the Boston Community Council, included several representatives of minority groups and civil rights organizations, including the NAACP, CORE, and Fair Housing Federation, the American Jewish Congress, and the Urban League. In all, fourteen of the thirty-six original appointees to the Advisory Council on Housing represented civil rights groups or community relations agencies. Sixteen represented the real estate and home building industry, two represented government agencies and one a university.[19]

The failure of the Commission to successfully coopt housing interests has made its enforcement task burdensome. Legal battles are more expensive, time-consuming, and nerve-wracking than educational conciliation. At the same time, the Commission was not bound by the need to preserve an atmosphere. When questioned about the possibilities of instituting procedural reforms, Chairman Mahoney made distinctions between housing and employment, suggesting that some policies could be implemented in the housing sphere that could not be implemented in employment for fear of threatening working relationships with the business community.

The success of cooptation in the employment sphere and its failure in housing is very interesting, for it both forces a qualification of the classic concept of cooptation and illuminates the concept of institutionalization. It is frequently stated that cooptation occurs when an agency lacks legitimacy; yet the Commission's failure to coopt the housing industry suggests that a certain minimal level of legitimacy is a prerequisite for cooptation. When those subject to the jurisdiction of a legal agency feel that their fundamental interests are in jeopardy, and when they have strong residual doubts about the moral force behind the agency's claim to interfere in their affairs, they will be unlikely to take the risks involved in being coopted. Rather, they will resist more strenuously, and will avoid actions that imply acceptance of the agency's goals or its legitimacy.

The necessary conditions for cooptation were present in the case of employment. The equal-treatment standard was already becoming accepted in many segments of the community; many firms had already integrated their labor forces. Business did not *want* the law, for they thought it might be a nuisance or that it would be enforced in an unreasonable manner. On the other hand, the law could be grudgingly accepted as long as there were some techniques for preventing enforcement from moving too far in front of emerging social changes. A comparable situation did not exist in the housing sector of the economy.

Thus, cooptation could occur in the employment sector because, during the classic era, the equal-treatment version of the equal-opportunity ideal was already undergoing a process of emergent institutionalization. Employers could afford to permit the law to make a contribution. Viewed in this light we see that cooptation is far from being an inexorable process which inevitably displaces goals and prevents institutionalization. Rather, when cooptation occurs it is an indication that institutionalization is already taking place; it is a device for moderating attempts to unduly accelerate the pace of social change.

The Work of the Commission

The activities of the Commission are by no means confined to council-sponsored studies and the investigation of complaints. A wide variety of informational, educational, and conciliatory endeavors are undertaken. Each year representatives of the Commission visit the offices of several hundred Massachusetts firms to hold conferences designed to

"minimize the possibilities of violation of the law by offering instructions, interpretations, answers to specific questions; and general information pertaining to the statutes; to review employment application forms and hiring policies and to obtain compliance with that section of the law which requires the posting of the summary of the law in a conspicuous place on the premises."[20]

In the five-year period, 1958-1962, conferences were held at 3,214 places of business. Similar conferences were held at 118 private housing developments in 1961 and 1962. Representatives of the Commission held conferences with, or spoke to, a variety of community organizations at a rate of over one hundred per year. Hundreds of persons visit the offices of the Commission each year seeking information about the law. There was an average of 630 visitors a year between 1958 and 1962.

During this same period, Commission representatives met with hotel and motel operators, with chambers of commerce, and with chiefs of police in dozens of Massachusetts communities. Annual surveys were made of the racial distribution in public housing projects. A survey was made of racial distributions in public schools. The advertising materials of over 1,000 places of public accommodation were checked each year. Spot checks were made of newspapers to catch violations of advertising regulations. Thousands of copies of the housing law were distributed through real estate boards. A teaching unit developed by the Commission was in use in many public schools.

The Commission endeavored to conciliate many problems in situations where it lacked technical legal jurisdiction. These activities were classed as "investigations without complaint" in the annual statistical report. During the first sixteen years of operation, 884 such investigations were conducted.

However, the core of the enforcement program was the investigation of sworn complaints. Almost without exception, the educational programs were merely informational. They were not used as a means of discovering remediable violations of a substantive nature. Only the complaint process mobilized the compulsive powers of law.

The importance of the dissemination of information about the law should not be depreciated. Knowledge is prerequisite to obedience. In law ignorance may not be a legitimate defense but it is nonetheless a cause of illegal activity. Further, the effectiveness of the promulgation of legal orders should not be underestimated. Some will institute changes on merely learning a new legal pronouncement.

Nevertheless, the impotence of purely educational devices in the face of powerful interests that shrink from the risks of change is well established. The self-confessed failure of antidiscrimination agencies with purely educational powers demonstrates the necessity of an enforcement process.

The failure of the "survey" method of enforcement is symbolized in the Commission's annual study of racial distributions within public housing projects. Year after year the Commission discovered and published information demonstrating a pronounced pattern of racial separation in some projects, yet the data showed little trend in the direction of less segregation.

The test of law's capacity to overcome intrenched opposition is to be found in an analysis of the outcomes of the complaint process. It is not that we are insisting upon "legal showdowns" as the only test of the agency's success.

139

It is rather that the legal process is more clearly illuminated in situations where the compulsive powers of law hover in the background than in situations where agencies, which happen to have legal powers, use purely educational procedures. In the case of the MCAD the complaint procedure is the relevant legal process.

The case load of complaints is not as large as the Commission's reports suggest. Between November 10, 1946, and December 31, 1964, roughly the years of Mrs. Mahoney's chairmanship, the MCAD processed 4,865 investigations of all types.

Table 8 provides an over-all picture of the total workload of the Commission but the figures must be interpreted with caution.

For example, the overwhelming concentration in the employment sector is a product of the longer time period during which the Commission has been working in employment and the large number of age cases, all of which concern employment. During the period of this study, 1959-1962, housing was a more significant segment. The Commission investigated 937 cases and, of these, 266 were housing investigations, 188 concerned public accommodations, twenty-three came under the Commission's jurisdiction in the field of education, and the remaining 460 were employment cases. Of these 937 cases, 613, that is, 65.4 percent, were cases in which race or color discrimination was in question, but at least half of them did not actually involve a complaint. They were merely part of the Commission's program of regulation of application forms.

The cumulative total of 4,865 cases reported in Table 8 includes not only complaints concerning religious and ethnic discrimination but also a large number of cases involving administration of a law prohibiting discrimination by reason of age. Since the statistical report lumps investigations without complaint, that is, the policing of application forms,

Table 8. Number of complaints handled by the MCAD between November 10, 1946 and December 31, 1964

Disposition	Employment	Private housing	Public housing	Public accommodations	Fair education	Total
Final order	2	10	0	2	0	14
Conciliated (after investigation and conference)	2860	297	11	240	16	3224
Lack of probable cause	890	162	4	144	11	1211
Lack of jurisdiction	55	29	0	13	0	97
Withdrawn by complainant	90	17	1	9	2	119
Total	3895	515	16	408	29	4865

and actual complaints, it is difficult to make an exact estimate of the number of complaints of racial discrimination that have been received by the Commission, An examination of a few sample years and of the internal patterns of the cumulative tables published by the Commission suggest that it received only 75 to 80 complaints of racial discrimination a year during Chairman Mahoney's tenure.

The annual reports of the Commission give one the impression of considerable enforcement activity and success. However, the various categories and breakdowns given in the annual reports hide as much as they show. The sketchiness and ambiguity of the statistical report is not a mere inconvenience to research. It is a vital element in the social process. The statistical procedures used in the annual report permit the Commission to control its visible output, to build its statistical record, and, thus, to protect itself from criticism.

Several devices serve this end:

1) *The ambiguity of "investigation and conference."* Two thirds of the complaints investigated by the Commission were classed as "resolved by investigation and conference." The category "investigation and conference" implies that some discrimination was found and eliminated. However, many of the cases classified as "investigation and conference" did not exhibit any evidence that an effective change had occurred. Many cases were moot; the respondent has purchased a settlement with an empty offer to a complainant who is not in a position to accept it. Relatively few of the cases classified as "investigation and conference" involved realistic victory for a complainant.

2) *The fusion of complaints initiated and received.* The Commission had the power to initiate complaints as well as to receive them. It did not make effective use of its initiatory power and this has been one cause of criticism by members of civil rights groups. The fusion of received and initiated complaints into one category has several effects.

142

Obviously, it fails to indicate the proportion of complaints that are initiated by the Commission. Secondly, it fails to show the nature of Commission-initiated complaints. The author examined more than thirty such complaints, initiated at one time or another between 1959 and 1962. All of them concerned violative employment application forms. None was concerned with substantive issues of employment pattern of employment policy. Commission-initiated complaints (which are a product of regular policing activity during periods when other activity is slack), permit the Commission to keep its case output high, and provide a large number of cases to place in the "investigation and conference" category. Received complaints in the employment field are generally dismissed for lack of probable cause. If the policing of application forms were excluded from the over-all statistics, the "investigation and conference" figure for the last several years before the emergence of the housing law would be closer to 10 percent than to 65 percent.

3) *The use of cumulative totals.* Until 1965 the Commission did not publish the totals for the year covered by the report; it cumulated all the cases since 1946. Thus, in any given category, the Commission could "ride" on previous accomplishments.

4) *Moot cases.* The legal category "withdrawn" fails to accurately reflect the number of cases in which complaints withdraw in effect by losing interest in the case, becoming lost to the Commission, or accepting an opportunity elsewhere.

5) *The use of totals instead of detailed breakdowns.* No given category of complaint, for example, race, religion, national origin, etc., was broken down by outcome and by institutional sphere. Thus, embarassing figures, such as the percent of complaints dismissed for lack of probable cause in employment, can be disguised.

It has been suggested that statistical reports often come to affect the performance that they are intended to measure. Organizations come to believe their own reports, and to accept statistical[21] distortions as pictures of reality. This tendency can be seen within the MCAD.

As the Commission struggled with the problem of defining to the public its successes and challenges, it wavered in its interpretations of the statistical record. In some contexts Commission personnel took a fairly realistic position. When asked to name the most serious problem in administering the law, Mrs. Mahoney and other officials often referred to the paucity of "good" complaints, a response which implies that discrimination existed but was not producing complaints. Such a response legitimized the Commission by asserting that it faced important problems. Yet, most of the time a decline in complaints, or a large number of conciliated cases, was taken as evidence for a decline in discrimination.[22] In general, there was a strong tendency both inside and outside the Commission to accept the figures in the statistical report as proof of the general capacity of the law to handle problems of discrimination and as evidence of successful administration of the law. In view of this uncritical acceptance of some rather general and vague numbers, it is necessary to examine a sample of cases more intensively.

Procedures for Processing Complaints

Since the major enforcement activities of the Commission are tied to the investigation and conciliation of complaints brought by aggrieved individuals, it is important to study the sources, targets, treatment, and outcomes of these cases in some detail. To lay the groundwork for this analysis we must first describe in a general way the procedures that are used to process complaints. In general the Commission followed the procedures established by the statute, but it

144

also established a number of policies that filled in the interstices of its legislative mandate and, in some instances, altered the procedures suggested in the law.

The Commission always placed great value on its educational and persuasive functions, so much so that even the procedures for handling formal complaints were tailored to the exigencies of a human relations perspective.

The enforcement process starts with a verified complaint. The complainant usually came to the office of the Commission where he made and signed a complaint, telling the story of his maltreatment in his own words, and giving the names of all parties and witnesses.

The MCAD representative who witnessed the complaint immediately gathered background data on the complaint. In employment, the complainant's age, work experience, education, appearance, and attitude were noted. In housing, the complainant's income was often recorded. The complainant was asked where he learned about the Commission.

The complaint was assigned to one of the three commissioners who was designated "investigating commissioner," and to one of the four investigators or field representatives who worked in the Boston area on employment and housing cases.

The field representative assigned to the case visited the respondent as soon as possible. He made contact with some responsible official, announced that a complaint had been filed and stated that it was his duty to investigate the allegations that had been made against the firm. There were no regularly followed formal rules or procedures for officially informing the respondent that allegations had been made against him, nor were there any rules for deciding at what level in the firm the investigation should proceed. In some cases, cases were handled entirely at lower levels in the firm. A case can be brought and settled without high-level officials within the firm ever knowing that there was any

145

dispute. This reflects the human-relations orientation of field representatives and commissioners, who justified the practice on the grounds that settlement of the dispute was the important thing; considerations of form were minor.

If the complaint was against an employer, the field representative collected general data on the firm. He learned the names of officers of the firm, the type of business that it was engaged in, and its affiliations with other firms. He tried to learn the racial distribution among employees. He inquired as to the firm's source of labor supply, the speed of turnover, the division of the labor force into departments and occupational categories, and the union affiliation of employees. He examined application forms. The field representative worked from a set questionnaire designed to provide the investigatory commissioner with useful background information which would provide knowledge as to the structure of the firm that might be useful in future negotiations. If a respondent was reticent about providing exact information about racial composition, he was not pressed. He was not, for example, asked to make a head count. In general, respondents were not forced to respond to any of these preliminary inquiries.

Background information in housing complaints was not always gathered in the same systematic manner for housing officials and owners tended to be reluctant to talk about the nature and extent of their holdings.

After obtaining preliminary information, the field representative investigated the complainant's particular allegations. He asked for the respondent's version of the incident. He interviewed witnesses and others named in the complaint, and, if there were relevant records, he asked to examine them. He might interview persons who were presently employed by the respondent or who lived in his buildings to determine their qualifications so that they might be compared with the qualifications of the complainant. He gathered all the information that seemed relevant and prepared a report of his investigations which was submitted to the investigating commissioner.

On the basis of the field representative's report, the investigating commissioner might dismiss the case for want of probable cause. Before formally closing the case, the investigating commissioner usually tried to bring the complainant to his office for a conference. He tried to explain the basis for his decision. He might tell the complainant that he had been treated unjustly but that there was no evidence that race was involved. He might clear up some misunderstanding that led the complainant to suspect discrimination. In some cases, commissioners counseled complainants, giving advice about how to apply for a job, how to behave during interviews, or how to act on the job. He might admonish the complainant to try to improve his behavior.

If circumstances warranted, the investigating commissioner might send the field representative back for further investigations, either to clear up ambiguities in the case or to investigate new allegations made by the complainant during the conference.

At the conference, the investigating commissioner would tell the respondent that there were some indications of unlawful practices and would give the respondent a chance to present a defense. Occasionally in employment cases, and frequently in housing cases, the respondent would bring legal representation to the conference.

The respondent might allege that the whole affair was just a misunderstanding and offer to make amends. He might insist that he was not guilty or allege that there was nothing he could do to remedy the situation. If the investigator thought there was good reason to believe that discrimination of some kind occurred, then he would try to suggest remedies and to persuade the respondent to accept them.

147

If there was an opening and the complainant was still interested in it, the commissioner might ask the respondent to offer it. If there was no opening or if the complainant had no interest in working for the respondent or renting or buying his property, the commissioner might ask for a written commitment to operate on a nondiscriminatory basis in the future. Occasionally, the respondent might be asked to apologize, or to write a letter of recommendation for a discharged employee, or to take some other affirmative action. Respondents were not asked to hire or promote a given number of Negro employees within a given time period, or to take steps to intergrate their holdings. They were not asked to reorganize their operations or to change their standards to give Negroes a better chance. They were only asked to consider all applicants on an equal basis and to afford equal treatment to all employees, tenants, and customers.

If a respondent was particularly obstinate and refused to accept the investigating commissioner's findings or his recommendations, a formal hearing might be called. Most respondents did not want the publicity of a public hearing, nor did they want to become involved in formal legal proceedings. They would rather settle the case on the Commission's terms, especially when settlement can be purchased at the price of a mere promise and without any affirmative action.

After the conference, the terms were explained to the complainant and the case was closed. Occasionally, a case was held open for a considerable period pending some follow-up to determine the extent of the respondent's compliance with the Commission's requests.

When a case was closed, it was classified as either "dismissed for lack of probable cause," "dismissed for lack of jurisdiction," or "closed after investigation and conference." The latter was a somewhat ambiguous category. There was no formal category termed "probable cause" found. Though the law says that conciliation is in order only after a finding of probable cause, there was not ordinarily any formal notification of such a finding prior to conciliation.

Officially, the category "closed after investigation and conference" implies that evidence of discrimination was found.[21] The category does not mean, paradoxically, that a conference was actually held. Sometimes, for example, a housing respondent would admit to the field representative that he had discriminated, or that there had been some misunderstanding, and would agree to offer a vacancy to the complainant. The case was closed and placed in the category "investigation and conference" without any actual participation by an investigating commissioner in the case. Formally, no finding of probable cause was ever made. Since the case was well settled the forms of the law did not seem to matter to Commission personnel.

Even when a conference was held, conciliation occurred without formal findings of probable cause. Commissioners did not like to explicitly state that they were finding probable cause. They found that it was easier to negotiate and to conciliate if the question of guilt was left open. They did not like to alienate the respondent by direct statements that implied a legal finding of guilt. In fact, commissioners sometimes used this as a bargaining point. A respondent might say that if a finding of probable cause was made, he would demand a formal hearing, but that he would cooperate if no finding was made. After conciliation, the case would be filed under the rubric "investigation and conference." What the respondent did not know is that he bargained for nothing. There was, in effect, no such thing as "a finding of probable cause." There were only two official categories, "no probable cause" and "investigation and conference," and the latter was ambiguous enough to hide the implication of guilt.

149

In other words, the complaint process as described in the statute did not correspond exactly to the day-to-day practice. In theory, the sequence was investigation, a finding of probable cause, conciliation, and finally the closing of the case. In practice, the sequence was investigation, followed by a decision as to whether conciliation would be worthwhile. Then, when the case was closed, it was classified as "no probable cause" or "investigation and conference" depending on whether evidence of discrimination was discovered and independent of whether conferences were actually held. In order to facilitate negotiation and avoid embarrassing respondents, the Commission allowed investigation and conciliation to merge into a continuous process, unburdened by explicit consideration of questions of guilt.

In some instances, the complaint process deviated even more radically from legal theory. Occasionally a complainant would bring a case as leverage in aiding him in bargaining with someone. In this case, he might ask the Commission to defer investigation pending his private efforts to settle the case. For example, after selling a house to a Negro, a builder delayed in completing construction of the house and in actually passing papers. The buyer filed a complaint to remind the seller of his rights under the law, but delayed investigation. Eventually the papers were passed and the case went into the file marked "closed after investigation and conference" though there was no investigation and no conference.

Some cases did not even appear in the records. A Negro might bring in a complaint against a firm with which a field representative was personally acquainted. The Commission representative might feel that he could secure a settlement more effectively by personal intervention without recourse to official procedure. There is no evidence to suggest that this was a frequent procedure but it did occur in at least two instances in housing since the passage of the law.

150

In general, Commission practice corresponded to the procedures contemplated in the statute. However, these procedures were adapted to circumstances whenever modification seemed appropriate. The guiding principle was successful settlement of the case. The goal of the procedure was solving problems in human relations. Legal form was secondary. The Commission was satisfied if it had contributed to clarification of a misunderstanding, obtained some benefit for the complainant, or received assurance that the respondent would abide by the provisions of the law.

The Commission had established a "game" which it could win without the opponent's losing. Field representatives spoke of a finding of investigation and conference as "winning" or "beating" a case. Such a case would appear in the Commission's official statistics as a success. Yet respondents did not give up much in many cases. Indeed, they would interpret the encounter as a victory, or at least a standoff. Thus, the Commission could build its record without creating a significant disturbance.

151

... a set of limitations grows out of the necessity of appealing to the individuals to set the law in motion ... for laws will not enforce themselves ...–[Roscoe Pound]

Sources and Targets of Complaints

Since the Commission has chosen to tie enforcement to complaints brought by aggrieved individuals, the social structure of enforcement is tied to the patterns of complaints brought to the Commission. The data for this chapter are provided by descriptive and statistical analysis of the fifty-nine housing and fifty-nine employment cases described in Chapter I.

The cases show that complaints originate at particular locations in the social structure and are directed at targets with particular locations and that the effectiveness of the enforcement process is limited by a set of social factors that produce a particular pattern of sources, targets, and types of complaints.

All 118 complaints were filed by particular individuals and alleged particular wrongs to them as individuals. However, for purposes of analysis the complaints can be divided into *individual* complaints and *group* complaints. Group complaints are complaints that were *filed* by individuals but supported in some way by one of the organized civil rights pressure groups that operated in the Boston area. These groups included the NAACP, the Urban League, CORE, and the various local fair housing groups that constituted the Boston Fair Housing Federation. A case is classified as a "group case" if the complainant was referred to the Commission by a group or if the case was initially developed by a group and sent to the Commission for litigation. Information on the origins of a complaint was available from several sources. The primary source was Commission records. The data sheet for each complainant has a space for noting who referred the complainant to the MCAD. The data sheets are incomplete and in some cases the complainant did not inform the Commission of his group "sponsorship." Interviews of Commission personnel, civil rights leaders and complainants supplemented the information from the data sheets.

Forty complaints, or about one third, were referred to the agency by organized groups working for equal opportunity and seventy-eight were brought by unaided individuals. Of the forty group complaints, twenty-six were housing complaints and fourteen were employment complaints. Group complaints accounted for 44.1 percent of all housing complaints and only 23.7 percent of all employment complaints which indicated that the various groups working for equal opportunity were more active in the housing field.

Group participation in housing cases was not only more frequent, it was more intensive. In employment, groups operated primarily as referral agencies. When informed of experiences of discrimination, they made a judgment as to whether a legal complaint was in order. In housing, groups worked directly with individuals seeking accommodations and, if discrimination was encountered, actively combatted it by direct action and by helping to prepare evidence for possible legal action.

There was some group effort in the employment field that was just as active as the fair housing work. However, it was not as extensive and did not produce any complaints before the Commission during the time period of the study. All group complaints in employment were simple referrals,

153

though a referral may be followed by pressure of other varieties. In contrast, of twenty-six group complaints in housing, only six were referrals and the rest complaints that were actively developed by groups.

The distinction between group and individual complaints is an important one. Group complaints can be shown to be of a qualitatively different type, and the greater prevalence of group complaints in housing accounts for some of the differences between the structure of the complaint process in housing and employment

A second mode of classifying the social source of complaints is provided by the social class of the complainants. Complainants can be divided into two status categories, middle class and working class. A complainant is middle class if he is in an occupation that is classed by the census bureau as professional, technical, managerial, official, clerical, or sales, or if he is a college or graduate student. All others are classed as working class. An unemployed complainant is classified according to the last job held.

Occupation is used as an index of social class for both theoretical and practical reasons. The theoretical reasons will become evident at a later point. The practical consideration is that occupation is the only index for which data was available for both housing and employment complainants. Educational measures are available only for employment cases.

It might be argued that the use of present occupation is inappropriate. Discrimination might temporarily reduce highly educated Negroes to low-status occupations while they use the legal process to seek employment commensurate with their qualifications. By this reasoning, either education or the occupational status of the job that the complainant is seeking would be a better measure of social class. This line of objection seems reasonable and would have considerable weight if there were, in fact, complainants who fit the criterion of not having an occupational status commensurate with qualifications. There was only one individual who met this criterion, a law school graduate temporarily working as a janitor while seeking work that would allow for the use of his legal training. His complaint was brought in the course of seeking employment in the management training program of an insurance company. One anomalous case would not seem to vitiate the classificatory scheme. Further, since occupational status is the only measure available in housing, occupation is the only index that permits comparison between institutional spheres.

According to the occupational criteria, seventy-five complaints were brought by middle-class persons and forty-three complaints were brought by working-class persons. The seventy-five middle-class complaints constituted 63.6 percent of all complaints. It should be remembered that this does not mean that sixty-three percent of all complainants were middle class. In a discussion of the complaint process the appropriate unit of analysis is the complaint. The class origins of the complaint is taken to be an attribute of the complaint, not of the complainant. Thus, if one complainant brings two complaints, his social class will appear twice in the computations. Throughout this chapter the case is the unit of analysis.

One of the hypotheses that guided this study was that employment complaints would be predominantly working class, and housing complaints predominantly middle class.

The avenue of legal complaint is not well suited to the middle-class individual seeking better employment opportunities because complaint to an outside agency will not produce or maintain good relations with middle-class colleagues. There is a strong bias in industrial management against what is called the "chip on the shoulder attitude." Middle-class occupations in industry tend not to be organized in opposition to management; they are either a part of

155

management or are coopted by management. Unionization of professional, technical, clerical, and managerial workers has been very slow. The same emphasis on colleagueship, cooperation, and social relations that makes union organization difficult, also forces Negro aspirants to middle-class status to avoid antagonistic or unfriendly actions, and complaints to legal agencies certainly qualify as antagonistic and unfriendly. A middle-class Negro might complain in anger or in desperation, but we would not expect him to bring a complaint as a realistic mode of improving his status.

Working-class complainants need not be as concerned with the consequences of fighting management. It is only another skirmish in the "class war."

In housing, one is not concerned with the kinds of permanent relations one is establishing with landlords or subdivision developers. Hence, the middle-class Negro is less constrained in his choice of techniques.

In sum, we would expect the incidence of middle-class complaints to be higher in housing than in employment because legal action is a more appropriate strategy for improving one's position in housing.

A second reason for expecting more middle-class complainants in housing derives from the variable structures of the markets involved. The middle-class Negro can hope that his possession of skills will induce management to treat him equally, since the competition for skilled manpower makes it unprofitable to exclude whole categories of potential employees. Thus, status can be improved by other techniques besides legal action. He can not have the same hopes in his search for housing. In the housing market, prejudice has a more disturbing effect on the supposedly rational forces of the market. In theory, the landlord or developer should not care where his money comes from. He would rather deal with a Negro than miss an opportunity for a transaction. However, prejudice and the fear of prejudice produce concern that transactions with Negroes will prevent future transactions with whites. The forces of the market, as perceived by the property owner, do not support the middle-class Negro. In employment, a Negro can develop one of the middle-class skills that are highly salable, and avoid the areas where discrimination lingers. In housing, he is cut off from virtually all the markets for high-quality accommodations.

The hypothesis that there is a higher incidence of middle-class complaints in housing is true.[1] Table 9 shows the incidence of housing and employment complaints by class. More than ninety percent of the housing complaints are middle-class, as compared to about one third of the employment complaints.

Table 9. Institutional sphere and class origins of complaints

Class	Employment		Housing		Total	
	Number	Percentage	Number	Percentage	Number	Percentage
Middle	21	35.6	54	91.5	75	63.6
Working	38	64.4	5	8.5	43	36.4
Total	59		59		118	

$\phi = 0.56$

A number of problems complicate the interpretation of these figures. The data used to test the hypothesis consist entirely of *incidence* of complaint. We can not use this data to say anything definite about the *rates* of complaint. Thus, we can not say for sure that middle-class persons respond with a legal complaint to a smaller proportion of instances of employment discrimination than instances of discrimination. To make a statement of that type, one must first know the rate of discrimination, which would

157

be very difficult to measure. Rates of *perceived* discrimination could be developed if appropriate surveys were taken, but no such survey was available for this study. Consequently, we cannot be certain whether a low incidence of complaint reflects a low rate of complaint or only a low rate of discrimination.

Nevertheless, it seems probable that the high incidence of middle-class complaints in housing does reflect a high rate of complaint. All areas outside of the ghetto are effectively closed to Negroes but it is middle-class individuals who have used legal techniques to try to move out. Working-class Negroes have not chosen to attack housing discrimination. Cheaper housing is available outside the ghetto, but is not open to Negro occupancy and working-class Negroes have not filed complaints to try to open it.

Similarly, in employment it is not likely that higher rates of discrimination exist in working-class than in middle-class jobs. Certain working-class jobs are closed by union restriction or tradition and certain middle-class jobs that involve supervision, or meeting the public, or elite status are also closed. If anything, discrimination increases as the status ladder is climbed.

Although fewer employment complaints are middle-class, the middle class is still over-represented in employment complaints. Only 26.6 percent of the nonwhite population of the Boston Standard Metropolitan Statistical Area (SMSA) were in middle-class occupations according to the 1960 census,[2] but 35.6 percent of complaints were brought by middle class persons. If we assume that there are no differences in rates of discrimination by class, then the rate of complaint is somewhat higher among the Negro middle class than the working class. Additional support for this view is given by the fact that the median years of education of complainants was 11 years compared to a median education of 10.5 years for the nonwhite population of the SMSA.

In sum, there seems to be a greater tendency for middle-class persons to complain than working-class persons, a difference that is exaggerated in housing where the factors that ordinarily restrain middle-class complaints do not operate. Because of ambiguities and uncertainties about rates we can not be certain that the differential incidence of complaints by class reflects the forces that have been suggested. However, one thing is certain. The class origins of complaints are different in housing and employment and this has consequences for the structure of the complaint process.

Later analysis will show that the two gross differences between the social sources of complaints in housing and employment have important consequence in their impact on the enforcement process. The complaint process in employment is conditioned by the fact that most employment complaints are brought by working-class individuals. Similarly the complaint process in housing is structured by the middle-class sponsored character of housing complaints.

Table 10 shows the number of complaints of various types alleging discrimination in employment. Complaints may allege that a firm's refusal to hire for some job was discriminatory, that a firm discriminated in failing to promote a qualified Negro to a better position, that a firm discriminated against a Negro employee in the terms or conditions of employment, or that an employee's discharge was discriminatory. Within each of these categories the particular job in question can be one of many different types.

Table 10 provides evidence for one of the major theses of this study: *The pattern of complaints did not correspond to the structure of discrimination.* By and large, the complaints did not attack the major bastions of discrimination. Rather, the complaints reflected the current structure of Negro employment; they tended to be directed toward areas where racial barriers had already fallen.

For example, eleven complaints alleged discrimination in

159

Table 10. Number of complaints of various types alleging discrimination in employment

Type of complaint	Position in question	Number	Percent
Hiring	Electronics assembly	6	
	Ship construction	6	
	Clerical-secretarial	6	
	Clerical IBM specialty	4	
	Unskilled labor	3	
	Mathematician-programmer system analyst	3	
	Gas station attendant	1	
	Airline stewardess	1	
	Nurse	1	
	School teacher	1	
	Salesgirl	1	
	Management trainee	1	
		34	57.6
Promotion	Electronics assembly (better paying job)	1	
	Electronics assembly (supervisor)	1	
	Records clerk (better position)	1	
		3	5.1
Terms and conditions	Electronics assembly	2	
	Other assembly	2	
	Unskilled labor	3	
	Nurse, physical therapist	2	
	Truck driver	1	
		10	16.9
Discharge	Electronics assembly	2	
	Other assembly	4	
	Unskilled labor	2	
	Skilled labor (carpenter, shoe worker)	2	
	Chambermaid	1	
	Nurse	1	
		12	20.3
Total		59	

employment as assembler in the electronics industry. The electronics industry is a young, modern, and growing industry with no traditions of racial exclusion in the industry and few current racial barriers. In an expanding industry that is experiencing needs for manpower recruitment, discrimination is not profitable. Consequently, Negroes were well represented as operatives in the electronics industry. In 1960, Negroes constituted 2.5 percent of the male operatives and 5.8 percent of the female operatives in the electrical equipment industry in the Boston SMSA. When these figures are compared with the proportion of Negroes in the experienced labor force of the Boston SMSA, 2.4 percent for males and 3.5 percent for females, it becomes evident that the Negro is by no means excluded from the industry. The comparison is all the more striking when the primary location of the industry in suburban areas far from centers of Negro population is taken into account. Yet, nearly 20 percent of the Negro employment complaints in the period 1959-1960 concerned employment as operatives in this industry.

By 1960, Negroes were over-represented in the general census category "operatives." Negroes accounted for 5.9 percent of female operatives and 3.8 percent of male operatives, yet fifteen complaints out of fifty-nine concerned employment as operatives.

Six complaints were filed alleging discrimination in shipyard work. Yet, shipbuilding work provided employment for at least 1,000 male Negroes in the SMSA.

Negroes were not well represented as mathematicians or secretaries. This is not necessarily a sign that these were areas of intense discrimination. Quite the contrary, mathematical and secretarial skills were in short supply and any Negro who was trained in these areas can surely find employment. The under-representation in these categories derives from the state of Negro training at the time rather than

161

from intensive discrimination. Other positions represented in Table 10 are similar in this respect. In 1960 the business machines specialty was in critically short supply, as were all clerical skills. Nurses also had a very salable skill. Negro participation in these occupations was no longer minimal; Negroes constituted 1.4 percent of the area's female clerical employees and 2.2 percent of nurses by 1960.

A few of the occupational categories shown in Table 10 represent statuses that were subject to a high degree of discrimination. The management hierarchies of private business were largely closed to Negroes. Only four tenths of one percent of the salaried managers and officials in private industry were Negroes in 1960. Hence the allegation of exclusion from a management-training program was a pioneering complaint. There were only twenty Negro secondary school teachers enumerated in the 1960 census out of a total of 4,357 teachers. The position of airline stewardess has been the subject of a great deal of controversy because airlines have been generally unwilling to hire Negroes in any flight capacities. Negro girls starting in the sixties have been able to get jobs in retail sales, but there is still a great deal of discrimination in this area. Filling station operators generally prefer white attendants except in Negro areas. It has been quite difficult for Negroes employed in industry to raise themselves above the assembly line level. The prejudice against Negroes in supervisory positions is still effective. Thus, the complaint alleging discrimination in a promotion to supervisor in an electronics plant had a pioneering quality.

However, these critical occupational categories account for only six complaints, only 16.3 percent of all hiring and promotion cases. A few of the complaints alleging discriminatory treatment or discharge might be considered to have had pioneering implications. Two of the terms and conditions cases concern the problems of the "shape up."

162

The "shape up" is the nonbureaucratic, somewhat arbitrary procedure by which employees are picked for referral to available jobs. Those who are not picked in the "shape up" do not work. The arbitrary, particularistic, personalistic way in which referrals are made tends to discriminate against Negroes who do not participate in the inner circles and networks of association that tend to govern the distribution of jobs. One complaint concerned a shape up for truck driving jobs, another a shape up among laborers in the controversial construction industry. In addition, one of the discharge cases was brought by a Negro carpenter who was suddenly not used on a project that he had been working on every day. Referral to carpentry jobs in the construction industry is on the same personalistic basis as the "shape up."

These three cases, together with the other six, make nine cases where the disputed occupational category was subject to considerable discriminatory pressures in Boston. The remaining fifty complaints did not place pressure on the current structure of opportunity. They involved the types of jobs that Negroes already held or jobs that Negroes were beginning to prepare themselves for and obtain in response to the demand for critical skills. In other words, the structure of complaints reflected the structure of Negro activity. Most activity is daily routine; only a little is pioneering activity on the racial frontier.

Complaints that were tied to the routine course of activity failed to produce inquiry into the areas where discrimination was the most prevalent. For example, according to the 1960 census there were no Negroes employed as linemen or servicemen for telephone, telegraph and power companies in the Boston SMSA. Negroes constituted only 0.5 percent of male salesmen in the area, only 1.0 percent of foremen and only 1.7 percent of apprentices. These were all areas where discrimination was evident, yet no complaints alleged discrimination in these occupations.

163

Promotion was one of the most crucial problems facing Negroes, yet only three complaints were brought alleging discrimination in upgrading and only one of these concerned promotion to the supervisory level. The consequence of treating anti-discrimination legislation as private law, concerned with conciliating the grievances of individual Negroes as they come to perceive discrimination in the course of their daily activities, is to predicate law enforcement on the limited experiences and selective perspectives of a segmented and isolated population.

In the housing sphere, complaints were more focused on real problems of discrimination. However, even in housing, complaints were directed toward some problems and not others. Table 11 shows the types of allegations made in housing complaints.

Table 11. Number of complaints of various types alleging discrimination in housing

Type of complaint	Number	Percent
Apartments		
Refusal to rent	50	84.7
Refusal to show	3	5.1
Eviction	1	1.7
Total	54	91.5
Homes		
Refusal to sell	2	3.4
Refusal to show	1	1.7
Eviction	1	1.7
Refusal to pass papers on sale	1	1.7
Total	5	8.5
Grand total	59	

A large proportion of the housing cases involved the rental of apartments. The one case alleging discriminatory eviction concerned a tenant who had just moved into the building.

Almost all of the cases were brought by Negroes attempting to move to different housing. No complaints alleged that ghetto landlords were charging exhorbitant rents or failing to maintain buildings in a proper state of sanitation and repair. Such cases would, of course, raise difficult legal and administrative problems, but the point is that the issue was never raised though living conditions in the ghetto are as much a part of the Negro housing problem as exclusion from white neighborhoods and buildings. The law has been used primarily by middle-class Negroes wishing to escape the ghetto and not by working-class Negroes seeking to improve ghetto conditions and, hence, these conditions did not come under the potential jurisdiction of the law.

Complaints may be filed against employers who already hire relatively large numbers of Negroes or against employers who employ relatively few Negroes. Similarly, in housing cases the accommodation under dispute may be in an integrated neighborhood or in an all-white neighborhood.

Cases alleging discrimination in employment tended to be filed against firms that already had a substantial number of Negro employees.[3] Nearly 56 percent of all employment complaints were against firms whose labor force was 3.0 percent Negro or more. More than a quarter of the respondents had more than 10 percent Negro employees at the time the complaint was filed. The mean percent Negro of all respondents was 6.6 percent.[4]

One reason for the preponderance of firms with relatively large numbers of Negro employees is that employees frequently allege that unequal treatment occurred on the job. A firm must hire Negroes before it can become a target for such complaints. Complaints alleging discrimination in ini-

165

tial hiring tend to involve respondents with fewer Negro employees. The mean percentage of Negro respondents in cases alleging discrimination in initial hiring was 5.2 whereas in cases where the allegation was one of discrimination against an employee, the mean percentage Negro is 8.7. Table 12 shows the distribution of Negro employees at firms that were targets of employment complaints.

Table 12. Number of employment complaints against companies already employing Negroes.

Percent Negro employees	All cases		Hiring cases only	
	Number	Percentage	Number	Percentage
0 - 2.9	26	44.1	20	58.8
3 - 9.9	18	30.5	7	20.6
10 - 19.9	9	15.2	5	14.7
20+	6	10.2	2	5.9
Total	59		34	
Mean 6.6				
Median 3.0				

In contrast, housing complaints referred almost entirely to nonintegrated housing. Only two complaints were brought concerning buildings that were already integrated. However, several complaints were directed against white buildings in predominantly Negro areas. There were eight complaints alleging discrimination in the rental of housing in Roxbury. Six of those accommodations were located at various addresses along Seaver Street, a Jewish pocket within the Negro ghetto that had remained Jewish despite its location in a census tract that had become nearly ninety-percent Negro. Three complaints concerned housing accommodations in the predominantly Negro areas of southeastern Cambridge. Six additional complaints referred to housing located close enough to the fringe of the ghetto so that the surrounding census tract was more than 3 percent Negro.

A large majority of the cases, forty-two in all, involved housing located in areas in which whites constituted more than 97 percent of the population. The prime targets were Back Bay (seventeen cases), Brookline (eight cases), "white" Cambridge (eight cases), and Brighton (four cases). The general direction of attempted movement in these cases is north and northwest from the established areas of Negro residency to the desirable apartment areas of Back Bay and Brookline. This presents an interesting contrast with the historic southwesterly movement of the ghetto toward Dorchester and Jamaica Plain. Only one case was brought in Jamaica Plain and none were brought in Dorchester. This serves to underline the pioneering quality of housing complaints.

No cases were brought in the South End, none in East Boston, none in North Boston and none in Allston. There was, in short, very little attempt to use the law to move into other areas of working-class housing.

Forty-eight of fifty-nine cases involved housing located in a diamond-shaped area with points in Roxbury in the South, Brookline in the West, Back Bay in the East, and Cambridge in the North. The other eleven cases involve housing in Watertown, Waltham, Lynn, Sudbury, Hyde Park, Randolph, and Jamaica Plain. With the exceptions that have been noted this was housing in middle-class white areas.

The median fraction of Negroes per census tract for all housing cases is only 1.0 percent. The distribution is given in Table 13.

In contrast with the employment cases the housing cases had a pioneering quality. Most complaints were brought in the pursuit of middle-class housing in white neighborhoods.

167

Table 13. Number of housing complaints in census tracts already
containing Negroes

Percent Negroes in tract	Complaints	
	Number	Percentage
0 - 0.9	29	49.2
1 - 2.9	13	22.0
3 - 9.9	7	11.9
10 - 19.9	0	0.0
20 - 49.9	2	3.4
50+	8	13.6
Total	59	
Median 1.0		

Only 17 percent of the cases were directed against housing that was clearly within the confines of ghetto areas, and of the remaining forty-nine cases, thirty-four concerned housing in middle-class residential areas such as Back Bay, Brookline, and suburban towns.

Employment cases, on the other hand tended to be brought against firms that already hired an average number of Negroes and to refer to working-class jobs that were not closed to Negroes.

Test of the Jurisdiction Hypothesis

One of the main hypotheses of this study is that groups tend to bring focused, strategic, pioneering complaints and that individuals tend to bring complaints that do not challenge the established social structure. Individuals bring complaints that reflect their limited experience whereas groups are able to generate complaints directed at significant targets. Thus, the Commission's access to significant targets depended on the cooperation of pressure groups.

We shall call a complaint successful if it causes a Negro to

168

obtain a housing or job opportunity which previously has been denied him. The Negro need not be the complainant in the case. Presumably, investigation of respondents' practices and policies could result in increased Negro employment, even if the complainant's case was without merit, or concerned treatment on the job, or discharge.

We shall call a complaint strategic when, if it were successful, it would produce a more even distribution of Negroes in the community. We are simply asking whether the targets of complaints are firms and neighborhoods that already include an average number of Negroes, or whether they are pioneering, strategic complaints against underrepresented firms or neighborhoods.

We would expect individuals to bring unfocused complaints, for the individual complains about experiences that occur in the course of his ordinary activity, and daily activity is shaped by an established social structure. One learns of job opportunities from relatives, friends, and neighbors; a network of primary-group ties channel information about openings. The individual Negro complains about treatment on the job or unfair dismissal, and Negroes tend to work where other Negroes already work. Similarly, Negroes often look for housing close to their friends and the established locus of their social life. Hence, individual complaints tend to reflect an established social structure.

Complaints brought by organized groups, on the other hand, reflect the aspirations of an avant-garde for fuller participation in the life of the community. Accordingly, they will have a more pioneering quality.

In short, group complaints will be strategic, individual complaints will not.

Sixty-six complaints are classed as strategic and fifty-two are classed as nonstrategic, according to the following operational definitions.

    a) A complaint against a firm in the central Boston

labor market is strategic if less than 5.1 percent of the employees of the firm are Negro. This is the Negro percentage of the population of the fourteen communities that are within forty-five minutes of central Boston by rapid transit.[5]

b) A complaint against a firm within the Boston SMSA but outside of the central labor market is focused if less than 0.4 percent of the employees of the firm are Negroes. This is the Negro percentage of the population of the other sixty-two communities in the Boston SMSA. We would not expect firms in outlying communities, far from centers of Negro population, to have as many Negro employees.

c) A complaint against a firm with branches throughout the SMSA is strategic if less than 3 percent of its employees are Negro. This is the Negro percentage for the population of the SMSA.[6]

d) A housing complaint is strategic if it is brought against a housing unit that is located in a census tract that is less then 3 percent Negro. It is assumed, and the pattern of complaints supports the view, that a complaint against a housing unit located in a census tract that is more than 3 percent Negro would serve, if successful, to fill in the gaps of the Negro ghetto, or to extend its boundaries, but not to reduce segregation.

It must be understood that a nonstrategic complaint is not *necessarily* an invalid complaint or a useless one. It is likely to be both, but it is *defined* as a complaint that could not produce a change in the established structure of uneven participation.

It may be argued that it is unrealistic to call a complaint unfocused just because a firm hires relatively large numbers of Negroes if the complainant is seeking a particular position that has no Negro representation. In abstract terms this is a legitimate objection. However, only two of the thirty-five nonstrategic employment complaints could be

170

considered strategic on the grounds that the particular job category involved might have been closed to Negroes.

It is clear that the definitions of strategic in employment and housing are not exactly comparable. There are more strategic complaints in housing (71.2 percent) than in employment (40.7 percent.) Part of this difference occurs because there is a more uneven distribution of Negroes in census tracts than in firms. If complaints were brought at random more housing complaints would qualify as strategic merely because of the highly skewed distribution of Negro residence. This is an unavoidable problem because there is no unit in housing that is exactly comparable to the firm in employment; the census tract is an arbitrary definition of the neighborhood.

It might be possible to develop a standard for the classification of housing cases that would make equal proportions of housing and employment cases classifiable as strategic. This would permit some types of comparisons, but would be undesirable from another point of view since housing complaints are more strategic than employment complaints. The data presented in this chapter indicate that the statistical difference between the two institutional spheres is not a mere artifact. The greater participation of groups and middle-class individuals tends to produce strategic complaints in housing.

Table 14 shows that there is a tendency for group-sponsored complaints to be more strategic. To test whether this association is an artifact, produced by the noncomparability of the definitions of "strategic" in the two institutional spheres, we must compute a measure of association separately for housing and employment. The association holds up rather well. For all cases the association is measured by $\phi = 0.42$. For employment $\phi = 0.40$ and for housing $\phi = 0.32$.

It might be argued that the association in employment reflects the fact that twenty-six of the fifty-nine complaints

171

Table 14. Group vs. individual origin and quality of complaint by institutional sphere

Complaint quality	Employment			Housing			Total		
	Individual	Group	Total	Individual	Group	Total	Individual	Group	Total
Strategic	13	11	24	19	23	42	32	34	66
Nonstrategic	32	3	35	14	3	17	46	6	52
Total	45	14	59	33	26	59	78	40	118
ϕ		0.40			0.32			0.42	
χ^2		9.44			6.04			20.82	
P		< 0.01			< 0.05			< 0.01	

allege discrimination in discharge or on the job. Since Negroes must be hired before such complaints can be made, many employment complaints will be classed as nonstrategic. Further, groups are not as likely to sponsor complaints alleging discriminatory discharge or unequal treatment on the job. Despite these considerations, the association between group origin and the focus of complaints holds up when only cases alleging discrimination in initial hiring are considered (see Table 15).

Table 15. Group vs. individual complaints and quality of complaint, hiring complaints only[a]

Complaint quality	Individual	Group	Total
Strategic	7	9	16
Nonstrategic	15	2	17
Total	22	11	33

[a] $\phi = 48$; $\chi^2 = 7.60$; $P < 0.01$.

Negroes are likely to seek employment at places where other Negroes are already employed. The racial composition of the firm's labor force will not necessarily dissuade Negroes from assuming discrimination and complaining to the Commission. Hence, the quality of complaints reflected the current patterns of Negro application and these patterns, in turn, corresponded to the current patterns of Negro employment. Groups, on the other hand, were more aware of the over-all patterns of discrimination, less caught up by the emotional impact of the experience of rejection, and able to operate more selectively in their choice of targets.

Since group cases in employment tend to be merely *referred* by groups rather than originated by groups, the strategic nature of group cases must be attributed to a screening process. However, the contribution of groups to securing strategic cases should not be denigrated. Groups such as the NAACP and the Urban League are actively working to increase employment opportunity and are keeping track of areas of resistance. In some cases it is necessary to wait for a litigable case to develop before legal action can be taken. When an appropriate complainant is discovered he can be referred to the MCAD. This is not a mere passive process. It is best described as an active process of low intensity. Its importance is underscored by this consideration: If there had been no groups informing prospective complainants of their legal rights (and in some cases persuading complainants to take action), the total number of strategic complaints would have been reduced by about one half, from twenty-four to only thirteen, whereas the supply of routine nonstrategic cases would have been cut by only 10 percent, from thirty-five to thirty-three.

In housing, where group efforts were more active and intense, groups supplied the Commission with about 55 percent of their strategic cases. Moreover, the greater activity of groups in the housing area helps to explain the greater number of strategic complaints. The evidence for this is that the strong tendency for strategic complaints to be housing complaints is less strong when we examine group and individual complaints separately. Table 16 shows that the tendency for housing complaints to be strategic is measured by $\phi = 33$, but for group complaints this association is only 0.13, and for individual complaints it is only 0.22. Neither of these lower figures are statistically significant.

Note that there is one cell in Table 16 that appears to be out of alignment. There is a tendency for housing complaints to be strategic even when brought by an individual. Nineteen of thirty-three (or 57 percent), of the housing complaints brought by individuals are strategic. This can be partially explained by the class differences in the origins of employment and housing complaints.

174

Table 16. Institutional sphere and quality of complaint

Complaint quality	All complaints			Group complaints			Individual complaints		
	Employment	Housing	Total	Employment	Housing	Total	Employment	Housing	Total
Strategic	24	42	66	11	23	34	13	19	32
Nonstrategic	35	17	52	3	3	6	32	14	46
Total	59	59	118	14	26	40	45	33	78
ϕ		0.33			0.13			0.22	
χ^2		12.85			0.68			3.78	
P		< 0.01							

Table 17. Social class and quality of complaint

Class	Employment complaints			All complaints		
	Strategic	Nonstrategic	Total	Strategic	Nonstrategic	Total
Middle	13	8	21	52	23	75
Working	11	27	38	14	29	43
Total	24	35	59	66	52	118
ϕ	0.32			0.36		
χ^2	6.04			15.29		
P	<0.05			<0.01		

Table 18. Social class and complaint quality

Class	Individual employment cases only[a]		
	Strategic	Nonstrategic	Total
Middle	7	7	14
Working	6	26	32
Total	13	33	46

[a] $\phi = 0.31$; $\chi^2 = 4.41$; P = < 0.05.

Table 17 indicates that middle-class persons are more likely to bring strategic complaints than working-class persons. Education and social status makes middle-class Negroes more interested in pioneering opportunities and more able to discriminate the targets of their efforts. The law was designed to facilitate complaints by removing them from the cumbersome and complicated procedures of the regular courts. Nevertheless, the effective use of legal procedures still presupposes a degree of sophistication on the part of the complainant.

There are not enough working-class cases in housing to study the relation between the quality and the class origins of complaints separately for housing cases, but as Table 17 shows the tendency that is evident within the whole sample holds up when employment cases are considered separately.

This association is not a spurious consequence of the fact that middle-class complainants tend to work through groups because the relationship holds even for individual employment complaints (see Table 18).

There is no reason to suppose that the preponderantly middle-class complaints in housing do not have the same tendency to choose strategic targets as their middle-class counterparts in employment. Accordingly, we may legitimately argue that the social-class factor combines with the group-activity factor to produce more strategic complaints in housing.

One way of summarizing this data is to contrast the modal housing complaint with the modal employment complaint. The modal employment complaint is not strategic and it is brought by a working-class individual. Forty-four percent of employment complaints are of this type compared to only 3.4 percent in this category in housing. In housing precisely the opposite case is modal. Thirty-seven and two-tenths percent of all housing complaints are strategic complaints brought by middle-class complainants via groups. Such complaints constitute only 10.2 percent of all employment cases.

Again, the consequences of waiting for complaints to be spontaneously generated in the community before activating the legal machinery is evident. In the absence of group organization to develop effective complaints, this strategy tends not to produce significant opportunities to make breakthroughs along the color line.

The relative ineffectiveness of the strategy of community generated complaints is magnified in those spheres where the use of legal complaint prevents the establishment and maintenance of continuing relationships. The role of law becomes one of arbitrating misunderstandings and lending legal weight to changes that are already being brought about by economic pressures.

Bases for Complaints

When a complainant comes to the offices of the Commission to allege that someone has discriminated against him, he must sign a verified complaint. This complaint contains a statement of the reasons for believing that discrimination has occurred. The complainant tells the story as he understands it in order to provide the Commission with initial clues as to how to carry out an investigation: A respondent is named, witnesses are suggested, and specific discriminatory acts are described.

The statements also provide an indication of what kinds of situations appear to Negroes to be discriminatory. This information may be used to examine our assumption that the limited perspective of the individual makes him an unsure judge of discrimination.

Analysis of the 118 cases under study shows that a wide variety of situations may appear to involve discrimination, ranging from blatant evidence of exclusion to mere whispers of suspicion. The various bases for complaint can be grouped into several general categories:

1) *Exclusionary statements.* The clearest indication of discrimination is a flat statement about Negro exclusion. Some Negroes report that they have been told, "We do not take colored" or "This is a white building," or "We don't like to mix-um," or "Of course, your race must be taken into account." In all, twenty-two of the cases involve allegations that someone overtly admitted that they were discriminating. In employment, discrimination is rarely so manifest; only three of the twenty-two cases of direct statement are employment cases.

In an additional four cases (all housing cases), the respondent was indirectly told that some opportunity was being denied on the basis of race. For example, in one case a man was looking for an apartment with the help of a real estate agent, Mr. W., who did a lot of apartment hunting for Negroes. A rental agent said to the man, "We don't take any of Mr. W's people."

2) *Tests.* In fifteen cases some claim of the respondent had been tested and found to be untrue before the complaint was filed. A white "ringer" was sent to the respondent to see if he received the same treatment as an unsuccessful Negro. Again this was a more frequent procedure in housing cases; only two of the fifteen cases were employment cases.

Tests can be made on an individual basis by friends of a Negro, or they can be done through the auspices of an organized group such as a local fair housing committee. Both of the employment cases involved individual tests. On the other hand, eleven of the thirteen housing cases were tested by groups.

Eleven of the tests proved that an opening existed when a Negro had been told that none were available. Three tests

179

discovered that the same qualifying criteria were not applied to the tester as to the original Negro applicant and one found different rental price quotations.

3) *Different treatment on discovery of race.* A frequent basis for complaint is that an individual is treated differently when he is seen in person than had been the case in prior dealings by telephone or correspondence. For example, one Negro woman was treated courteously on the telephone when she called inquiring about an advertised vacancy. She was told that the apartment was still available and invited to come and make an inspection. Upon arrival she quickly inspected the apartment and announced that she would take it, whereupon the real estate agent began to try to discourage her by suggesting another building and, finally, by telling her that the apartment was taken. A sudden shift in attitude upon discovery of an applicant's race was a motivating factor in seventeen housing complaints and in only two employment complaints.

4) *Specific unequal treatment.* In some cases the complainant is able to make specific allegations of unequal treatment without performing an artificial test. The complainant observes that particular white people with known qualifications are hired, or promoted, or given a housing accommodation, and he is not. The complainant makes the judgment that his qualifications are equal and concludes that he is an object of discrimination. A claim of unequal treatment may be termed *specific* only if the complainant makes reference to particular white persons and makes specific references to his assessment of his own and the white person's comparative qualifications. Vague statements that whites are treated better should be placed in a different category. One must have an "insider's" knowledge of a situation to make such a charge. The "specific unequal treatment" charge is often made by a worker who is dissatisfied with his treatment in comparison with other people

who work with him. For example, one woman was waiting her turn as mechanical machines replaced manual machines in the order of the seniority of their operators. When it was her turn for the next mechanical machine, she was skipped over in favor of the next white person in the line of seniority.

Of the eleven cases alleging specific unequal treatment, ten were employment cases. In housing cases one is seldom personally acquainted with the other applicants for an accommodations, if, indeed, he knows that such alternate candidates exist. Accordingly, if he is to demonstrate specific unequal treatment he must use an artificial test procedure. On the other hand, the artificial test procedure has very important advantages over the natural situation in that it provides more conclusive evidence of discrimination. The advantages of testing are not unlike the advantages of experimental technique over naturalistic observation in scientific method. They are the advantages of control. The complainant can mold the characteristics of the real or imaginary tester to the qualifications to which the respondent has committed himself. He can be sure of the visible characteristics of the test individual. In the natural case the complainant runs a greater risk of misunderstanding the nature of the standards that are being applied and of being mistaken as to the qualifications of the white person.

5) *Evidence of false statements.* In twenty-two cases the complainant rested his assumption of discrimination, in whole or in part, on evidence that he was not being told the truth. In these cases proof fell short of either a natural or artificial test situation. In nine of them the complainant discovered evidence that an opening or vacancy existed after he had been told that it was filled. For example, one man was told that an apartment had been taken and that the new tenants would move in the first of the next month. The man watched the apartment on the first and saw no

181

one moving in. When return visits did not produce evidence of occupancy, he concluded that he had not been told the truth.

Several complainants noted that an advertisement for a supposedly filled opening continued to run in the newspaper and concluded that the position had not been filled after all. In twelve cases complainants inferred discrimination from the fact that they were told contradictory stories, and in six of these the contradictory stories concerned the availability of openings. One official would describe an opening and send the applicant to another official who would claim that there was no such opening.

Both housing and employment are fairly well represented in the "evidence of untruth" category. Thirteen housing cases and nine employment cases are included.

6) *General evidence.* One possible ground for inferring discrimination is notable for its unexpected infrequency. One might suppose that the lily-white character of a building or a firm might frequently be cited as grounds for assuming discrimination or that the hiring of only white persons on a given day when both races are represented among the applicants, would be mentioned frequently. In fact, only three cases of the former are to be found and two of the latter. All five are employment cases.

It could be argued that over-all pattern of Negro participation is frequently an element in the total gestalt that spells discrimination to the complainant, but that it is not frequently cited since racial composition is not, in itself, proof of discrimination. In housing cases that argument is frequently valid. However, as we shall see, *none* of the bases of complaints cited in verified statements are "in themselves" proof of discrimination. All are mere indicating signs. Further, it should be noted that complaints are frequently made against firms with demonstrably integrated work forces or real estate holdings. The evidence suggests

182

that the infrequent citing of general evidences of discrimination may be taken at face value. Complainants make their allegations on the basis of sociological investigations. In fact, this is the reason that so many complaints are ill-founded. They reflect the limited perspective of an individual with a particular position in a social structure.

7) *Suspicious or unfair treatment.* In sixty cases evidence is cited that falls into one of several categories that can be lumped into the general class "suspicious and unfair treatment." The complainant is subjected to treatment that seems either racially motivated, or unfair, or both. There may be no direct evidence that he is being lied to, or any evidence that any white persons have been or would be treated differently in similar situations. Nevertheless, the respondent's behavior seemed unjust, or impolite, or insincere and seemed to be motivated by discriminatory intent.

In seven of these cases the complainant was a victim of what could be called "frustrated expectations." For instance, one man was led to believe that he had done rather well on a qualifications test and felt that he had been encouraged in the personnel interview. Later he was turned down via an impersonal and rather vague letter. He assumed that his race caused some higher-ups in the company to veto his employment. Frustrated expectations are more frequent in employment; only one of the seven instances occurs in a housing case.

Another common experience is the "run around." The applicant is sent from one person to another, avoided, and subjected to unaccountable delays and frustrations. His application is "lost," his appointments "forgotten," his request is "in process." The "run around" frequently accompanies other evidences of discrimination and is particularly common in the housing field where it is specifically reported in sixteen cases.

In ten employment cases and in six housing cases, complainants were disturbed by the fact that the reasons that they were given for their failure sounded "fishy" or "flimsy." They simply didn't seem believable.

A very frequent basis for making an employment case is a simple feeling that one hasn't been treated fairly. A Negro who is accorded treatment that he doesn't feel he deserves may attribute a discriminatory motivation to that treatment. Twenty-one employment cases allege "unfair" treatment of this sort. This is quite infrequent in housing, occurring only two times in fifty-nine cases.

Six cases of this sort were associated with racial slurs or other racial incidents[6] on the job, helping to give the situation a racial cast. One typical case of "unfair treatment" occurred when two men were dismissed for fighting on the job. One was white and one was Negro and the fight had been over alleged racial slurs. It didn't seem fair to the Negro that he should be fired when the other man was at fault. On the other hand, since both men were fired, a case could be made that firing both was a universalistic procedure.

On occasion the line between unfair and discriminatory treatment becomes even more blurred as in the case of one complainant who filed a complaint alleging discrimination and citing the fact that he "was not rehired even though four other Negroes were."

Other types of suspicious treatment include being discouraged from going through with an application, attempts to steer the applicant into a different slot from the one applied for, making an application and not receiving a return call, and insisting on seeing an applicant in person.

In general, these more vague indications of discrimination are found more frequently in employment (thirty-eight cases), than in housing (twenty-two cases), the "run around" being the major exception.

The various situations that suggest discrimination to Negro complainants vary in the degree to which an assumption of discrimination seems to be justified. When a Negro applicant is told "We don't accept Negroes," he has good reason to suppose that he is facing discrimination. On the other hand, a feeling that one's treatment has been undeserved may reflect a discriminatory situation, or it may reflect some other type of injustice, or it may be based on mere lack of comprehension of the total gestalt of the situation. The categories of perceived evidence of discrimination may be combined and arranged in a series to form an a priori scale of degrees of sound evidence of discrimination.

A Negro who is excluded from an opportunity, and is told that all Negroes are excluded, bases his perception of discrimination on very strong evidence.

A test also produces sound evidence of discrimination, but a test can produce a mistaken impression. It is possible that testing can fail to ferret out all the possible failures of communication that may be involved. It may be that an applicant is told that a vacancy does not exist when in fact a vacancy does exist. To tell an applicant that there is no opening is often a "tactful" way of saying that he does not meet the standards. It may be that the "standard" that the applicant does not meet is a skin-color standard, but it may be a bona fide standard. Furthermore, change can intervene between the original unsuccessful attempt to acquire an opportunity and the successful white test. Testing is a powerful tool for the production of evidence, but it is fallible.

Change upon discovery of racial identity amounts to a test in reverse. The opportunity is first offered to someone who is presumably white, then withdrawn when the factor of race is introduced. Both testing and change constitute evidence of actual differential treatment. For purposes of developing a series of degrees of soundness of evidence the two categories can be combined.

Perception of unequal treatment in a natural setting is

a somewhat less sound base for assuming discrimination than a test or a sudden change in attitude upon discovery of race; judgment of the relative qualifications of one's own qualifications relative to others may be distorted by self interest. Further, the standards upon which decisions have been made may be imperfectly understood.

Still, in the "specific-unequal-treatment" category, the complainant is reporting and comparing the treatment of specific Negroes and whites; he is not merely reporting treatment that seems false, or suspicious or unfair, or calling attention to apparent lies or to racial imbalance in the composition of the work force. Within the latter categories of evidence, actual evidence of false statements and actual evidence of racial imbalance, although not demonstrating unequal treatment, indicate a better case than mere suspicious or unfair treatment.

This makes, in all, five degrees of evidence of discrimination. Each complaint can be classified according to its strongest element. In the figures given above many cases were included in more than one category. For example, in one case a man was stalled and avoided before finally being told that no colored would be allowed in the building. This case was counted in the "direct statement of exclusion" category and under the rubric "run around." In Table 19 each case is counted only once and classified according to the strongest and soundest element of evidence that the complainant produced to justify a charge of discrimination. Thus the case of a person who is merely avoided at first and later is directly excluded, is classed as a case of first degree evidence. This procedure provides a table that better represents the quality of evidence generally adduced by complainants.

Table 19 produces several striking features and comparisons. In the first place, in more than one third of all cases, the complainants' allegations are based entirely on treat-

Table 19. Distribution of bases for complaints by degree of soundess of evidence of discrimination

Category	Housing		Employment		Total	
	No.	%	No.	%	No.	%
Class 1 Statement of exclusion	23	39.0	3	5.1	26	22.0
Class 2 Test, change on discovery of race	20	33.9	3	5.1	23	22.0
Class 3 Specific differential treatment (no test)	1	1.7	9	15.3	10	8.5
Class 4 Untrue statements General evidence	8	13.6	1	17.0	18	15.3
Class 5 Suspicious or unfair	7	11.9	34	57.6	41	34.7
Total	59		59		118	

ment that the complainant considers suspicious or unfair. However, these cases are highly concentrated in employment where they constitute well over half of the cases brought. Only a little more than one tenth of the housing cases have such a minimal initial foundation. In contrast, nearly three quarters of the housing cases fall into the three most firm categories, whereas only one quarter of employment cases were so firmly grounded.

Let us call the five numbered classes by which the cases have been categorized "credibility classes" and the number of the class of any given case the "credibility score" of that case. Low scores indicate high credibility, since the most reasonable cases are designated "first class" and the least sound cases are designated "fifth class." The mean credibility score of all housing cases is 2.26 and employment cases have a mean credibility score of 4.17.

187

The firmer foundations of housing cases have three sources. In the first place, discrimination in housing is more blatant and overt, less subtle; people are willing to openly exclude Negroes, and thus there is a greater frequency of housing cases in category 1.

Housing cases are also more frequently found in category 2. Part of this difference is due to the greater preparation of cases by testing in housing, which in turn may be attributed to greater group participation in housing cases.

The third factor is more difficult to demonstrate, but is probably a very important factor. It could in theory, account for all the difference between housing and employment. Perhaps there is less discrimination in employment than in housing and employment complaints are objectively less well founded. This could account for their subjective ambiguity for, where objective discrimination is more frequent, it will result more frequently in experiences that provide good evidence of discrimination. The fact that subsequent investigations of employment complaints by the Commission have shown that many are of very poor quality would seem to support this interpretation of the relative weakness of employment cases.

However, the poorer objective quality of employment cases can not entirely explain the lower rates of "firm" cases in employment. Firmness is not a mere consequence of the objective truth of a set of allegations; it also reflects the extent to which a case has been prepared before it is filed with the Commission. The importance of this factor can be demonstrated by comparing the credibility of individual and group complaints. We predict that group complaints would be more credible than individual complaints since specialized groups would, in order not to waste their limited resources, push cases that were well founded, eliminate weak cases, and prepare cases as much as possible. We find confirmation of this hypothesis in housing where group cases have a mean credibility score of 1.92 and individual cases a mean score of 2.54. Further examination reveals that this difference stems primarily from a high frequency of group cases in category 2. These cases are primarily "test" cases, suggesting that the greater participation of groups in testing procedures accounts for the individual vs. group difference in credibility (see Table 20).

Table 20. Individual and group housing cases by firmness category

Category	Number of cases	
	Individual	Group
1	15	8
2	5	15
3	0	1
4	6	1
5	7	1
Total	33	26
$\overline{X}$	2.54	1.92

In employment the mean credibility score is 4.16 for individual cases and 4.21 for group cases and the hypothesis is not supported.

The failure of the hypothesis in the employment sphere may be attributed to the quality of group participation in employment cases. The pressure groups in employment operate as passive referral agencies rather than active initiating agencies. They do not participate in testing procedures or other case-improving activities such as badgering a respondent until he makes a discriminatory remarks. There were no group tests in employment as against eleven in housing. Nevertheless, the success of the test of the hypothesis in the housing sphere suffices to indicate that objective differences in discrimination rates do not completely account for the greater credibility of housing cases; intensive

189

group participation produces more credible complaints.

It had been expected that credibility would also be associated with social class. Upper-status persons might be presumed to have more insight into the evidentiary requirements of a good case. However, few substantial and no consistent differences in credibility between social classes were found. Apparently all social classes assumed that further investigation will produce enough evidence to create a viable case. Professional and managerial workers were as likely to file on the basis of suspicion and unfair treatment as lower-status workers.

In order to prevent future confusion, it should be pointed out that this is a separate question from the question of whether upper-status complainants are keener at distinguishing apparent from real discrimination. The latter question is not to be answered by looking at the nature of the evidence originally provided by the complainant, but by the information that emerges from the subsequent investigation by the Commission. Middle-class complainants and lower-class complainants may be equally willing to bring cases of unfair treatment to the Commission, but middle-class complainants may still be better at distinguishing mere unfair treatment from racially motivated unfair treatment.

When complainants assume discrimination on the basis of relatively weak evidence we would suppose that their assumption would prove false in a relatively large proportion of cases.

A finding of "probable cause" (that is, a determination by the Commission, after investigation, that there is probable cause for crediting the complainant's allegation) is not a perfect index of the actual existence of discrimination in a case. However, acceptance of the commissioners' findings of probable cause as indicative of actual discrimination, and the commissioners' findings of no probable cause as indicative of mistaken accusations, seems preferable to any attempt to "second guess" the commissioners' findings on the basis of examination of secondary accounts of the actual investigations.

This being the case, it is difficult to test the hypothesis in the sphere of employment where only eight out of fifty-nine cases resulted in a finding of probable cause, and of those eight cases, three did not involve a finding of racial discrimination. Nevertheless, the remaining five cases had a mean credibility score of 3.20 compared with a mean score of 4.23 for cases that were dismissed as being without probable cause. In firmness classes 1, 2, and 3, where actual evidence of unequal treatment or direct statements of exclusion had led the complainant to file with the Commission, one case in five resulted in a finding of probable cause, but in categories 4 and 5, where the complainants' suspicions arose out of mere evidence of untruths or unfair dealings, only one case in about twenty (4.5 percent) eventuated in a finding of probable cause.

In housing, where 62.9 percent of cases were found to have probable cause, the hypothesis can be more firmly grounded. Cases which are initially well founded are much more likely to prove well founded after Commission investigation. The mean credibility score of probable-cause cases is 1.62 compared to 2.84 for cases dismissed for lack of probable cause. Probable cause was found in nearly three fourths (72.7 percent) of cases in credibility classes 1, 2, and 3, and in only one third of the cases in credibility classes 4 and 5.

Table 21 summarizes the relation between the firmness of the basis for assuming discrimination and the frequency that allegations of discrimination are credited by the Commission.

It is striking that even in credibility classes 1 and 2, where the complainant's assumption of discrimination

191

Table 21. Percentage finding of probable cause by institutional sphere and credibility class

Credibility class	Percent probable cause		
	Housing	Employment	All cases
1 + 2 + 3	72.7	20.0	59.5
4 + 5	33.3	4.5	11.9
All cases	62.9	8.5	35.6

seems quite reasonable in view of his pointed treatment, the case is frequently dismissed as lacking probable cause. This occurred in 27.2 percent of the cases in these categories. Several possible explanations can be adduced to account for this. The complainant may be lying; he may not have received the treatment he alleges. Complainant prevarication could account for two or perhaps three of the cases, but generally speaking the complainants' stories were not destroyed by the investigation. It might be supposed that the Commission refused to make a finding of probable cause even where discrimination was clearly present. Again, this might account for a few cases, the precise number depending on what the observer means by "clearly present." But there is another force at work. *The mechanisms for allocating persons to occupational and residential roles or niches are so constituted and structured as to regularly produce situations which give the appearance of discrimination, or which are easy to interpret as discrimination, but which do not involve any discrimination in the legal sense of the word.* This is an important point and deserves treatment in some detail.

Let us start with two examples of cases that looked very strong from the point of view of the complainants, but turned out to be without substance.

In one case, the complainant, a young professional man, was seeking an apartment. A friend told him of an apartment for rent in Cambridge. The complainant called about the apartment and was told to hurry over to inspect it. The complainant arrived within an hour but was told on arrival that the apartment was already rented. He was suspicious but left without complaint. Two days later, he called anonymously and asked about the same apartment. This time he was told that it was still available. Convinced that he was being excluded on account of race, the complainant filed with the Commission. On investigation, the Commission learned that while the complainant was on his way over, someone else interested in the apartment had agreed to take it. However, the new tenant had upon closer examination discovered roaches and other inconveniences and decided to back out. Accordingly, the apartment was returned to the market. In an interview, the author discovered that the respondent owned integrated buildings, was active in an integrated evangelical sect where she worked closely and intimately with Negroes, and had very strong views on the immorality of discrimination. Not a shred of evidence of discrimination could be uncovered.

The apartment market is fluid and unstable. Since openings come and go quickly the time element in testing permits some mistakes to be made.

In another case, a complainant was turned down with discriminatory intent but the situation could not be defined as discrimination from a legal point of view. In one case, an applicant was told by an agent that "he couldn't rent to colored or it would have to be all colored. The white tenants would move out. It doesn't make any difference to me but . . . etc."

Investigation revealed that the complainant had too many children and too small an income to meet the respondent's clear standards. The apartment was in a mixed area and was finally rented to a qualified Negro applicant. Since the applicant did not qualify and the apartment utlimately went to a Negro, the complaint was dismissed as without probable cause. Legally, there is more to discrimination than intent. At least as the Commission interprets the law, it is not illegal to turn someone down on the basis of race and to tell him that you are turning him down on grounds of race if you also have legitimate grounds of refusal. In sum, the structure of allocation involves the application of standards. In many cases Negroes are turned down under circumstances indicative of discrimination, but who would not qualify even if discrimination were not present.

Similarly, each of the categories of bases for assuming discrimination can be shown to be potentially fallacious. The ordinary course of business will inevitably impinge upon some individuals as apparent discrimination. A number of structural and procedural features of the allocative process permit mistaken impressions of discrimination:

1) The allocative system is based on the concept of qualifications. Openings are distributed to those who have the appropriate qualifications. The anti-discrimination law protects this feature of the allocative system and puts the burden on the complainant of being qualified for the position in question. A high level of unfair and unjust treatment with overtones of racial animosity will probably produce feelings of discrimination, yet the situation is not legally discrimination if the complainant does not have the qualifications for attaining or keeping the opening in question.

2) Because of the requirements of human relations technique, tact, and fear of creating unpleasant situations, references to qualifications are taboo in many situations. It is common procedure to tell an applicant that an opening does not exist in order to avoid unfavorable comment upon his qualifications. The author once sat for an hour in the office of an apartment rental agent and watched a parade

of applicants being alternately welcomed and told that nothing was available. Low-status people, students, and groups of unmarried applicants were turned away by the receptionist with the explanation that nothing was available. The agent boasted as to how well his receptionist could recognize and discourage unacceptable applicants. Yet, this agent owns and manages several integrated buildings; he did not personally discriminate. A businessman might tell a Negro that nothing was available to accomplish a discriminatory purpose, but, on the other hand, a group of Negro students would have been turned away at this office with the "no-vacancy" story, not because they were Negroes, but because they were students.

A total of thirty-nine cases, or one third of all the cases studied, rested at least in part on evidence that openings existed where it had been claimed that they did not. Yet, false statements about openings are made every day as an ordinary element of business practice.

3) For any given position in the system there are multiple persons with at least minimal qualifications. Hence, an applicant may correctly feel himself to be qualified for the opening and yet fall short of the qualifications of other applicants. In the absence of information about the whole range of persons available and competing, the complainant may feel discriminated against and file a complaint that would fall in a category such as "frustrated expectations," "unbelievable reasons," or "unfair treatment."

4) The system is highly mobile. Openings quickly appear, disappear, and reappear as persons move from position to position. This produces contradictory stories over time that are easily interpreted as having racial motivation. Often, public notices of openings do not change as rapidly as the actual situation. Advertisements continue to run and notices stay in windows after openings are already filled.

5) One of the most common forms of organizational

195

maladjustment is failure of communication. When there is an internal failure of communication a contradictory face is presented to the outside world. Twelve cases were based in part on such contradictions, yet, contradictions can have normal structural sources.

6) One form of failure of communication is failure to successfully communicate company policy with respect to race. Subordinates may commit discriminatory acts in ignorance of, or contravention of, well-established company policy. Acts expressing the personal prejudice of unauthorized individuals may be interpreted by outsiders as expressions of a firm's official position. Of course, a firm has some responsibility for the acts of its employees, but there are some limitations. A Negro who concludes that a firm does not hire Negroes because a janitor so informed him may well be mistaken. If the Commission, upon investigation, finds that many Negroes are employed in many capacities, a finding of probable cause is unlikely.

7) Other kinds of lies besides lies about openings are used for various administrative or political purposes. The cases show the Commission's policy on lies to be clear. One is under no obligation to refrain from telling lies to Negroes if it is not done with discriminatory intent. If it is a part of ordinary business practice, it is someone else's ethical concern.

8) Ordinary administrative routine, developed to meet internal problems of organization, seems often to the outsider to be needless red tape. To the Negro, needless red tape can be interpreted as a purposeful imposition of racial obstacles, in short, "the run around."

9) There are many sorts of injustice in the world. Bureaucratic impersonality, personal animosities, the rigid application of rules, and disrupting events can produce injustices in the absence of any racial antipathies. Furthermore, situations often seem unfair to someone who is hurt, where an

outside observer, with his detachment, and his broader perspective on the whole situation, would see no injustice. A Negro who has experienced countless racial snubs in the past is likely to interpret each new real or perceived injustice as another experience of discrimination.

The ambiguity of events permits Negroes to blame discrimination for their troubles. Hence, some complaints represent a projection of one's own deficiencies onto the outside world. On the other hand, the same ambiguity permits the opposite type of distortion. A Negro may wish to protect himself from discrimination by denying that it exists. He may easily construct a reasonable explanation of apparently unequal treatment. In consequence, potential complainants may not perceive discrimination. One of the functions of civil rights groups is to convince potential complainants that they may be experiencing discrimination.

In short, personal experience is too difficult to interpret to provide an adequate indicator of the presence or absence of discrimination. Yet, unless groups intervene with corrective perspectives, the Commission's patterns of jurisdiction depend on the individual's limited capacities to judge the meaning of his treatment.

When the initial step in enforcement is left to the minority groups that experience discrimination, the job of locating discrimination goes to those who are its chief victims. Are the victims of discrimination well situated and equipped to uncover discrimination? How does the Negro know that he is experiencing discrimination? The complainant comes to make an allegation of discrimination when his personal experiences impinge upon him in a certain way. He does not conduct sociological investigations, he simply goes about the business of finding and keeping a job or a residence. In the course of this everyday activity, he experiences a variety of kinds of treatment. As an outsider to the organizations that affect his treatment, he must make inter-

197

pretative guesses as to what motivates that treatment. When the treatment does not seem completely above board, when he is told lies, when he is insulted, when injustice besets him, he is likely to blame racial discrimination. In a community where discrimination is prevalent, the blame is likely to be well placed. On the other hand, the ordinary operation of the structures of allocation regularly produce experiences that could be interpreted as discrimination. Consequently, many allegations of discrimination turn out to be mistaken. When law enforcement is tied entirely to individual complaints the Commission is forced to work with relatively poor and ill-founded complaints.

This was a more serious problem in employment where discrimination was subtle, covert, and concentrated in certain industries, occupations, and firms, than in housing, an institutional sphere where discrimination was more blatant and widespread, and where organizations were actively at work, seeking to locate discrimination and to develop evidence of discrimination.

It cannot be said that discrimination is so rampant that it does not matter how one goes about developing complaints. The evidence in this chapter has shown that complaints developed by individuals whose structural position provides limited perspective are objectively poor. They tend to be based on mere suspicion, they are quite likely to eventuate in a finding of "no probable cause," and they tend to be made against the very firms that do not discriminate.

Judicial intervention is possible only if there were ample evidence to show that petitioner was rejected solely because of his color.– [New York Supreme Court]

The only way to determine the matter of color is to determine whether these men were worse or better than all of those considered for promotion to the position of steward.– [New Jersey Commission of Education]

Equal and Reasonable Treatment

In Chapter III the legal definition of discrimination was termed the "equal-treatment standard." However, closer examination of the work of the Commission reveals yet new ambiguities in the equal-treatment standard. To most officials, the legal meaning of the term "discrimination" seems clear. Asked what "discrimination" means, officials will reply that it means unequal treatment:

Q. What is discrimination? How do you know when you have a case of it?
A. That's easy. It's unequal treatment. Where the person is treated the same way as a white person there is no discrimination.[1]

In practice, however, commissions frequently use a somewhat different standard that implies a subtly different definition of discrimination.

Consider the case *In re Jeanpierre,* decided by the New York Supreme Court in 1956.[2] Jeanpierre, a Negro had originally filed a complaint with the New York State Commission Against Discrimination in February 1955, alleging that he was refused employment as a flight steward by Pan American Air Lines by reason of his race. The case was dismissed as without probable cause, whereupon Jeanpierre appealed.

These were the facts. At that time no scheduled airline operating in New York employed Negroes in any flight capacity. Jeanpierre testified that he had been told that he met the basic standards; he was qualified in French, had a high school diploma, and American citizenship. He alleged that attempts were made to dissuade him from seeking employment in a flight capacity. He was told that flying was dangerous and bad for the ears, and that he would be subject to racial discrimination. He was offered a higher paying job as "cargo representative," but his original application for a position as flight steward was turned down. In the course of the investigation it was discovered that the complainant had a very spotty past work record consisting of eighteen employments over the previous sixteen years as "salesman, kitchen utility man, waiter, sandblast operator, clerk typist, machine operator, guard, special deputy sheriff, and French tutor." On that basis a finding of no probable cause was made.

The court's comments are worthy of quotation.

There are several suspicious circumstances . . . which at least would require further inquiry by the commission in this particular case were it not for the petitioner's unimpressive if not wholly irresponsible work record. *Here an avenue of escape has been opened for Pan American* by the petitioner's own past history. Judicial intervention is possible only if there were ample evidence to show that petitioner was rejected *solely because of his color.*[3]

Despite evidence of a discriminatory employment pattern, of specific attempts to discourage the applicant, and of evidence that he was otherwise qualified, the *complainant's case was dismissed because his employment record was not good, even though respondent was willing to hire him in another capacity and no evidence was heard as to the past work histories of men actually hired as stewards.* Clearly, by the court's reasoning, this is not a case illustrating application of the standard of equal treatment. The issue is not how whites in a similar situation are treated, but whether there is evidence that other justifications besides race can be reasonably put forth as a basis for the complainant's treatment. By this reasoning, a complainant, in order to prevail, must be virtually perfect in all respects. He must meet a theoretical rather than an actual standard. In view of the well-known sociological principles about the differences between formal rules and organizational reality, the Negro is placed at a severe disadvantage. He must compete against a theoretical set of standards, divorced from the real world.

Compare the reasoning of the Jeanpierre case with the reasoning in a similar case from New Jersey, *Thompson v. Erie Railroad.*[4] Thompson and a co-complainant were applying for the position of steward on the dining cars of the Erie Railroad. They were waiters-in-charge and were seeking promotion. Again, no Negroes had been employed as stewards up to that time. Thompson and his co-worker were not promoted, but a Caucasion was made steward during the period that their applications were in effect. The railroad argued that the complainants were not qualified, that they made mistakes in record keeping, that they had been subject to disciplinary action in the past, and that they were generally unreliable. Nevertheless, the Commission of Education, in disposing of the case, decided in favor of the complainants, arguing that

as bad as the record of these men ... may appear to be, unless it can be shown that the record of those appointed over them or in their place is better than that of these men, then the question of the color of the complainant is still a matter of concern. The only way to determine the matter of color is to determine whether these men were worse or better than all of those considered *for* promotion to the position of steward.[5]

The commissioner was in a very good position to make an appropriate comparison for the complainants had been working for some time as waiters-in-charge, a position virtually identical in duties and responsibilities to the position of steward. He found that the complainants performed their duties as well as the stewards. Both made mistakes. The commissioner refused to apply an abstract set of standards to complainants; he insisted on inferring the effective standards from the actual treatment of white stewards.

In the case of *Thompson v. Erie,* the equal-treatment standard that Chairman Mahoney speaks of was clearly applied. *In re Jeanpierre,* on the other hand, illustrates the application of a different standard, a standard we shall denote as the "reasonable-treatment standard." The appropriate question is not, "How is a white man treated in similar circumstances?" but "Would it have been reasonable to treat the complainant as he was treated if he had been white?" Is it reasonable to refuse to hire a white applicant for the position of flight steward when he has a spotty job history? Yes, past job stability is a reasonable job qualification; hence it is permissible to apply the standard to Negro applicants.

The cases decided by the MCAD include some cases decided by the reasonable-treatment standard and some cases decided by the more rigorous equal-treatment standard.

In one case, a Negro electronics worker was dismissed from employment for allegedly making improper and obscene remarks to a white female co-worker. As she walked by his work space on the way to the drinking fountain he would make remarks such as "Boy, I would like to if I could."

202

The worker felt he was suffering from discriminatory treatment and complained to the Commission. The Commission's entire investigation was designed to determine whether the alleged incidents had actually occurred. No attempt was made to discover what treatment had been accorded white persons for similar offenses. No attempt was made to assess the customary level of informal banter between employees. The question was, Is it reasonable to dismiss an employee who makes obscene statements to female employees? Yes, clearly it is, and the only task of investigation becomes deciding whether the statements have been made. In this case the evidence was that the complainant did make the statements and the dismissal was allowed to stand.

Clearly, the Commission's belief that cases are decided by applying the standard of equal treatment was not entirely accurate. In many cases the investigators did not seek the type of evidence that would allow the investigating commissioner to apply the equal-treatment standard, indicating that they have a different standard in mind. Commission personnel were generally unable to verbalize this alternative standard, but when it was suggested to Chairman Mahoney that the standard of reasonable treatment as outlined above was applied in some cases, she readily agreed.

In other cases, the strict standard of equal treatment was applied. Whenever an unsuccessful Negro applicant's qualifications are compared systematically to the qualifications of successful white applicants as a basis for reaching a decision in a case then the standard of equal treatment has been applied. For instance, a Negro man was refused a position as clerk-typist. He was told that the only positions open were for stock boys. Investigation revealed that there were three successful applicants for the position of clerk-typist, all female. All of the girls hired had more education (one year of college) than the unsuccessful male. On balance, the Negro applicant had had more experience. The respondent was an insurance company with quite a large number of clerical employees, but no Negroes were employed outside of maintenance positions.

The investigating commissioner concluded that the complainant was as well qualified as any successful applicant, that experience was more important than formal education for that type of position, and that a finding of probable cause was in order.

As a practical matter it makes a great deal of difference whether a commission is regularly applying a standard of equal treatment or a standard of reasonable treatment. If the reasonable-treatment standard is consistently applied, then the law protects only virtually perfect specimens. Respondents have an "avenue of escape" as the New York court put it. They can scrutinize a Negro applicant until they discover some disqualifying feature. Effective use of the law to break down racial barriers would be predicated on careful selection of prime complainants since an ordinary, naturally produced complainant would probably have a regular share of human defects.

Accordingly, analysis of the conditions under which the different standards are used is in order.

The first task is to establish the relative proportions of equal-treatment and reasonable-treatment cases. Categorizing the cases according to which standard was used involves a measure of subjective judgment. Nevertheless, the basic criteria for objective classification can be explicitly stated. If a case turns upon evidence concerning the comparative treatment and/or comparative qualifications of the complainant and similar white persons, then it is an "equal-treatment" case unless a decision is made against the complainant despite clear evidence of unequal treatment. The standard of equal treatment also applies where a finding of probable cause is based on admitted discrimination. On the other hand, if the relevant evidence that would make it possible to decide the case on the basis of comparative qualifications or comparative treatment is not produced, or if a decision is made against the complainant in the face of clear evidence of unequal treatment, then it is a "reasonable-treatment" case. If a case does not *and could not* turn on matters of comparative treatment and qualifications, then it is not classified in either category. Cases can not be classified when they are decided upon jurisdictional grounds, when they are withdrawn, or when the evidence indicates that there was no opening for which the complainant could have been considered. (In some cases no investigation was completed; the cases became moot by virtue of the conclusion of some satisfactory arrangement between the parties before the investigation was completed.) Fifteen housing cases and eleven employment cases could not be classified for these reasons.

Among employment cases, twenty-one were decided on the basis of equal treatment. These included all but one of the five cases where probable cause was found.

Twenty-seven cases were decided on the basis of the standard of reasonable treatment and probable cause was found in only one of these cases. An unsuccessful applicant for a position as airline stewardess was deemed by the Commission to be qualified for the position, but the decision was not based on comparison of the applicant's qualifications with the qualifications of successful applicants or working stewardesses. Instead, the investigating commissioner treated the grounds for rejecting the applicant as untrue and unreasonable. The girl was, in fact, attractive, personable, and otherwise qualified. The airline's minor criticisms of the applicant's facial features and figure did not reasonably justify elimination from competition.

Ten of the reasonable-treatment cases can be placed in a separate category because they involve some indirect evidence that the respondent followed a policy of equal treatment. In these cases no direct evidence of the treatment of white persons in similar circumstances was considered, but the general employment patterns of the respondent were considered evidence of their generally equal policies. Where Negroes are employed in the department in question or are widespread throughout the firm, the allegations of unequal treatment in the case at hand tend to lack credibility.

It should be noted that none of the reasonable-treatment cases were so classified because the commissioner made a finding of no probable cause in the face of clear evidence of unequal treatment. In general, use of the reasonable-treatment standard reflects unwillingness to generate the necessary evidence to apply the equal-treatment standard, not unwillingness to take facts into account once they are known.

The equal-treatment standard was used more frequently in cases involving disputes about initial hiring and promotion than in cases involving treatment on the job or discharge. Of twenty-nine cases of initial hiring and promotion, seventeen were decided by the equal-treatment standard. Of nineteen cases of treatment on the job and discharge, fifteen were decided by the reasonable-treatment standard (see Table 22).

Table 22. Equal - vs. reasonable-treatment standard by case category.
Employment

Standard	Hiring	Promotion	Treatment	Discharge	Total
Equal treatment	15	2	3	1	21
Reasonable treatment	11	1	6	9	27
Total	26	3	9	10	48

Use of the equal-treatment standard was more frequent in housing. Twenty-eight cases involved equal treatment compared to sixteen cases where the reasonable-treatment standard was applied (see Table 23).

206

Table 23. Equal - vs. reasonable-treatment standard by institutional sphere

| Standard | Institutional sphere[a] | | | | | |
| | Employment | | Housing | | Total | |
	No.	%	No.	%	No.	%
Equal treatment	21	43.6	28	63.6	49	53.3
Reasonable treatment	27	56.4	16	37.4	43	46.7
Total	48		44		92	

[a] $\phi = 0.20$; $\chi^2 = 3.68$.

The greater prevalence of the standard of equal treatment in housing can be attributed to two causes; the greater blatancy of discrimination in housing and the activities of pressure groups. In seven housing cases the classification of cases in the equal-treatment category rests on the respondent's admission that he was discriminating, a circumstance that occurred on only one occasion in an employment case. When a respondent's past behavior has been too blatant to cover with false excuses, he frequently admits the fault and hopes for the best. In eleven housing cases the Commission was provided the evidence for use of the equal-treatment standard by tests performed by organized pressure groups, but no employment cases were based on such tests. (On only one occasion did a group test fail to induce the commissioner to apply the standard of equal treatment.)

Of the sixteen reasonable-treatment cases, six were further supported by general evidence that the respondent maintained integrated properties (though in three of those six cases the filing of a complaint preceded the integration of the respondent's property).

As in the case of employment, the classification of most of the reasonable-treatment cases turns on the lack of production of the relevant evidence. However, in three instances reasonable-treatment cases are so classified because findings of no probable cause were made despite clear evidence of unequal treatment. For example, in one case a respondent's claim that a Negro was excluded because she had children was upheld despite the presence of children in the building.

It is important to examine the use of the standards. When did the Commission apply the equal-treatment standard and when did it apply the reasonable-treatment standard? The basic prerequisite to the application of the equal-treatment standard is a body of evidence on the comparative treatment and qualifications of whites and Negroes in similar situations. Accordingly, the major factor encouraging the use of the equal-treatment standard is the ready availability of such evidence. Fifteen of the twenty-one employment cases where the equal-treatment standard was applied were complaints alleging discrimination in initial hiring. In all fifteen cases, the qualifications of the complaint could be readily compared with the qualifications of successful applicants, or if there were no successful applicants, with the qualifications of other unsuccessful applicants. On the other hand, cases of treatment on the job and discharge generally involve unique situations and evidence of treatment of white persons would necessarily be inferential and drawn from analogous situations.

In the initial hiring cases, the comparison was usually quite simple and objective. Test scores, number of years of experience, and previous work records were available and easily compared. In only one case did the decision turn on something relatively intangible, namely, complainant's arrangements for taking care of children.

There is a preponderance of large, bureaucratic employers represented in these cases. Twelve of the fifteen firms involved had more than one hundred employees and at least one full time personnel officer. Six had over 1,000 employees. Six were insurance companies or banking institutions and four were large manufacturers of equipment. Seven had given written tests to all applicants, including the complainant. Bureaucratic firms regularly make decisions on the basis of the qualifications of applicants and keep records of the test scores and applications of all applicants. When a firm operates in a bureaucratic manner, it is relatively easy for the Commission to apply the standard of equal treatment.

If this reasoning is correct, then why did the Commission apply the less rigorous standard of reasonable treatment in eleven cases involving initial employment, including ten cases where the respondent was a bureaucratic employer with over one hundred employees? One answer is that investigating commissioners did not require the same level of evidence to exonerate a respondent who had a demonstrably good record of fair treatment. Six of the eleven cases involved two employers who frequently receive complaints and who have a large number of Negro employees at a variety of levels. Four of the cases were filed by complainants who seemed poorly qualified and the investigating commissioner was unwilling to force the issue by examining the character and qualifications of other employees. The eleventh case was the airline stewardess case mentioned earlier, where the Commission thought the applicant's treatment unreasonable. In all eleven cases, application of the equal-treatment standard would have required extensive investigation beyond the most easily available evidence. Given the general circumstances surrounding the cases, that is, "good" employees and substandard applicants, the effort did not appear to be justified.

An illustrative case will serve to clarify these points. A Negro girl applied for a secretarial position with an electronics firm. She was told that her test scores were good and the company seemed impressed. She was told to wait. Two weeks later a phone call informed her that someone within the plant was being given the job. The firm did not hire very many Negroes, only five out of 1,100 employees. However, the firm was located a long distance from any centers of Negro population and the five Negro employees were in engineering, technical, and secretarial positions. In fact, the complainant was introduced to the firm by a Negro friend who worked there as a secretary.

Investigation by the field representative assigned to the case revealed that the girl would have been hired if she had not had bad references. She had done very well on the tests of skill and aptitude, but the previous employer alleged, partly on the basis of a poor attendance record, that she was "not industrious." Hence, she was turned down and another girl hired. The field representative talked to the previous employer and determined that the references were deserved and not themselves the result of prejudice, whereupon the investigating commissioner dismissed the case for lack of probable cause. The firm's general use of references was not investigated. Were otherwise excellent prospects usually turned down on the basis of bad references or were references usually consulted only in borderline cases? Were other employees engaged despite bad references? These were apparently not deemed relevant lines of inquiry. Yet the white girl who was finally given the position was a former employee who had had "some attendance problems" during her previous employment with the firm. A representative of the firm stated that "she deserved another chance."

Nevertheless, given the fact that respondent did have one Negro secretary and given the fact that to press this case would be to press the respondent to accept a potentially poor employee, the investigating commissioner elected not to push the case any further.

Without necessarily alleging that respondent was discriminating in this particular case, or that the Commission did not properly dispose of the issue, we can still raise questions as to the possible consequences of such a policy. When the author asked businessmen how they would go about discriminating without running afoul of the Commission, they frequently responded that they would search intensively until they found some disqualifying feature in the applicant's background, for example: "I'd make a long list of the requirements you could go into to find a disqualification especially school records and former work and references that you wouldn't check as carefully in a white."

Consistent application of the reasonable-treatment standard whenever a Negro applicant had a surface disqualification would permit firms to hire a few token Negroes and to limit and control all other Negro employment through manipulation of qualifications.

The unwillingness of the Commission to use the standard of equal treatment to support or protect an apparently substandard applicant is shown clearly in the cases involving dismissal where nine of ten cases were decided on the basis of the reasonable-treatment standard. In one case two employees were discharged for fighting each other. One was Negro, one white. Obviously the Negro and white were treated equally and the equal-treatment standard applies. In the remaining nine cases information about how whites were treated was not readily available. In all cases there was a plausible reason for the dismissal indicating an undesirable employee, and, in all cases, the complaints were dismissed for lack of probable cause.

The same considerations apply to the promotion cases and to the terms of employment cases. Only when evidence about comparative treatment is readily available *and* the complainant appears to be beyond reproach was the equal-treatment standard applied.

The process of allocating persons to housing vacancies is not as bureaucratically organized. It does not ordinarily

211

involve a comparison of the relative qualifications of a number of applicants. Usually the first minimally qualified applicant is accepted. Nor do housing agents keep extensive records about applicants who are turned down. The housing market is, in effect, a series of spot transactions between renters, purchasers, owners, and agents. Hence, arguments often revolve around priority of application and the absolute qualifications of Negro applicants, not the relative qualifications of several applicants. Further, it is often difficult to determine what basis has been used in the past to turn down white applicants. This leaves only two convenient bases for applying the standard of equal treatment except in cases where the respondent admits guilt. One can either compare the qualifications and treatment of the unsuccessful Negro applicant with the qualifications and treatment of persons who actually live in the housing in question, or one can observe the respondents' treatment of test applicants who are similar to the unsuccessful Negro except in color. In housing, as in employment, when the respondents' standards seem reasonable, the Commission is reluctant to seriously question them through systematic inquiry into the characteristics of persons living in the apartment or development. Nor is the Commission fond of the test process, though some field representatives occasionally perform tests unofficially. One might conclude from this that the equal-treatment standard is seldom applied except in cases of admitted guilt. In fact, leaving aside cases of admitted discrimination, the equal-treatment standard was applied in twenty-one instances. Of those twenty-one applications of the standard, eleven were made possible because civil rights groups performed tests which demonstrated unequal treatment. Two involved tests made by Commission personnel.

The structure of the allocation process in housing makes testing an efficient means of demonstrating discrimination. The relative simplicity of the qualification for entry into a housing accommodation, and the tendency of owners and agents to accept the first qualified applicant immediately, makes testing a simple operation. However, Commission personnel have shied from testing; it smacks of entrapment. Field representatives did occasionally attempt tests of the validity of some claim made by the respondent; there were five such attempts recorded among the records of the fifty-nine housing cases in the sample. By and large, the Commission accepts the tests of complainants and civil rights groups, but does not try to test on its own; at least one commissioner has forbidden testing by field representatives.

In all, thirteen cases of equal treatment involved tests. Those thirteen plus the seven cases of admitted discrimination account for all but eight of the equal-treatment cases. In five instances flagrantly different treatment of the Negro applicant upon discovery of his racial identity was considered to be conclusive evidence of differential treatment, and in the remaining three cases easily available records showed that the successful applicant was as well qualified as the present tenants.

On sixteen occasions the Commission elected not to generate the necessary evidence for applying the standard of equal treatment. Two of those are probable-cause cases in which the investigating commissioner deemed the respondent's behavior unreasonable. A respondent's claim that he did not accept single girls in the first floor of a building and another respondent's claim that an applicant was refused because his complaint to the Commission proved that he was a trouble maker were not accepted as reasonable. In the remaining fourteen cases, there was some deficiency in the applicant's qualifications and the Commission elected not to press the respondent as to how universalistically the relevant standards were applied. In six of those fourteen cases, further investigation was discouraged by evidence that the respondent had integrated holdings.

In sum, for both housing and employment the conditions

for the application of the equal-treatment standard are the same. Basically there are three such conditions:

1) Information about the treatment of whites in similar situations must be available or easily discoverable.

2) Application of the equal-treatment standard must not put the Commission into the position of protecting or supporting an undesirable complainant.

3) Application of the equal-treatment standard must not put the Commission into the position of attacking a respondent with a generally good record.

Occasionally when conditions 2 and 3 are clearly met, the Commission will make relatively detailed inquires about comparative treatment that go beyond the immediately available facts.

The author had supposed that the Commission would tend to apply a more rigorous standard in cases brought or referred to the Commission by organized groups. It was thought that the group that brought the case would act as a watch dog, motivating the Commission to investigations of maximum rigor. This hypothesis did not prove correct in the employment sphere where group participation was not intensive. Table 24 shows no relation between the origins of the case and the standard applied.

In housing the hypothesis was confirmed. Table 24 shows that a case brought by a group was much more likely to be decided by the equal-treatment standard.

The data permit us to go beyond the general statement that cases brought by groups are more likely to be decided by the equal-treatment standard. The specific mechanism by which the process works can be delineated. It is not a simple matter of group pressure for rigorous consideration of the case, for if that were so, then we would expect the relationship to hold in employment as well as housing. Rather, groups force the application of the equal-treatment standard by supplying the relevant information for applying

214

Table 24. Standards applied by origins of case, individual vs. group

Origin of case	Employment[a]			Housing[b]		
	Equal treatment	Reasonable treatment	Total	Equal treatment	Reasonable treatment	Total
Group	4	5	9	17	4	21
Individual	17	22	39	11	12	23
Total	21	27	48	28	16	44

[a] $\phi = 0.01$.

[b] $\phi = 0.34$; $\chi^2 = 5.10$; $P = < 0.05$.

215

the standard through testing. If information about how white persons were treated in similar circumstances is clearly presented to the Commission, they cannot ignore it. Testing provides information that would otherwise go unregarded. Thus, it is not the mere participation of groups that makes the difference, it is the quality of participation. In employment, group participation is limited to referral of cases to the legal agency. In housing, group participation includes active preparation of the case and the production of evidence according to techniques that the Commission is unable or unwilling to use.

The hypothesis that it is the phenomena of testing that accounts for most of the difference between group and individual cases in housing can be supported by removing all of the cases involving group tests from Table 24. The relationship between the origins of a case and the standard that is applied is reduced to an insignificant level (see Table 25).

Table 25. Standard applied by origin of case in housing; group tests excluded

Origin of case	Standard applied[a]		
	Equal treatment	Reasonable treatment	Total
Group	6	3	9
Individual	11	12	23
Total	17	15	32

[a] $\phi = 0.17$; $\chi^2 = 0.92$.

Table 26 summarizes the association between the standard applied and the outcome of the case. Since the equal-treatment standard is a more rigorous standard, we would expect to find more findings of probable cause when it is applied. In employment four of the five probable-cause cases were consequent to the use of the equal-treatment standard. In housing, twenty-eight of the thirty cases of probable cause

Table 26. Equal- vs. reasonable-treatment standard and the outcome of the case

Institutional sphere	Outcome of case		
	Probable cause	No probable cause	Total
Housing[a]			
Equal treatment	28	0	28
Reasonable treatment	2	14	16
Total	30	14	44
Employment[b]			
Equal treatment	4	17	21
Reasonable treatment	1	26	27
Total	5	43	48
All cases[c]			
Equal treatment	32	17	49
Reasonable treatment	3	42	45
Total	35	59	94

[a] $\phi = 0.90$; $\chi^2 = 81.18$; $\underline{P} = {<}0.01$.

[b] $\phi = 0.25$; $\chi^2 = 3.0$.

[c] $\phi = 0.61$; $\chi^2 = 34.50$; $\underline{P} = {<}0.01$.

were cases where the equal-treatment standard was applied. In only three cases altogether was a finding of probable cause made through an application of the reasonable-treatment standard. On the other hand, the equal-treatment standard was applied in seventeen cases where no probable cause was found. However, all seventeen of those cases were employment cases. In other words, *in housing, every single application of the equal-treatment standard resulted in a finding of discrimination!*

The tendency for the application of the reasonable-treatment standard to produce a finding of no probable cause is not difficult to comprehend. A finding of probable cause under those circumstances would mean that the investigating commissioner has found the respondent's alleged standards to be quite unreasonable. In view of the law's protection of the right to establish qualifications, the commissioners were understandably reluctant to make such findings. Nor is it difficult to see why the application of the equal-treatment standard to employment cases led sometimes to conciliation and sometimes to dismissal, for sometimes analyses of comparative qualifications was to the complainant's advantage and sometimes it was not.

It is a little more difficult to see why the use of the equal-treatment standard was always associated with a finding of probable cause in housing cases. Would not comparative analysis sometimes lead to the discovery that the complainant was, in fact, less qualified than the successful applicant? Close examination of the equal-treatment cases reveals the source of the uniform findings of probable cause.

Only five housing cases were actually based on comparative analysis of qualifications. Remember that several equal-treatment cases were so blatant that the respondent or one of his agents confessed, and that many involved tests showing clear evidence of unequal treatment. In other cases there was flagrant and undeniable evidence of unequal treatment arising from different treatment of the complainant when he was seen in person. Only three equal-treatment cases were actually based upon comparative analysis of qualifications and it so happens that all of them were cases where probable cause was found. Presumably, a larger number of such cases would show more variability, but in the other fifteen cases where a finding of probable cause could have been based on comparative analysis of qualifications, the investigating commissioner either did not go beyond a judgment of the reasonableness of the respondent's behavior or found no probable cause in the face of clear evidence of unequal treatment.

In sum, because of the blatancy of discrimination in

housing, and because of the relative informality of the process of allocating persons to housing accommodations, housing cases seldom turn on ex post analyses of comparative qualifications. Many cases could rest on such analysis, but it would require a militant posture on the part of the Commission and extensive analysis of the present tenants in a building or other uncomfortable investigations. In consequence, if a housing case did not involve blatant discrimination, or if a civil rights group did not actively push it by testing, it was usually dismissed.

A prime determinant of the outcome of the case was the standard that was used in determining whether a case exhibited discrimination. The equal-treatment standard is a rigorous standard that demands absolutely equal treatment. Undesirable Negroes must be treated in the same manner as undesirable whites. The reasonable-treatment standard only demands that a respondent show some reasonable cause for his treatment of the complainant. It permits respondents, and businessmen in general, an "avenue of escape" from the strict requirements of the law through the manipulation of standards.

The data indicate that discrimination is seldom found unless the equal-treatment standard is used. Use of the equal-treatment standard ordinarily occurs only under a set of specific conditions. The requisite kinds of evidence must be quite obvious, the complainant must be of excellent character, and there must be no evidence that the respondent runs an integrated operation. These conditions are most frequently met when the case has been brought by a group that has actively worked to produce evidence of unequal treatment.

Since groups are able to stimulate the use of the standard of equal treatment and the equal-treatment standard produces findings of probable cause, it follows that groups are able to secure findings of probable cause in a larger proportion of cases. Probable cause was found in 80.8 percent of the housing cases brought by groups and in only 53.3 percent of the housing cases brought by individuals (see Table 27).

Table 27. Findings of probable cause by origin of case in housing

Outcome	Origin of case[a]				
	Group		Individual		Total
	No.	%	No.	%	
Probable cause	21	80.8	16	53.3	37
No probable cause	5	19.2	14	46.7	19
Total	26		30		56

[a] $\phi = 0.29$; $\chi^2 = 4.70$; $\underline{P} = \; < 0.05$.

The standards: differences between commissioners. It was often alleged in the community that some commissioners were more militant than others and that this was reflected in their treatment of cases. One commissioner in particular was seen as particularly militant. This commissioner also thought of himself as one who pushes cases hard.

Four different commissioners handled employment cases.

Table 28. Use of equal- vs. reasonable-treatment standard by individual commissioners in employment

Commissioner #	Standard	
	Equal treatment	Reasonable treatment
1	10	6
2	5	9
3	5	6
4	1	6
Total	21	27

220

Table 28 shows the frequencies with which each commissioner applied the standards of equal and reasonable treatment.

Commissioner No. 2, who was thought to be more militant, actually used the equal-treatment standard less often than two of the other commissioners, and Commissioner No. 1 emerges as the principal user of the equal-treatment standard.

In an interview, Commissioner No. 2 said that his militancy was more pronounced in housing. Table 29 supports his statement, Commissioner No. 2 was a much more frequent user of the equal-treatment standard in housing.

Table 29. Use of equal- vs. reasonable-treatment standard by individual commissioners and outcome of case in housing

Commissioner #	Standard used		Outcome	
	Equal treatment	Reasonable treatment	Probable cause	No probable cause
1	9	8	11	10
2	14	5	19	6
3	5	3	5	3
Total	28	16	35	19

The use of the standard of equal treatment is related to finding probable cause. Hence we would expect Commissioner No. 2's militancy to be reflected in a higher proportion of findings of probable cause. Table 29 indicates that Commissioner No. 2 did in fact find probable cause more frequently.

The Rules of Antidiscrimination Law

We have stressed the generality of the provisions of the law. Discrimination is not defined in detail, and the prob-

lems of what would constitute sufficient evidence of discrimination are not discussed. It is up to the Commission
to decide the finer points in the context of the litigation
that it passes upon.

In view of the Commission's self-conception, its emphasis
on human relations, conciliation, and education, rather
than on legal exegesis, it is not surprising that the rules of
antidiscrimination law have never been formally spelled out.
The formal interpretations of the Commission have been
limited to the problems of pre-employment inquiry. Even
the few cases that go to formal hearing do not result in
extensive legal formulations and the vast majority of cases
are settled by the investigating commissioner without any
accompanying written decision. When the case is closed,
the complainant and respondent merely receive official notification of closure together with a statement as to whether
the case was closed after investigation and conference or
dismissed for lack of probable cause. Official notice is so
brief as to allow for some confusion as to the outcome of
the case. Some respondents think that they were officially
found innocent where, according to the Commission's reck-
oning, probable cause was found and the case was closed
after successful conciliation.

A disposition sheet is attached to the file for each case.
The sheet includes a section marked, "reasons for disposition," wherein a brief comment is made as to the basis
for closing the case. The meaning of the term "reasons for
disposition" turns out to be somewhat ambiguous. Sometimes reasons for classifying a case as either "no probable
cause" or "investigation and conference" are given, but
sometimes only reasons for closing the case are given, without any justification for closing the case in any particular
manner. Thus, under the heading "reasons for disposition,"
we might find the statement, "complainant can no longer
be located." The disappearance of the complainant may, in

fact, justify closing a case, but it would not necessarily be a basis for dismissing a case as being without probable cause.

The reasons given for disposition are very brief and are not intended to provide an exhaustive account of the processes of reasoning that led to the decision in the case. In fifteen cases the reason given for disposition is the simple statement that the complainant's allegations could not be substantiated. In the cases closed after investigation and conference the reasons given for disposition were that the respondent had taken some action that would demonstrate a willingness to comply with the law, but no explanation was given for why the investigating commissioner thought that the respondent had or had not discriminated against the complainant. In other words, the reason given for disposition was that the case had been successfully conciliated and no reason was given for the decision as to probable cause. Hence the Commission's "rules of antidiscrimination law" must be inferred from their behavior. Since the verbal explanations of their decisions are so meager and sketchy, they must be supplemented by inferences based on their decisions in combination with the facts of the case.

Inferring rules of law from observation of how commissioners treat cases is an undeniably risky procedure. Although, it is not entirely unlike the process of legal reasoning that jurists use in inferring the *ratio decidendi* of a case from the judge's decision in combination with his recital of the facts of the case,[6] we must guard against too close an identification of the determination of the rules of law within a precedent system and the determination of the rules of the MCAD. Commissioners do not study each other's cases in search of binding principles for the disposition of their own cases. In fact, given the flexibility of this type of administrative procedure, commissioners are not necessarily even bound by their own previous decisions in other cases. Since commissioners are not trying to establish or develop a set of rules of law, their treatment of cases is relatively informal and casual. They do not try to report all the considerations that go into making a decision; they do not give any indication of what facts they considered relevant to the dispute. In analyzing a published legal case, the jurist knows what facts the judge considered to be a basis for his decision. Thus, he can specify the limits of the general rules that the precedent established. In the case of analyses of MCAD decisions, one has only the decision of the investigating commissioner and the facts of the case *as reported by the field representative* assigned to the case. One doesn't know what the investigating commissioner's findings of fact were. Hence, any inference as to the rules of law he was applying must rest on the observer's guess as to which of the field representative's discoveries formed the basis of the commissioner's findings.

Furthermore, cases do not ordinarily turn on the simple application of a single legal rule. The investigating commissioner sees a case as a complex set of circumstances to be judged according to a complex set of considerations. Any attempt to deduce a rule of law from a case runs a risk of tearing a feature of the case from its total context, thus distorting and oversimplifying the commissioner's reasoning processes.

For these reasons the following outline of the "rules of antidiscrimination law" must not be seen as a presentation of a set of systematic legal rules developed by the Commission, but as a list of guiding principles which commissioners, by their statements and their behavior, seem to have followed fairly consistently.

Rule 1: *Nothing in the law prevents a respondent from applying legitimate standards of qualification or reasonable standards of performance to either prospective or actual employees, renters, or purchasers.* By "legitimate standard" is meant a standard that does not have as its intent the

224

exclusion, limitation, or restriction of Negroes in general or a Negro complainant in particular.

Rule 1 is the rule most frequently used by commissioners in their explicit comments on the disposition sheet. The complainant's absolute or relative lack of qualifications, or his unsatisfactory on-the-job behavior is specifically cited as a reason for disposition twenty-six times. It is more frequently cited in employment cases than in housing cases by a ratio of twenty-one to five. Experience, performance on qualifying tests, references, attendance, morality, obedience to superiors, quality or output, and promptness were upheld as legitimate standards in employment cases. In the housing cases, number of children and income were held to be appropriate bases for excluding applicants.

There are a number of other cases where qualifying standards were not mentioned on the disposition sheet, but they in effect, support the right of employers and housing allocaters to establish and apply standards of qualification. Some of these cases uphold the right to base personnel decisions on relatively subtle and intangible qualifications such as "leadership ability" and (in the case of a prospective school teacher) the quality of the schools attended by the complainant.

The Commission rarely quarrelled with a standard established by a respondent, although in some cases the Commission challenged a respondent's good faith in applying a standard. In one case, the Commission did not believe that the respondent was serious about a rule that first floor apartments could not be rented to single girls, but the Commission did not necessarily object to that rule in the abstract. In only two instances were the respondent's standards clearly challenged. The obviously illegal requirement that tenants not be the sort of people that complain to the Commission was rejected, and, in a more interesting case, the Commission seemed suspicious of airline stewardess qualifications that apparently called for the rejection of applicants with noses "too flat" or lips "too full."

In sum, the Commission allows a wide latitude to businessmen in setting appropriate standards and does not press or otherwise harrass respondents if the complainant can be shown to be substandard and there is no other blatant evidence of discrimination. Respondents can not establish qualifications that are obviously quasi-racial in character, but they can base rejection on subtle bases that are likely to be correlated with race.

One qualification that can bear a subtle relation to race is the requirement that workers be able to "get along" with fellow workers on the job. Six of the cases in the sample involve complainants who had been dismissed or otherwise disciplined for squabbling with fellow employees or for failing to harmonize with their immediate superiors. The complainants felt that there were racial elements in their troubles, but none of their complaints were upheld. The complainants' troubles were attributed to "personality clashes" over which the Commission had no jurisdiction.

In one case, a hotel chambermaid was discharged by the hotel housekeeper for alleged tardiness, inefficiency, and early quitting. In the process, she was called a "black nigger." In dismissing the case, the investigating commissioner gave as the reason for disposition, "Investigation could not prove or disprove the charge of discrimination because of color. The fact that respondent housekeeper was difficult to please was evident." The evidence in the case was ambiguous and contradictory. Some informants saw the complainant as a good worker, others did not. That the complainant could not get along with the housekeeper and that their arguments came to have racial overtones was clear. On the other hand, it appeared that the other Negro chambermaid had no difficulty. The commissioner concluded that there was no racial discrimination involved.

At the same time, it is clear that the housekeeper was not without fault. In effect, the commissioner's hands were tied. The racial element in "getting along" is too intertwined with other elements of personality and interaction to be clearly separated. Hence, the law is not able to do much to lighten the racial burden that Negroes must shoulder as they try to work together with prejudiced white fellow workers.

The Commission was also unable to challenge the particularistic preference for members of the owner's family, or for the relatives and friends of current employees. Since Negroes are excluded from the network of primary group affiliations that work to the advantage of groups that are already in an advantageous position, these sorts of particularistic standards may be seen as related to race.

The practical implication of Rule 1 is that successful breakdown of racial barriers through legal action will ordinarily require an eminently well-qualified and unobjectionable complainant. It is also clear that businessmen can be relatively safe as long as they practice the more subtle forms of discrimination which involve the manipulation of standards to limit, select, and selectively place Negro applicants.

Rule 2: *Charges of discrimination will not be credited where there is clear evidence that the respondent's general policies have produced a well-integrated work force or integrated property holdings.* The commendability of the general racial patterns of a respondent was cited ten times as a reason for dismissing a case. Nine of those ten cases were employment cases. Rule 2 appears as a background factor in at least nine additional cases, including five housing cases. It is difficult to estimate the exact number of times that an investigating commissioner was influenced by an over-all racial pattern. The over-all pattern for each case was known by the investigating commissioner but it is not always clear whether the general pattern had an important

227

bearing on the disposition of the case. This much is clear: a commissioner rarely pressed an individual case when there was clear evidence of a high degree of integration. Only two exceptions could be found. Probable cause was found once when there were no Negroes in the particular job category in question even though Negroes were employed extensively in other categories.[7] In another case probable cause was found even though respondent owned integrated buildings when there were no Negroes in the particular building mentioned in the complaint.

An over-all pattern of integration is not a sure defense, but it is a very powerful one. In consequence, many complaints are doomed to failure since, as we have seen, there is a tendency for complaints to be filed against firms that have already broken the color line. Of the five findings of probable cause in employment cases four were in the category labelled "strategic" and in the thirty-one nonstrategic cases probable cause was found only once.

Another practical consequence of Rule 2 is to hinder the use of legal action to break through various types of limitations in Negro employment and housing, including tokenism, selective placement, and quotas.

No attempt was made to determine whether there were any general practices that would tend to lead to Negro exclusion. The entire case turned upon investigation of the comparative qualifications of the complainant and the various successful and unsuccessful applicants. In six other cases filed against firms where Negro employment was minimal, (constituting less than 1 percent of all employment) no probable cause was found five times.

The degree of integration of a respondent's various real property holdings is rarely brought out in the investigation of the cases. The extent and location of holdings is often a closely guarded secret. Nevertheless, it is possible to say that at least eight cases in which the respondent owned no integrated properties were dismissed for lack of probable cause.

Rule 3: *A finding of probable cause requires clear evidence that the complainant himself was subjected to intentional discrimination on the basis of race.*

The Commission will not make a finding of probable cause entirely on the basis of evidence of respondent's general policies if no evidence of specific discrimination against the complainant can be produced. The only exception to this rule concerns application forms. In three employment cases, the commissioner found probable cause on the grounds that respondent had used application forms that asked illegal questions about age. This suggests that it is possible to use the complaint as a basis for general investigations of respondent's policies. However, in the cases studied, such general investigation never produced a finding of probable cause on any grounds related to racial discrimination.

Rule 4: *The best evidences of intentional discrimination are overt discriminating statements, confessions of discrimination, artificial testing of complainant's policies, and flagrant, inexplicable changes in treatment accompanying the discovery of complainant's racial identity.*

If investigation reveals any of the four types of evidence listed in Rule 4, a finding of probable cause is highly likely. General evidence for this statement may be drawn from Table 29 which shows the relation between findings of probable cause and the credibility rating of a complaint. Complaints in credibility classes 1 and 2, tend to involve the types of evidence listed in Rule 4. Class 1 and 2 produced findings of probable cause in thirty-three of forty-six cases, leaving only thirteen possible cases in which no probable cause was discovered despite apparently high quality evidence. In these cases, investigation revealed holes in the complainant's story, or reasonable explanations for the complainant's treatment.

The best evidence that Rule 4 is important in deciding cases is that twenty-six of thirty-five probable-cause cases rested on one or more of the categories of evidence mentioned in the rule.

Of the nine exceptions to the rule, seven are cases resting on comparative analysis of qualification. Comparative analysis of qualifications can not be classed as one of the best evidences of intentional treatment because of the large number of cases in which the Commission elected not to develop evidence about comparative qualifications. This suggests that the commissioners do not believe that evidence of comparative qualifications is necessarily good evidence of discrimination. The place of comparative analysis of qualifications is stated in Rule 5, a corollary to Rule 4.

Rule 5: *When evidence deriving from comparative qualifications is available and indicates unequal treatment, that is good evidence of intentional discrimination. However, such evidence is available only in certain situations and will not be produced if respondent has a reasonable explanation for complainant's treatment.*

Rule 6: *Probable cause will not ordinarily be found if it can be shown that no opening or vacancy existed at the time the complaint was filed.*

The absence of a job opening was specifically cited eight times as a basis for dismissing complaints and three additional cases turned on the absence of an opening.

Usually, the elimination of an opening or vacancy *during the course of the investigation* affects only the probability of achieving meaningful redress. Probable cause can be found even though the opening disappears. However, the disappearance of the opening sometimes disheartens a commissioner and he comes to feel that there is no purpose in continuing the investigation. For example, in a case involving a promotion, the job was abolished in the course of the investigation and the investigating commissioner cited this as a reason for dismissing the case. However, there was other evidence tending to indicate that the complainant was not well qualified.

There is one notable exception to Rule 6. A Negro college professor applied for an apartment in Brookline. He was told that the vacancy was taken. The local fair housing committee tested and found that white testers were allowed to see the apartment and were not told it was taken. Investigation revealed that the apartment had been rented; the complainant had been told the truth. The person who had rented the apartment had not made a deposit and the owners of the building were developing a list of substitute tenants to take the apartment if the initial rental did not work out. The case demonstrates that the fact that a vacancy does not exist is not conclusive if it can be shown that the complainant was treated differently than white persons. Thus, if it were a landlord's practice to show a model apartment even when no apartments were available for occupancy, then he must extend that opportunity to white and Negro applicants alike.

In the absence of a test, the respondent's claim that no vacancy was available would sound quite reasonable. Thus, the group test bolstered what otherwise would have been a weak, deficient case.

Rule 7: *Nothing in the law requires that Negroes be told the truth, or the real reasons for their treatment.*

If, for reasons of business practice, a respondent has misinformed a complainant, the complainant is likely to suspect discrimination. However, if it can be shown that the misinformation was not given with discriminatory intent, the respondent will not be penalized. There are no cases where probable cause was found simply because a respondent had told a lie. On the other hand, on three occasions a respondent readily admitted to making false statements. For instance, in the case of the Negro girl who was turned down for a secretarial position because of her poor references, the firm told the girl that she was not being hired because the job was going to someone within the company. The story was not true, but one does not expect a firm to divulge the contents of confidential references.

Rule 8: *A respondent is responsible for the discriminatory acts of his employees. He is responsible for the discriminatory acts of anyone charged with the showing of accommodations.*

Probable cause has been found in housing cases where discriminatory acts were traced to rental agents, to janitors, and to janitors' wives. On the other hand, when a person is told that colored are not accepted by a tenant or a neighbor, the landlord is not responsible.

Rule 8 means that the heads of organizations must not only have a nondiscriminatory policy; they must insure that this policy is known and practiced throughout the organization.

Implications. It is sometimes alleged that antidiscrimination laws create administrative agencies which interfere with the normal course of business. The rules of antidiscrimination law, as they have been developed by the MCAD, do not involve any interference in the course of business activity. They clearly limit the Commission's critical role to judging whether there has been intentional discrimination against particular complainants. Nothing in the cases indicates that the Commission acted on the basis of a critical attitude toward a firm's racial composition, the racial composition of a respondent's property holdings, the actual but unintentional consequences of his personnel practices, the nature of his standards of qualification, or his administrative procedures.

The Commission found probable cause only when there was clear and, in fact, flagrant evidence that a complainant has been treated unlawfully. Most of the cases of discrimination that the Commission was willing to fight involved admitted, confessed discrimination or overpowering evidence of outright exclusion of Negro applicants. If a firm made a practice of hiring on the basis of comparative qualifications and kept records of past personnel dealings, then the Commission used those records to determine whether the respondent's standards had been applied without discrimination, but in almost all cases it was the respondent's standards that were relevant, not the Commission's. Only when the businessman's standards clearly indicated some racial preference did the Commission interfere. The rules of antidiscrimination law suggest an agency that tries to limit its official legal role to enforcement of the strict legal rights of complainants so as to minimize interference with the business community's pursuit of its legitimate goals. It hopes in this way to maintain the respect, cooperation, and good will of the business community. It is hoped that appropriate attitudes on the part of businessmen should, in turn, provide a suitable atmosphere for the Commission's educational and persuasive efforts.

On the other hand, the policies expressed in the rules of antidiscrimination law, seem to imply an assumption that problems of discrimination can be abstracted and separated from the over-all structure of employment and housing as social institutions. That is a mistaken assumption and therein lies the great weakness of the legal avenue to the elimination of discrimination.

The law is oriented to the remedy of intentional discrimination against individuals. A firm can be innocent of any intention to exclude Negroes, and at the same time, engage in procedures and practices that, in effect, limit Negro employment. A firm can be legally innocent of intentional discrimination against an individual complainant and yet practice many types of discrimination outside of the range of the specific complaint. The successful prosecution of an individual complaint depends on a complex combination of fortuitous circumstances. An opening must be available, the particular complainant must qualify better than all others under the respondent's special set of standards, and evidence to prove unequal treatment must be available. In theory, it might be possible to extend the surveillance of firms beyond the purview of the individual complaint, to use the complaint to unlock the door, as it were, to extensive investigations of a firm's practices and policies. In practice, the Commission only went beyond the complaint to police written policies and application forms. The only organizational requirement that was made of respondents was that their official policies be communicated throughout the organization. General patterns of Negro exclusion, discriminatory recruitment techniques, and evidence of selective placement, were not treated as evidence of probable cause in order to justify a conciliation program.

The emphasis on the particulars of the complainant's allegations has the consequence of limiting the potential effectiveness of the complaint process. The complainant's case often turns on more or less accidental factors that may be unrelated to the main features of the respondent's racial policies.

In short, although the Commission's policies purported to be oriented to human relations, they were, in effect, legalistic, for in accepting the individualistic, voluntaristic framework of traditional law, the organizational settings of human relations were obscured.

234

CHAPTER VIII. THE COMPLAINT PROCESS: III. THE

OUTCOMES OF COMPLAINTS

If it comes to a law case it's their ball game.—[Former respondent in a case before the MCAD]

Terms of Conciliation

How successful has the Commission been in securing positions and accommodations for complainants? Since the Commission reserved its legal powers for use on behalf of particular aggrieved individuals, it is important to examine the incidence of successful prosecution of individual cases. Is it true, as the former respondent said, that if it comes to a law case it is the Commission's "ball game?"

The Commission is hampered in its attempts to secure realistic benefits for complainants by the fact that many cases become moot in the course of investigation and conciliation. Either the vacancy in question becomes filled, or the complainant loses interest in filling it. In some cases the vacancy is filled before the complaint is even filed. In other instances the complainant has no interest in the position; he files the complaint in anger rather than in the hope that he will personally benefit. In one case the complainant expressed his disinterest in actually accepting an apartment in the sworn complaint itself, for all to see, including the respondent. Sometimes the Commission did not discover that the complainant was not interested until after they had secured an offer from the respondent. In other cases the Commission lost track of the complainant and was unable to find him.

235

At least sixty-seven cases were moot for one reason or another. This constitutes 57 percent of all the cases in the sample and represents a minimum estimate of the number of moot cases. Many of the cases that were dismissed for lack of probable cause did not provide any information on whether the complainant was still interested.

The problem was most serious in housing. In employment, most of the cases were without foundation; their moot quality did not add more problems. In housing on the other hand, the difficulty is quite crucial, since many cases of real discrimination became irremediable when they become moot, and at least three quarters of all housing cases were moot. A total of forty-five housing cases were so classified, including eighteen cases in which the complainant refused a housing accommodation.

Before legal provision for interlocutory relief was established in 1961 a landlord could stall until the accommodation in question was rented or sold to a third party. This difficulty loomed very large in the eyes of civil rights workers and was the main justification for the amendment permitting injunctive relief when such a situation threatened.

A few cases illustrate the dilatory pattern. A recent arrival to Boston was unsuccessful in his search for middle-income housing. At one building he applied directly to the superintendent and was told that he must apply to the owner personally. The owner avoided him for a considerable period. When finally cornered, the owner said that the apartment was taken. Then the applicant applied to the rental agent who said that all apartments were taken and that everyone who handled rentals was on vacation.[1] During the investigation the respondent insisted that the particular apartment in question had been rented. His attorney delayed in making records available to the Commission. Finally, when the apartment *was* rented, records were made availa-

236

ble and the case was settled on the basis of a letter promising no future discrimination.[2] It was never clear whether the apartment was rented at the time the complainant applied, but there are indications that it was not. The person introduced as the new tenant seems to have been a relative of a prominent realtor who had connections with respondent's firm.

In another case a realtor who was building a series of adjacent apartments promised to rent to a Negro applicant, then immediately converted the only vacant apartment to a model unit so that the complainant would have to wait for another building to be constructed.

Although a pattern of delay is apparent in several cases, relatively few cases became moot because the opening in question was filled in the course of investigation and conciliation. Far more frequently the case became moot because the complainant took advantage of another opportunity during the interim.

Of course, the high rate at which complainants drop out reflected both respondents' own delays and the delays in the legal process. A complainant must work and live somewhere while the process runs it course. He would be foolish not to accept an opportunity on the assumption that legal action will ultimately secure his original desire. On the other hand, many complaints were actually moot from their very inception.

The limitations that the moot quality of complaints impose on the terms of conciliation are apparent in Table 30. Time and time again the Commission was forced to rely on mere promises to refrain from discrimination in the future or upon empty offers to complainants who were uninterested.

The terms of conciliation fall into four main categories:

1) *Accepted position.* The first column of Table 30 shows the number of cases that resulted in the complainant or

Table 30. Number of cases conciliated by MCAD and terms imposed

Finding	Position accepted	Offer to complainant	Promise to obey law	No terms	Total
Housing					
Probable cause	11	12	11	3	
No probable cause	2	4	2	14	
Total	13 (22.0%)	16 (27.1%)	13 (22.0%)	17 (28.8%)	59
Employment					
Probable cause	1	4	0	0	
No probable cause	4	2	0	48	
Total	5 (8.4%)	6 (10.2%)	0	48[a] (81.4%)	59
Grand Total	18 (15.3%)	22 (18.6%)	13 (11.0%)	65 (55.1%)	118

[a]Includes three cases of change in application form to conform to requirements of the age law.

some other Negro accepting an apartment or house or job or some other tangible benefit. As is shown in the table about 15 percent of the cases achieved that measure of success. Six of the eighteen cases that resulted in tangible benefit were cases dismissed as without probable cause. The filing of the case brought about capitulation even though it failed from a legal standpoint. In all but six of the cases the beneficiary of the respondent's action was the complainant himself. Twelve of the cases involved obtaining occupancy of apartments, two entailed obtaining employment, two improving the conditions of work, one securing a promotion, and one passing papers on a house.

2) *Offer to complainant.* The second column shows the number of cases settled on the basis of an offer to provide some benefit to the complainant. For nineteen of the twenty-two cases of this type, there is clear evidence that the offer was turned down. In the remaining three cases, the offer had not been accepted at the time the case was closed. Those three cases might belong in the first category, but there is no available evidence that the respondent's offer was ever accepted.

3) *Promise to obey the law.* In thirteen housing cases the terms of conciliation were simply that the respondent promised to obey the law in the future. If the case was moot, then no specific offer could be made to the complainant and the Commission was limited to extracting general promises. In ten of those thirteen cases the case was moot because the complainant was not interested in moving into the accommodation in question. That leaves only three cases where the respondent blocked action by renting the apartment.

4) *No terms.* In sixty-five cases there were no terms of conciliation. All but three of these were cases dismissed without probable cause. Three housing cases were dismissed after investigation and conference in which the commis-

239

sioner was unable to secure any kind of action from the respondent. For example, an apartment house was sold during the conciliation process, leaving no course of action open to the Commission. In one case an army officer was evicted from a rental home in a subdivision. The army had rented a block of houses for their officers, some of whom were Negroes. The owner of the subdivision decided to evict the Negro tenants on the grounds that the remaining homes in the development were difficult to sell when Negroes were living in the neighborhood. The army countered by canceling all leases. From the Commission's point of view, the case became moot and they withdrew.

This case is interesting because it illustrates the Commission's unwillingness to go beyond the issues in the complaint. The Commission did not obtain a promise that the homes would be sold on a nondiscriminatory basis, let alone a commitment to advertise the homes in a Negro newspaper, or list them with a civil rights agency.

When the individual case became moot the Commission was satisfied with general promises. They did not demand broadened bases of recruitment, restructuring of the personnel process, broadened advertising, or cooperation with civil rights groups, though such terms of conciliation are not unknown to some legal agencies.[3]

There was little cooperation with other civil rights organizations. For example, when the Commission developed a commitment to abide by the law they did not publicize the commitment so that it could be tested by other agencies. Informal lines of communication operated in a few cases. Field representatives sometimes privately informed civil rights groups of a respondent's good intentions, but there were no systematic techniques for exploiting the commitments developed by the complaint process. On one occasion a commissioner informed a respondent that he would send a couple over to test his promise to rent on a nondiscriminatory basis, but there is no evidence that he carried out the threat. In general, the Commission put the testing of commitment in the same category as testing to prove guilt. It was all right if civil rights groups wanted to do it, but the Commission would neither test, nor be an accessory to testing.

A few types of conciliation terms do not appear in Table 30. In some instances the respondent was required to post a notice concerning the provisions of the law, or to instruct his employees to abide by the law. Application forms were changed in some cases by the removal of discriminatory questions. In general the terms of conciliation did not go beyond the individual case, except to extract general promises to obey and instruct, and to cease obvious violations.

Of the thirteen housing cases classified as "accepted position," eight were sponsored by groups.

The relatively high proportion of group-originated cases in this category merely reflects the capacity of groups to produce probable cases of discrimination. Groups have not been able to exert diffuse pressure to force stringent terms of conciliation. Among probable cause cases, there is only a very slight, insignificant tendency for group cases to be associated with the most successful category of cases (see Table 31).

Table 31. Group vs. individual origin of case and success in conciliation with housing complaints

Probable - cause cases	Individual	Group[a]	Total
Position accepted	7 (33.3%)	4 (25.0%)	11
Other terms	14 (66.7%)	12 (75.0%)	26
Total	21	16	37

[a]$\phi = 0.09$; $\chi^2 = 0.30$.

In sum, if we define a successful complaint as one that leads to a more even distribution of Negro participation in social life, then successful complaints were rare events. Of the 118 cases studied only eleven met that criteria. Only nine housing cases and two employment cases were both strategic and successful.

The Commission's focus on the solution of the immediate issues raised in the complaint dissipated its energy because of the frequency with which those immediate issues became moot.

When the issues became moot the Commission did not go beyond general and superficial demands for promises to abide by the law. Since these promises were not tested, the Commission lost jurisdiction over the offense when the case became moot.

Groups have been shown to be successful in producing complaints against significant targets and complaints that eventuated in a finding of probable cause. However, once a finding of probable cause has been made, groups have been able to produce only a slightly higher proportion of cases conciliated on strict terms.

One of the most persistent complaints voiced against the Commission was that investigation and conciliation proceeded at too slow a pace and that this was the major source of the problem of moot cases. At first glance this seems a valid charge for cases often remained open for over a year. Closer examination shows that time is indeed a significant dimension of the process, but that the Commission was proceeding more rapidly than some suppose. The commissioners were aware of the vital importance of prompt investigation. If the complaint process is tied to resolving the particular grievance of the complainant, it follows that it is very important to proceed with conciliation before the vacancy in question is filled, before a discharged worker has been replaced, or before a punitive suspension has run its course. Commissioners pushed field representatives to complete investigations as quickly as possible and sometimes expressed displeasure and frustration when investigative reports seemed overdue.

Information about the duration of the process was gathered from the record of investigation. The timing of four intervals was studied:

1) The period from the discovery by the complainant of discrimination to the docketing of the complaint;

2) The period from the docketing of the complaint to the first field investigation by a representative of the Commission;

3) The period from the first investigation to the end of investigation and conciliation;

4) The period from the end of investigation and conciliation to the formal closing of the case.

It might seem useful to divide the investigation process into two separate periods, one of investigation and one of conciliation. However, such a division would not correspond to the reality of the Commission's procedures for it is not possible to say when investigation breaks off and conciliation begins. The two imperceptibly merge; field representatives often begin conciliatory attempts before formal meetings occur between a commissioner and the respondent, and investigation continues after conciliation begins.

Table 32 shows the median time elapsed during the four periods for employment and housing.

It is clear that the sooner the Commission can reach the respondent to start an investigation the more the chance of helping the complainant. For conciliated housing cases the median time elapsed during period 1 was three days and the median time elapsed during period 2 was two days. For cases dismissed for lack of probable cause the corresponding periods are seven and five days respectively.

At the same time the Commission can not be made to

243

Table 32. Median time elapsed during the complaint process (number of days)

Period	Employment	Housing
Period 1,		
Discrimination to docketing	6	4
Period 2,		
Docketing to start of investigation	6	3
Period 3,		
Investigation and conciliation	17	23
Period 4,		
Dormant period before final closing	13	51
Sum of the medians of periods 2,3,4	36	77
Sum of the medians	42	81

bear the entire brunt for delay. As much time elapsed between the time discrimination was recognized and a complaint was filed as passed between docketing and first investigation. Delay in reporting discrimination can be fatal. In housing, if discrimination was reported within ten days, probable cause was found in 71 percent of the cases. If reporting was delayed beyond that ten-day period, as it was in fourteen of fifty-nine cases, findings of probable cause decline to 43 percent.

In this respect civil rights groups are often offenders. In housing, groups take more time to report cases than individuals. No doubt this time is spent in preparing the case, but extended delay is dangerous nevertheless. The median time taken by a group to report a case is seven days. Individuals report in median time of three days. In five cases in which groups failed to achieve a finding of probable cause the median time elapsed before reporting was eleven days whereas in nineteen successful group cases the median time was four days.

Investigation and conference proceed reasonably rapidly. Once begun, it was usually completed within three weeks. Conciliation agreement was reached in cases of probable cause in a median time of twenty days from the beginning of the investigation.

The long dormant period following investigation and conciliation makes cases seem to take a very long time. Actually, the case is in effect closed but it is left officially open while the Commission awaits compliance or in consideration of the possibility that a new case will be brought, in which case the old case can be used as evidence in the new one.

The Consequences of the Process

In 1952 the MCAD surveyed complaints of discrimination that had been settled after investigation and conference during the previous three years.[4] Two hundred and seventy employers were checked. Only twenty-six of the firms showed an increase in the number of minority-group members employed. Thirteen of the firms showing an increase had employed some minority-group members before complaints were filed. The other thirteen had had no minority-group employees. At the time of the follow-up the twenty-six firms were employing 1,770 minority-group members out of a total of 17,370 employees. This represented a thirteen-fold increase in minority-group employment. Only 124 minority-group members had been employed prior to the Commission's enforcement efforts.

The Commission's figures indicate that the filing of a complaint might possibly have produced spectacular results. In some cases successful negotiation led to substantial gains in opportunities for minority-group members. On the other hand, such cases appear to be rather rare. In a three-year period, only twenty-six firms actually increased minority-group employment. Less than 10 percent of the firms where discrimination was found were able to demonstrate changes in the patterns of minority-group employment. The overwhelming majority of "investigation and conference cases" produced no long-run change.

245

The Commission's findings though they are quite old, are consistent with the information gathered by the author in 1962. Forty-seven former respondents in Commission cases were interviewed in an effort to assess the impact of the complaint process.

The results of these interviews must be approached cautiously. The twenty-seven former respondents in employment cases and twenty former respondents in housing cases do not constitute a random sample in any sense. All of the respondents and correspondents in the cases analyzed in this chapter who could be located were approached. Nine employers and eighteen realtors or property owners refused to be interviewed. Many of those who consented to be questioned were not entirely candid in their answers and others refused to answer individual questions. All were informed that answers would be treated in strictest confidence but suspicions were not always completely allayed. It is not easy to interview respectable businessmen about violations of the law. Many suspected that the author was using research as a ruse to gather information for one or another of the civil rights organizations in the area, or that information would leak to such organizations.

Accordingly the following data allow only a few tentative approximations. Nevertheless, some responses were extraordinarily consistent from one respondent to another and permit interesting insights into the legal process.

None of the former employment respondents thought that they had "lost" a case brought against them! The respondents in four of the five probable-cause cases were interviewed. All thought that they had won the case. One "defeated" respondent said:

Sometimes the colored people here treat me terribly. The case was no case at all. If it had gone against me I would have taken it to court. It was a silly case. It's a case of the weak person claiming color because they can't fight their own badness. I think it's a confession of weakness. I should charge discrimination myself. These people use the law to protect themselves. The Commission treated me fair. It was all fair. No one treated me badly; I came out all right.

Another said

The case was dismissed. They went through all kinds of records and applications in a formal series of thorough investigations. They did an outstanding job; fair and thorough.

In view of the fact that all informants thought that they had been successful it is not surprising to find that all thought that the Commission was fair in its enforcement activities.

A few sample comments are revealing:

They [the Commission] are very good. By and large they are conciliatory, moderate, and don't presume guilt . . . They made an honest effort.

Yes, we had a case; there was no cause; the case was dismissed. A very fabulous man came. He said he had to investigate. He was very apologetic and told me of all the phony cases he had investigated.

We have no complaints about the Commission. They exonerated us and I think they did a fine job.

Two girls at the——plant applied and weren't hired. They claimed that white girls were hired before and after them . . . No work was open. A very nice girl came out here to investigate. When she found out she didn't follow through . . . I was treated fairly.

Only two complainants had minor criticism. One thought that an investigation had been too thorough considering that the charge was "obviously false." This informant said that the Commission was not as "bad" in this regard as SCAD in New York. Another respondent thought that it was not fair for the field representative to ask for an application form without announcing his purpose.

Complaints from the Commission were not viewed as catastrophic occurrences. In fact, the law was not very salient to these respondents. Even those who saw problems of discrimination as a salient segment of their work experience did not see the state law or the state commission as the most important source of their problems. Federal anti-

247

discrimination programs, the activities of pressure organizations, or pressures within their own firms were seen as more significant guarantors of a policy of nondiscrimination. In six cases, respondents were not even aware that complaints had been lodged; the complaint process had not been imprinted in the organizational memory. In one case, an informant confessed that he had not really been aware that there was a case until the author interviewed him. He said that he had never made the connection before between the investigation that had been held and the existence of a state law against discrimination.

The informality of investigations failed to impress respondents with the requirements and the compulsive powers of the law. None thought that they were discriminating according to their conception of that word. They did not feel threatened by the law or the Commission. Some felt threatened by militant civil rights advocates who tried to press what they considered illegitimate conceptions of nondiscrimination, but none felt that the Commission exerted this type of pressure.

Twenty-two of the respondents responded to the question, "Has your firm ever changed its policies or practices as a result of the fair employment practices law or the activities of the MCAD?" Nineteen said, "No." Three said that they had modified application forms. None mentioned any other changes.

Overdrawn conclusions from this information must be avoided. In the first place many did not know whether legally induced change might have occurred at some time in the past. Secondly, informants seem reluctant to credit the law with power to affect change, preferring to stress the role of economic and moral factors. Thirdly, some of these respondents had actually offered tangible benefits to particular complaints as a consequence of Commission investigations. Nevertheless, it can be said that there is no

248

clear evidence to indicate that employers regard the law as a serious threat or a powerful force.

In contrast, respondents in housing cases found the Commission ominous, threatening, and very salient. Sixteen out of twenty saw the law as operating against their interests and rights. Most of these stressed the possible financial loss that could accrue if Negroes were to become tenants in their buildings, or residents in their developments.

Seaver Street ten or twenty years ago was mostly Jewish people but over the years Negroes were moving in. We had the property for five years, paid 117 and sold for 102. We bought it with no Negroes in and sold with no Negroes in. When we put it on the market no one was interested in it to buy it.[5]

I think it is unconstitutional because it tries to make businessmen into do-gooders at a cost of loss on investment. You put Negroes into a place and you lose the whites.

People say "I won't move up there—you've got niggers in there." When they moved out we rented five of those seven apartments in three months. In the previous two years and four months we had rented only one. We lost $17,000.

Others stressed the right of management to protect tenants from undesirable applicants. Negroes were alleged to bring in noise, undesirable cooking odors, unpleasant and dangerous friends, and careless habits.

Some of the more sophisticated realtors realize that loss on investment follows Negro occupancy only under special circumstances. They are aware of the "color tax" and the special profits that can be made from conversion to Negro occupancy. These men tend to stress the right to the property owner to decide for himself what "type" of property they would like to own:

The value I speak of is not the value of the market place but the value in the intangible sense of the value of a well coordinated operation. Private properties are almost human beings; they must be groomed; they have their own personalities.

Another realtor had a similar but more bluntly stated view:

When the time comes that I have to collect my rent in ten installments per month with a bullet proof vest, I'll sell out.

Twelve of the informants had been involved in one or more investigation and conference cases, but as in employment, respondents feel that they won the case. Sometimes they believe that they purchased victory by making an offer to the complainant or by writing a letter stating their intent to comply with the law, but such capitulation was interpreted as victory because there was no official punishment or formal finding of guilt. None of the informants spoke of losing to the Commission.

The belief that one prevailed can soften perceptions of the enforcement agency. Some respondents expressed attitudes parallel to those of the employers quoted above. For example:

I have no criticisms—they believed me.
I was treated fairly. They found that the fellow had made a mistake.

On the other hand since some respondents purchased "victory" at a price, we find outspoken critics among realtors who have been involved in Commission cases. Six informants criticized the Commission's administrative procedure. Some were particularly unhappy about the apparent combination of judgment and prosecution in one role. "_____ was judge, jury and everything and I told him so.

Others objected to the Commission's attempt to force respondents to sign papers saying that they promised to do what they must do under the law, and to the fact that insincere and unfounded complaints were allowed to take up valuable time.

Respondents in housing cases were more likely to see the law as controlling their behavior than respondents in employment cases. Employers did not believe that the law or the MCAD forced them to any action that they would not take in the absence of the law. None of the discriminatory or quasi-discriminatory elements of business policy seemed threatened.

In contrast, some realtors and property owners described the compulsive powers of the law and of action under the law.

I had an old piece of property down in the Boston University student area. A colored person came to rent it and my superintendent told him the vacancy was filled. It wasn't. I would have condoned it, but I don't want anything like this, so I let them move in. As I was saying, as a lawyer I couldn't fight it.

Yes, we've integrated many places since the law went into effect. We obey the law; we have no choice, we are watched like hawks . . . How could we evade it. The law is black and white—there is no gray. You have to rent to Negroes and that is it.

Six respondents said that they had changed practices since passage of the law. In some other cases respondents issued new instructions to employees, but in at least six cases buildings were actually integrated.

Other respondents insisted that the law had not made them change. Seven respondents admitted discrimination. They were divided as to whether the law might change their practices in the future. One worried realtor said:

We do have a problem. We have colored people coming in and owners will say don't send them down. Our practice is to ask the owner and go according to what they do. I'm somewhat worried it will get me into trouble. We try to avoid trouble by saying that nothing is listed or we give a higher price. If it comes to a law case it's their [the Commission's] ball game.

Another man seemed less worried. His opinion shows a firm grasp of the role of civil rights organizations in law enforcement.

The law doesn't mean anything and won't change anything until economics makes it change . . .

I don't put the amount of rent in the ad so that I can say no to Negroes by quoting a higher price. You can pay the bastards off anyway . . .

It's economics that does it. The only thing that might get me is if CORE and the NAACP ganged up and sent seventy-five people a day down those steps [pointing to steps leading to his office].

This man (and others), had successfully stalled off the Commission with a letter of good intent:

Sure, I signed a piece of paper for the Commission. It doesn't mean a damn thing.

Those who are really intent on excluding Negroes were quite willing to sign false papers, or to commit other immoral acts to protect their right to choose tenants and buyers:

We don't discriminate, that is, we haven't been caught. I lie, cheat, and steal to do it. It's made a crook out of me and all the others in the profession.

Housing respondents were aware that their real enemy is not the Commission, but the civil rights groups that can invoke the power of the law.

When they speak of being "watched like hawks" they are not referring to supervisory activities on the part of the Commission. They are referring to the activities of fair housing groups and other organizations that might force a showdown at any time. In the words of one realtor:

—— keeps coming in here because he's trying to get me and he will sooner or later. I can't lie forever.

Given the nature of the available data, a definitive statement on the types, the extent, and the sources of law evasion is not possible. However, a few gross differences between housing and employment seem well established. Employment respondents did not find the law salient or threatening. The most serious sources and types of employment discrimination had not been challenged. The MCAD was viewed as a fair and honest board that merely regulates the misunderstandings that arise despite the good intentions of management.

Housing respondents were more likely to have practiced flagrant discrimination and they were more likely to desire to continue to discriminate. The MCAD was either viewed as unfair in itself or as subject to the unfair demands of Negroes and pressure organizations. The machinery of law was seen as threatening and powerful. Some violators felt that they can continue to violate for some time, but that in a showdown they will lose. A substantial number appeared to be willing to continue to discriminate on the assumption that relatively few victims will complain to the Commission. They were willing to risk a few confrontations with the Commission to protect their perceived interests. Others had already integrated property in response to the pressures of the law.

Summary and Conclusion

The data on the structure of the complaint process show that when the enforcement process is tied to the goal of justice for the aggrieved individual, the capacity of law to produce social change suffers accordingly.

Jurisdiction. The ultimate prerequisite to social change through law enforcement is jurisdiction over violations. The enforcing agency must obtain access to the condition that it is attempting to remedy. The MCAD has relied almost entirely on complaints brought to it by aggrieved individuals. Reliance on complaints will provide for effective jurisdiction only if three conditions are met: (1) Victims must experience violations in the course of their activities; (2) The violations of law must be flagrant and thus easily recognizable by victims; (3) Victims must be willing to use the procedures of law as a means of remedying violations.

We have seen that those conditions were more closely approximated in housing than employment. Housing discrimination is more open and less subtle than employment discrimination. At least one segment of the Negro population, the middle class, was actively engaged in attempts to

253

crash the barriers of segregated housing, and was willing to use the law as a weapon in the assault. In employment, those who were engaged in the struggle for greater opportunity seemed willing and able to take advantage of the liberalizing push of economic change and unwilling to utilize legal techniques to attack discrimination in sectors that have been insulated from economic pressures.

Thus, reliance on the complaints of aggrieved individuals as the sole avenue of jurisdiction over offences was relatively effective in housing and relatively ineffective in employment. At least a portion of the greater success in attaining jurisdiction in the housing sphere stems from the activities of civil rights groups that were organized to facilitate the search for housing. They developed efficient techniques for recognizing discrimination, and they funnelled significant cases to the legal agency. The policy of justice for aggrieved individuals is effective only because groups provide an organizing effort that serves as a functional equivalent or substitute for initiation of complaints by the Commission.[6]

Interpretation of the law. The establishment of jurisdiction over alleged violations is a necessary but not a sufficient condition of enforcement. The Commission must be able to establish that discrimination occurred according to some set of rules and standards that define the offense.

The Commission's interpretations of the meaning of discrimination stressed the right of employers and housing allocaters to establish reasonable qualifications. This is in accordance with statutory provisions. In some cases, however, the Commission's decision did not go beyond a judgment of the reasonableness of the complainant's treatment. This occurred quite frequently when the type of evidence that could establish the actual inequality of the complainant's treatment was not readily available. When such evidence is unavailable, or for some reason is not produced, the Commission fell on an assessment of the complainant with reference to the respondent's alleged standards. This places a heavy burden on the complainant; he must be exceptionally well qualified in order to prevail. Again, reliance on the character of the individual complaint seems less effective than an over-all appraisal of the nature and consequences of the respondent's policies and procedures.

As in the case of the problem of jurisdiction, civil rights groups made a contribution of overcoming this obstacle. Groups were willing and able to generate the information that is prerequisite to the use of the rigorous standard of equal treatment. Civil rights groups need not worry about whether they are putting themselves in a position of supporting an applicant who appears to be substandard. The commissioners must be concerned about this problem for they feel that the legitimacy of the agency must be maintained. They do not wish to take action that appears to denigrate the right of management to establish reasonable qualifications. Civil rights groups are not constrained by this problem of legitimacy. Given the Commission's official commitment to the equal-treatment standard, they cannot ignore evidence of unequal treatment when it is presented to them. Accordingly, civil rights groups are in a position to transcend the limitations that derive from the human weaknesses of individual complainants.

More evidence of the commissioners' tendency to concentrate on justice for the aggrieved individual is provided by their habit of treating cases as if a complaint only establishes jurisdiction over the particular violations alleged. They did not maintain this position consistently, for they went beyond the limits of the complaint to police such matters as application forms and written policy, that is, the symbols of discrimination. Yet, they did not use analysis of over-all patterns of Negro participation as a lever for encouraging reevaluation and modification of established policies and practices that may be discriminatory in effect, if not discriminatory in intention.

Enforcement. Once jurisdiction has been established and

discrimination proven, the power of the Commission to remedy the situation remained problematical. Again, there is an important limitation consequent to exclusive focus on the issues of the individual complaint. When the complainant did not wish to use the complaint as a realistic avenue to a substantive benefit the Commission usually limited its efforts to attempts to secure untested verbal commitments.

Nevertheless, given jurisdiction over a probable case of discrimination, and given a "live" complainant, the power of the Commission to compel a settlement was well established. In no case of this type did the Commission fail to secure the capitulation of the respondent. A formal hearing was necessary in only one of these cases. The twin moral pressures provided by the norm of equal opportunity and the norm of conformity to law, made most respondents anxious to settle within the confines of the privacy of the conciliation process. The experiences of other antidiscrimination commissions has been similar. In view of the probability that continued public defiance will ultimately fail (given the compulsive powers of law), there is little point in opening one's self to the additional sanctions of public condemnation and, more recently, attacks from militant pressure organizations.

Thus, insofar as the complaint process has shown signs of weakness in the past, it must be attributed to the effects of social structure on the acquisition and maintenance of jurisdiction over offences and to the problems of collecting sufficient evidence under established standards, not to the inability of the Commission to prevail in a power showdown.

From this point of view, the weaknesses in the process seem to be remediable rather than inevitable. Effective organization of community support can strengthen the process by stepping in to plug the holes caused by weak policies. On the other hand, the weakness of the policies themselves stem from the limitations of the Commission's power position. Stronger policies are conceivable, but it does not follow that the Commission would have had the realistic power to implement more militant policies even if they had been viewed as desirable. The law gave the Commission ultimate power in any particular show-down because the Commission had access to the power of the state, but its continued access to that power is always problematical and depends on the success with which the Commission can institutionalize its position and its views.

CHAPTER IX. AN INTERPRETIVE OVERVIEW:

1946-1962

. . . before the law was passed they weren't as willing to listen to reason—[A civil rights worker]

During the period 1946 to 1962 the Boston community experienced a measure of racial harmony. According to the theory of institutionalization, the resolution and suppression of conflict that characterized this period should be attributed to the successful institutionalization of social values. According to this theory the social integration of a community is not to be attributed to a mere physical suppression of disruptive demands. It is to be seen as a consequence of the development of integrative interpretations of social values and the establishment of these interpretations through the reshaping of the patterns of interests in the community and the development of implementive apparatus.

The Boston experience illustrates several elements of the theory of institutionalization as it was developed in Chapter I. In subsequent chapters we have seen how particular versions of the ideal of equal opportunity, supported by the organized advocates of change, came to have the force of law and how organizational apparatus developed to implement the new legal norms. At the same time, it is clear that the newly legislated norms did not totally transform the structure of the community. The attempt to establish these norms met with a number of deeply intrenched structural obstacles. The activities of the MCAD can be viewed as a

258

compromise between the advocates of complete institution-alization and the forces demanding protection of interests vested in the established social structure.

During the first sixteen years of its existence the MCAD played an integrative role in the community by achieving an equilibrium between the forces of institutionalization and the forces of the conditions of institutionalization. The conditions of institutionalization—established ideology, es-tablished interests, and obstacles to jurisdiction—were at-tacked with sufficient vigor to meet the most pressing de-mands in the community, but not so militantly as to en-danger the precarious foundations of the equal-treatment standard.

As subsequent efforts have shown, this equilibrium was not ultimately stable and Chapter 10 will suggest a Com-mission struggling to achieve a new equilibrium in the face of more insistent demands for change and more substantial threats of disruption.

Demands for new interpretations of the ideal of equal op-portunity now confront the community; demands for more sweeping and militant enforcement now confront the Com-mission, but the roots of these demands lie in the problems of institutionalization that the foregoing analysis has un-covered.

The following resumé outlines a few of the major findings and implications of the preceding analysis of institutionali-zation during the classic era.

The role of values. The structure of opportunity in the Boston community could not be predicted from the value premise of equal opportunity. There was both intentional and structural exclusion of Negroes from a number of eco-nomic roles and residential locations.

Some would say that the presence of discrimination shows that the value system is without consequence, but the his-tory of equal opportunity in Boston indicates that abstract values and norms can play a significant role in shaping social action.

The mobilization of "lip service" values during the legislative battles over the passage of civil rights statutes put the defenders of the status quo on the defensive, and in so doing, closed off a number of possible avenues of effective counterattack. Prejudice is often a powerful weapon in group conflict. Bias is one of the main sources of support for both active and passive discrimination,[1] but the social mobilization of values can prevent those who would prefer to maintain discrimination from making effective use of appeals to prejudice.

The effective organization of the symbols of value consensus allowed the champions of equal opportunity to secure passage of an enforceable law against discrimination, and the law once passed gave civil rights forces access to the power of the state, permitting a shift in the balance of power.

Law also solidifies the moral position of the forces advocating the implementation of equal opportunity. Those who would continue to discriminate find themselves even more on the defensive than they were in opposing the original passage of the law. The normative force of legally established ideals is apparent in the unwillingness of respondents to challenge complaints at public hearings. Defendants have regularly surrendered at informal meetings to avoid the publicity of open legal battles.

In sum, values do not "institutionalize themselves," but actors who seek to implement values can use value consensus within the community as a weapon, whereas those who would resist are bound by the operation of "moral estoppel." "Estoppel" is a legal principle that operates to prevent a person from alleging or denying what he has, by his own previous action, admitted or implied. There is an analogy in social process, for participation in a community

260

comes to imply acceptance of its ultimate values. Deviance occurs, but the deviant by virtue of his claimed membership and his past claims to the rights of membership, is estopped from defending himself by challenging ultimate values. Some types of resistance imply such a challenge, and in consequence, resistors find avenues of counterattack difficult to find.

Interpretations. Institutionalization is complicated by the existence of variable interpretations of the meaning of social values. Persons who agree on a value in the abstract may differ radically as to the binding obligations that acceptance of the value implies. Thus, value consensus may be accompanied by normative dissension. Furthermore, various normative interpretations of a value have variable capacities to integrate the community, to command assent within the community, and to transform an established social structure.

Several alternative interpretations of equal opportunity were found in the Boston community. Some businessmen, interpreting equal opportunity in the context of the value of economic rationality, believed that Negroes should not be excluded from roles that Negroes can perform without detriment. This interpretation can command considerable assent with the business community. Moreover, in stressing economic rationality, it presents a powerful argument to a businessman who has been intentionally and unreasonably excluding Negroes from all participation in his firm. However, its dynamic potential is limited because acceptance of the "racial-qualifications" approach does not force the businessman to accept Negroes in the face of risks of economic loss and, of course, it does not encourage the businessman to take active steps to overcome structural discrimination.

The racial-qualifications approach allows little leverage on the status quo. In fact, the followers of this approach feel obliged to adjust to prejudice whenever it is expressed in

261

market forces. Since racial prejudices affect the preferences that determine market forces, the racial-qualifications standard fails to drive a wedge between prejudice and discrimination.

The limitations on the capacity of this standard to produce change affect its capacity to stabilize relations between the races. A standard that tends to preserve the status quo will ultimately prove unacceptable to the forces of social change. The Negro vanguard refuses to be judged by the average characteristics or the "acceptability" of the race.

The equal-treatment standard requires that each individual be treated on his own merits, without regard to his race or the possible reactions of others to his race. He must be judged by the same standards as all others. If whites are judged by loose and low standards, then the same loose and low standards must be applied to nonwhites.

The equal-treatment standard was the dominant interpretation of equal opportunity among the white liberals and Negroes who engineered the passage of the original fair employment legislation, and the MCAD officially subscribes to this doctrine.

In practice, the MCAD sometimes has applied a somewhat different standard. In some cases a judgment was made on the basis of an assessment of the "reasonableness" of a respondent's action. According to the reasonable-treatment standard, Negroes must be treated in a manner and according to standards which would be reasonable in the case of white employees or customers.

The reasonable-treatment standard is less effective than the equal-treatment standard. It leads to the dismissal of more cases and to fewer attempts to negotiate change. It is not acceptable to civil rights advocates because it permits employers, realtors, and landlords to fall back upon the racial-qualifications approach, that is, to insist upon higher standards for members of less "acceptable" races.

The equal-treatment standard permits more leverage on

the established social structure than the racial-qualifications approach; equal treatment prevents businessmen from responding to prejudice as it is expressed in the market or in their perceptions of the market; it demands that businessmen take risks, and in some cases, losses, in order to implement the ideal of equal opportunity.

Equal treatment harmonizes rather closely with the individualistic strain in American values. The standard of equal treatment demands that each actor be treated equally by every other actor. However, it does not demand that the system as a system treat everyone alike. Thus, the businessman bears no collective responsibility for the effects of inequalities that are beyond his control.

There is still a strong element of the value of economic efficiency in the equal-treatment conception. All must be treated by the same standard and the standard must not be racial, but the standards themselves need not be chosen so as to ensure the inclusion of Negroes. They need only faithfully reflect the exigencies of efficiency and profit. Similar criteria govern the selection of techniques of recruitment and of methods of regulating the procedures regarding personnel. If such methods are efficient they need not ensure the selection or promotion of Negroes.

Because of its individualistic emphasis, the implementation of the equal-treatment standard fails to uproot the collective and structural sources of unequal participation. Thus, when substantive equality is not forthcoming, the advocates of change come to reject the equal-treatment standard and to demand affirmative action to ensure the Negro a fair share of the wealth and comforts of the community. Advocates of the fair-share standard may demand a quota, or they may demand some other action, such as a reorganization of the recruitment or allocation process, the establishment of training programs, or systematic searches for candidates for promotion.

The various versions of the fair-share approach offer the

most leverage for change, but they are difficult to articulate with traditional conceptions of equal opportunity. In some cases, discrimination against whites is implied. Further, businessmen resent the intrusion of noneconomic criteria, and they resent the demand for the assumption of collective responsibility within the private sector.

The demand for a fair share began to emerge during the period in question but the officials of the MCAD remained true to the old faith. There is little evidence that conciliators, in the course of their negotiations, went beyond the requirements of equal treatment.

Ironically, the most vigorous enforcement activities initiated by the Commission were directed to the elimination of the symbols of discrimination. Application forms were systematically screened and purged of all reference to race and color. Businessmen came to believe that any sort of racial record keeping was illegal and immoral. Many businessmen accepted "color blindness" as a moral obligation, but color blindness can also be used as a defense against those who wish to look beneath the surface to the underlying structure of the allocation process. Elimination of the outward signs of color consciousness can prevent effective control of a conscious program of equalization.

The possibility of mediating racial conflict through the institutionalization of common values is still in doubt. Value consensus is not enough; an emergent consensus at the normative level is necessary. The Negro will demand a normative interpretation that will permit change in the established structure of opportunity, but the most dynamic interpretations may be difficult to reconcile with other elements of the value tradition.

The threatened impasse suggests a point of far-reaching theoretical importance. The institutionalization of one social value cannot proceed without reference to other values in the system because sets of values are organized into

264

systems. Normative interpretations must not only meet the exigencies of enforceability and the need to mediate conflicting demands and interests, they must also be legitimate in terms of the other values in the system. Legitimacy implies not only compatibility with the content of other values, but also the absence of serious threats to the institutional structures that embody other values. In the case of equal opportunity, implementation faces an important hurdle in the form of the imposing edifice of economic organization that has been founded on the concept of economic rationality in the market place.

Ideology. Conceptions of the social world support particular interpretations of values, and, in turn, social norms influence perceptions of social reality. Although the author's empirical investigations did not focus on this "ideological" dimension of the problem, a few brief observations are appropriate.

The "fair-share" approach, with its demand for affirmative action, sometimes reflects a sophisticated understanding of the structure of the allocative process. In fact, one of the strengths of the demand for affirmative action is that it can be grounded in sound conceptions of the nature of the social order. In contrast, the "racial-qualifications" and "equal-treatment" conceptions are often associated with selective and distorted conceptions of the world.

The racial-qualifications approach is often supported by over-generalized beliefs about the detrimental consequences of the acceptance of Negroes. The advocates of the racial-qualifications standard tend to believe that property values invariably decline when Negroes move into an area, that vacancy rates increase when Negroes move into an apartment house, and that Negroes will prove unacceptable to fellow workers, customer, or clients. They are likely to accept the assumption that prejudice will always be expressed in behavior. Conversely, they are unlikely to recognize the power of structured situations to inhibit the expression of prejudiced attitudes. In the jargon of social science, believers in racial qualifications are prone to the fallacy of "psychologism."

Another type of individualistic fallacy is associated with the equal-treatment concept. Faith in the efficacy of equal treatment is often supported by the "atomistic" fallacy. Society is conceived as a set of isolated individuals, each competing according to standards of excellence. Each is rewarded according to his own efforts and achievements and the advantages and barriers that facilitate or impede success are either minimized or entirely neglected.

In some instances the demand for a fair share is also grounded on an individualist conception of the world. Some demand a fair share or other affirmative action not because they recognize the structural sources of unequal participation, but because they overestimate the degree of intentional discrimination by individuals. It is naïvely assumed that if the equal-treatment standard were really in force, Negroes would be receiving a fair share. The fact that Negroes are not receiving an equal share is taken as proof that there are individuals of ill will in high places who exclude Negroes out of sheer prejudice.

According to this view, the advocates of a fair share must demand quotas or similar arrangements because that is the only method by which discriminators can be prevented from hiding behind outward protestations of innocence. The demand for a fair share is justified as a demand for a tangible measure. There may be an element of truth in this view. It is difficult to institutionalize values if it is not possible to tell whether or not a person is complying, and for this reason, there may be a drift toward interpretations that permit a ready standard for the measurement of compliance.

On the other hand, there are means of measuring compliance under an equal-treatment standard. In many types of situations the testing method described in Chapter 7 provides a measure of compliance. Testing permits controlled comparison of the treatment of whites and similar Negroes by a method comparable to experimental design in science. In other situations analysis of the comparative qualifications and treatment of whites and Negroes in natural situations permits measurement of compliance by a technique comparable to the comparative method used in social and natural history.

In sum, the demand for a fair share may be supported by ideological exaggeration of the intentional element in discrimination and ideological magnification of the difficulty of proving discrimination under the equal-treatment standard.

Ideology is not the only base for the fair-share concept. The demand for affirmative action may also be grounded on recognition of the structural sources of unequal opportunity. The support of realistic conceptions of social reality is an important component of successful institutionalization. Ultimate values cannot be demonstrated by the methods of science, but the conditions of implementation can be studied objectively. Thus, the normative implications of values are subject to rational criticism in terms of their practicability. Just as the proponents of civil rights measures justify their cause by documenting the relative deprivation of the Negro group, so they can support their normative demands by documenting the necessity of particular types of remedial action.

A person who is committed to American values is committed to both equal opportunity and a rational, realistic approach to the world. If such a person can be shown that his normative interpretations are founded on unrealistic, disprovable conceptions of reality, he faces a dilemma. He is put on the defensive just as one who would deviate from the concept of equality is placed upon the defensive. Thus, conceptions of reality can come to have the same dynamic force as value conceptions. Once allegiance to a set of values and norms has been established, the generation of facts becomes an important element in the process of influence.

We observed this dynamic process in operation in the relations between the MCAD and the civil rights groups in the Boston area. The Commission, in order to avoid supporting second-rate complainants, and in order to build and maintain the good will of businessmen, slipped on occasion into the weak, "reasonable-treatment" interpretation of equal opportunity. The reasonable-treatment standard seemed appropriate to commissioners who believed in the basic good will of respondents. One who assumes that official organizational blue prints correspond to day-to-day practice is likely to accept the application of purely theoretical standards of Negro candidates. Civil rights organizations, by using testing procedures, produced facts which compelled the Commission to apply the stronger standard of strict equal treatment. Tests can show that the rules and standards which a respondent claims to be using, reasonable as they might sound, do not correspond to the less rigorous criteria that are usually applied in the press of day-to-day business.

Through a similar dynamic process the advocates of equality for Negroes, by calling attention to the deeply rooted structural obstacles to equal opportunity, can lend factual support to the demand for affirmative action. Indeed, from the perspective of the theory of institutionalization, the growth of recognition of structural obstacles to equal participation is a condition of successful institutionalization.

Power and legitimacy. One of the conditions of institutionalization is that the members of the community come to have an interest in compliance. The passage of a law purports to support institutionalization by giving potential deviants an interest in avoiding legal penalties. The legislature granted the MCAD the power to secure fines and prison sentences for willful and persistent discriminators. In theory, it should no longer be in the interests of businessmen to discriminate for, whatever the costs of nondiscrimination, they are probably not equal to the possible costs of being caught and punished. However, businessmen may assume that they will not necessarily be caught, and that if they are caught, they will not necessarily be punished. Thus, the extent to which passage of the law actually restructures the patterns of interests in the community depends in part on the vigor and comprehensiveness of enforcement programs.

We cannot assume that an agency will invoke all of its legally defined powers in its enforcement programs. Social analysts have called attention to the fact that theoretical legal power may not coincide with actual social power. The forces of opposition do not simply wilt when they fail to block passage of legislation. Since the same legislature that unwillingly passed the statute must also provide funds to support the agency, and since statutes may even be repealed, a new agency must come to terms with the forces that opposed its creation.

The leadership of the MCAD was very successful in engineering its permanent acceptability. Its strategy was to pursue a policy of moderation, conciliation, and persuasion. A reasonable attitude, a meticulous concern for fairness, and an almost diffident willingness to forego interference with the normal course of business procedure contributed to the development of a large store of good will within the business community.

In several respects the moderate policies of the Commission involved abstention from the use of several potential legal powers. For example, the Commission was unwilling to undertake a program of Commission-initiated complaints, to go beyond the confines of the individual complaint, to apply the standard of strict equal treatment, to test with white "ringers," to use the power of publicity, or to demand various types of affirmative action.

The Commission utilized the device of cooptation. Representatives of regulatees were given a semiofficial status on community councils that were created to symbolize business acceptance of the law, to translate the Commission to the business community, and to sponsor research and educational projects.

Reliance on the cooperation and good will of regulatees may involve costs since the agency is forced to avoid actions and policies that threaten continued cooperation. For this reason some commentators have assumed that cooptation is a "zero-sum" process; what the enforcement agency gains in stability and protection it must give up in effective social power.

To accept the zero-sum assumption is to deny the social power of *legitimacy*. If the zero-sum assumption is literally true, then the moral leverage exerted by the backers of the law during the campaign for passage was for naught. Did the power of the opposition, temporarily muzzled by a campaign of moral suasion, re-emerge to foil enforcement? The implication of the zero-sum theory is that the balance of social power cannot be permanently altered by moral pressures.

It is clear that the MCAD assumed a compromise stance. In coming to terms with the effective social power of the interests they sought to regulate, they did not exploit their potential legal resources to the full. However, before assuming that this demonstrates the futility of law in the face of established interests, we must remember that the Commission's policies earned for it the respect of the business community. By avoiding threats to business values they secured and maintained a legitimate status. They were not viewed in the community as dangerous and impractical radicals who would over-ride all other considerations to provide special help and protection for a minority of the citizenry. Thus, when the Commission made impeccably legitimate demands, respondents were unable to counter-attack by alleging the illegitimacy of the enforcement agency. In consequence the Commission was able to retain the moral offensive and to exert telling moral pressure on respondents who, in the absence of the law, would have continued to pursue flagrantly discriminatory policies. This study has set forth ample evidence that most cases brought to the Commission did not produce substantial and long-run changes. Nevertheless, there were *no* examples of cases in which the power of a respondent prevented the Commission from correcting flagrant discrimination. On many occasions the Commission failed to effect a remedy in the face of one or another realistic obstacle, such as loss of interest on the part of the complainant; but the Commission was rarely, if ever, defeated by the sheer obstinacy of a powerful opponent.

The protection of stability and legitimacy through compromise is an inescapable condition of successful enforcement. One may still ask whether an enforcement agency has been more moderate than the balance of power requires. All of the commissions established in the late forties and early fifties pursued moderate policies in their early years, but, in recent years, some state commissions have been able to take advantage of their more secure status to respond to the new demands of a larger, more vocal, and better organized Negro community. As the civil rights movement has gained more moral momentum, civil rights agencies have been able to muster countervailing power in the community in support of more militant programs of enforcement. In

271

Massachusetts, the original leadership maintained for a long time the moderate policies that were established in an era when civil rights agencies had a less secure position.

Some observers have noted the tendency of official civil rights agencies to compromise and the power of representatives of the status quo to block behind the scenes what they avoid resisting openly and have concluded that the creation of a civil rights agency is a fraud. Such agencies merely assuage the community's guilt, and by creating the appearance of a solution, prevent constructive action and real social change.[2] This view may apply to some cases of social conflict; everyone is aware that committees are sometimes created for less than sincere purposes. However, as applied to Northern civil rights agencies endowed with legal powers, this view does not accurately represent either the history of the passage of the statutes or the potential power of an agency, once firmly and legitimately established, to take increasingly militant action. The creators of *ersatz* committees sometimes receive more than they bargain for.

Jurisdiction: antidiscrimination law as private law. The confrontation of those who do not wish to comply with new standards is an important element in institutionalization. When established patterns of activity and interests run counter to emerging norms, it is necessary to actively confront strategic violators, if only for exemplary purposes. Only in this way can the enforcement process effectively transform the structure of interests.

The mere power to sanction violators is not sufficient; if violators believe that the enforcement agency holds the ultimate power should a showdown ever occur, but that a confrontation is unlikely, they are unlikely to change, especially if they perceive the risks and the costs of change to be high.

In employment, the complaints brought to the Commission failed to give the Commission jurisdiction over the

272

most discriminatory firms, the occupations closed to Negroes, or the various structural conditions that tend to lead to the exclusion of Negroes.

The Commission emphasized justice for the individual complainant, but the complaints of individuals reflect the established patterns of everyday life. Individuals bring complaints against the very firms that offer the most opportunity to members of their ethnic group and they complain about the types of jobs in which they have already been employed.

The Commission was hesitant to extend its critical eye beyond the purview of the issues in the individual case. They wished to know if the complainant was justly treated; but the inequalities that are built into the structure of organizations and of the larger community escaped the jurisdiction of the Commission.

In a word, *the Commission treated antidiscrimination law as a system of private law, designed to adjust disagreements that arise within an established social order.* The vast majority of disputes that arise within a system of private law do not challenge the social order. Litigants seek redress for grievances that arise through misunderstandings, divergent interpretations of situations and other points of friction. The importance of legal machinery in equilibrating social maladjustments should not be deprecated. The provision of a meaningful avenue for the redress of the personal difficulties of a group that is subject to numerous frustrations and to perplexing, threatening experiences contributes to social stability. At the same time we should not expect the typical disputes of private law to provide leverage for change. If law is to be a significant instrument of social change, it must come to have jurisdiction over significant, strategic targets in the social structure.

Some firms are more strategic targets for legal action: firms whose policies are visible and influential in a par-

273

ticular industry, firms offering employment that is highly visible to the public, firms offering types of employment into which Negroes could easily move, and firms whose policies are historically exclusive are strategic targets of legal action. But comprehensive jurisdiction over such targets implies a purposive, directed, and systematic enforcement program. It implies the conscious utilization of law as an instrument for the implementation of collective policies.

In sociological terms, the use of a private-law approach implies a relatively *undifferentiated* state of legal development. In relying on complaints brought by the Negro community, the MCAD tied the structure of enforcement to the structure of the Negro community and its established patterns of participation in the economy. When a commission initiates enforcement activities that purposively reflect the actual patterns of discrimination in the community, it breaks the bonds that tie its activities to external and irrelevant processes.

The MCAD also viewed the housing statutes as creating a system of private rights. However, in the housing sphere an organized body of civil rights advocates did regard the law as an instrument for the implementation of collective values. Organized groups, in bringing significant complaints, gave the Commission jurisdiction over strategic targets, thus compensating for the static elements in the Commission's private-law approach. Groups can, in effect, transform a private-law system into a public-law system and assist in the differentiation of the legal process.

The role of groups. Groups not only provided the Commission with access to significant targets, they played an important role in building cases against respondents. The MCAD, sensitive to its dual role as both prosecutor and judge, avoided some of the more aggressive investigative techniques. Civil rights groups did not operate under similar constraints. They were willing to trick respondents into

274

differential treatment, thus providing the evidence required for application of the rigorous equal-treatment standard.

Group organization created the moral atmosphere that facilitated passage of the civil rights statutes. The advocates of passage did not merely point to a value tradition, they created the organizational symbols of community support for the value tradition, and they organized the symbols of the commitment of the community to its implementation.

The law, once passed, reinforced the community atmosphere that had facilitated passage and groups began to take advantage of the solid power of legal legitimacy. Law enforcement was not limited to the official activities of the MCAD. Negro and civil rights agencies continued to exert direct pressure on behalf of their goals, and their direct activities were greatly facilitated by the power and legitimacy provided by the law.

Pressure groups need not make direct reference to the law to utilize its leverage. The author asked a representative of a pressure group whether he threatened employers with legal sanctions:

We like to use reason, not force. It isn't right to talk reason out of one side of your mouth and the law out of the other, but before the law was passed they weren't as willing to listen to reason.

Other civil rights workers were unanimous in their agreement with this conception of the role of law in their activities. Few made direct reference to the law or direct threats of legal action, but all report that their work has been facilitated by the law. Groups have been very successful in this work. In many areas they have opened more opportunities than the Negro community can utilize in its present state of education and training.

The importance of group support was evident from our analysis of the legal process. But the direct contribution of groups to the official enforcement process is only a part of their total impact and, by the same token, because of the

275

enforcement activities of groups, the official activities of the Commission created only a part of the impact of the law.

Education and enforcement. The Commission insisted that its own implementive activities were not limited to the formal processing of investigations and complaints. They rightly called attention to their extensive educational activities.

The institutionalization of a value or norm requires a restructuring of interests through the imposition of sanctions. Restructuring can take two forms: Either acting units are taught to pursue new goals, or goals are left constant and the *situation* is changed so that goals must be pursued in a certain manner. The former process, which may be termed *socialization,* operates by teaching units to sanction themselves. The latter process is termed regulation and operates by arranging sanctions so that the actor must follow a given course of action in order to achieve his ends and avoid costs.

The distinction between socialization and regulation corresponds to the distinction between education and enforcement. The educational policy of the Commission contemplates the socialization of the business community. They wish to encourage business to accept nondiscrimination as a goal. The MCAD's emphasis on the educational goal is not to be dismissed as mere compromise of the enforcement powers of the Commission. Socialization, because it bypasses the problem of access, has a special advantage as a restructuring technique. It is not dependent on constant oversight by a relatively small staff of state officials who lack close touch with daily decisions in the economic arena. There was sense in the Commission's decision not to rely entirely on penalties in a vast effort to make the costs of discrimination outweigh whatever benefits might be involved.

Criticism of the Commission for relying on education *rather* than enforcement is misplaced. Clearly, the Commission did not rely on either one alone. The limitations of the Commission's policies are more clearly seen if we view the consequences of cooptation on *both education and enforcement.* Insofar as cooptation and compromise forced the Commission to tie the enforcement process to the complaint process, enforcement was distorted. As we have already noted, the Commission was prevented from applying sanctions to significant targets.

The cooptation of the educational program involved more subtle but no less significant compromises. Socialization is control that operates through changing actors' goals, but there is no evidence that the Commission was able to, or has even sought to change business goals. The profit motive was accepted by the Commission as the entirely legitimate goal of business. The core of the educational message was not "social responsibility," it was that self interest is not served by discrimination. Nondiscrimination was said to reflect the ultimate exigencies of efficient use of manpower and the possible ill effects of integration were minimized. The educational program of the Commission sought to combat the racial ideologies that distorted perceptions of interests. It is not that the value theme was neglected, or even underplayed, it is just that the convergence of values and economic rationality was made the central message.

As a propagandistic technique the reliance on established business goals seems appropriate. Certainly it gave the argument resonance in the business community and helped to legitimize the Commission's position. On the other hand, the argument may reinforce the "racial-qualifications" definition of discrimination.

Education designed to show that nondiscrimination is not good business can be very important, especially where racial ideology is rife in the community, but it has limitations. When the apparent risks of integration are high, such arguments are unlikely to produce change.

277

The importance of education is clear. However, the assimilation of an educational program to the perspectives of business may be ineffective. If education is limited to attempts to elucidate the underlying structure of costs, it may be only partially successful for in some cases the market does not effectively sanction discrimination with economic costs, and persuasion is unlikely to produce convictions to the contrary. In those cases either complete education, (in the sense of a transformation of goals), or strict enforcement is necessary.

Housing and employment. It is somewhat surprising to note that the enforcement activities of the MCAD were more vigorous and successful in housing than in employment. The MCAD by no means eliminated discrimination in housing but it was able to place Negroes in previously all-white buildings and neighborhoods, and to convince the owners and allocators of housing that significant dents could be made in established patterns of segregation. In employment on the other hand, there were few cases of strategic breakthroughs and employers did not view the law or the Commission as compelling them to do anything beyond what they already did.

It seems paradoxical that the Commission was able to accomplish a difficult task with more success than an apparently easier task. Discrimination in employment, though it was substantial in some spheres, was not as prevalent, direct, flagrant, and intentional as housing discrimination. Opposition to the law was more determined and more aggressive among realtors and property owners than among employers. Housing allocators had more public sympathy and support for their discriminatory practices than employers. The relative success of the legal process in the housing field flies in the face of a popular, commonsense view of law. At first glance it would seem to be much more difficult to regulate activity in spheres where deviance is

278

more common and opposition more intense. In one sense it was easier for the Commission to deal with employment discrimination; it was more comfortable. However, this study has shown that "difficulty" has several dimensions. The popular view is incomplete. Let us contrast housing and employment as social institutions in an attempt to isolate the factors that support and the factors that upset the predictions of popular theory.

The differences between employment and housing do *not* appear to be due to the fact that the housing law was new and the employment law was old. One might suppose that regulation under the employment law was more aggressive, effective, and produced more friction in earlier days and that passage of the housing law forced the Commission to divert resources and attention from the employment law. To examine these possibilities the author inquired about the Commission's experiences in the early years. According to officials who had been with the agency since its inception, "employment was never like housing." Also, all of the employment cases for the year before passage of the housing law (1958) were examined. These cases were very much like the cases in 1959 and 1960 and provide no evidence that the housing law diverted attention from discrimination in employment.

The differences must be attributed to differences in the social character of the two institutions. The fundamental difference between employment and housing lies in the citizen's views as to the nature of the social relations involved. In an industrial society employment is perceived to be an impersonal relationship. Work relations are not intimate, and the work force does not perceive itself to be a solidary group. In contrast, the neighborhood has a more communitarian quality. Even though neighbors might actually see each other less than co-workers, residence in a common location seems to imply more intimate contact,

279

more personal relations and less instrumental attitudes. Neighborhoods are perceived to have a communal character and to imply common membership in a solidary group.

Because of the more intimate character of association within a neighborhood, prejudice has a more profound impact on perceptions of market forces in housing.[3] In contexts where human relations are intimate and communal the acceptance of other races is more threatening. As race becomes more salient it comes to have more effect on perceptions of market forces.

Economic decision makers, insofar as they are rational, act so as to maximize their access to resources. They do not wish to cut themselves off from productive resources or from consumers. It is not rational, from an economic point of view, to refuse to use qualified Negroes, nor is it rational to refuse to sell to Negroes. On the other hand, if the decision maker believes that to use or to sell to Negroes results in cutting off supplies of white workers or customers, then he must weigh that loss against the losses that accrue from discrimination. The same considerations apply in employment and housing. Both employers and property holders are trying to maximize the stock of workers and customers. The difference between employment and housing lies in the perception of the tipping point. Employers believe that within an impersonal work setting, employees and customers will accept relatively large numbers of Negro workers. As many as 50 or 60 percent of the employees within a given department can be Negroes without substantially affecting the availability of white workers. However, according to employers, it is important not to go over the tipping point, thus cutting oneself off from the white labor market.

Housing allocators, on the other hand, are more likely to see the relatively intimate and communal character of the neighborhood, the housing development, or the apartment house as an absolute bar to Negro occupancy. The tipping point is perceived to be one family: if one Negro family is allowed to move in, the apartment or development will become unacceptable to such a large portion of the white market that it is not economic to accept customers from the Negro market. The exclusion of Negroes becomes the lesser of two costs, unless it is believed that the entire building or development can be easily converted to Negro occupancy. Such perceptions may be unfounded and biased by racial ideologies, but as perceptions they have a profound impact upon action.

Thus, resistance to integration is stronger among housing allocaters than among employers. If we were to base our conception of the law's capacity to produce change entirely upon the structure of economic interests, we would predict that law would have more capacity to affect employment discrimination. Such an inference is inadmissable because the character of relationships within the housing sphere has other consequences as well.

In the first place, since discrimination in the housing market is more flagrant and pervasive, it is easier to discover and prove. Further, the relatively communal character of the organization of housing makes discrimination easier to demonstrate. The basic qualification for living in a residential community is a willingness to accept the obligations of membership and to live by the standards and precepts of the group. Employment is likely to involve complex sets of technical qualifications and particular types of training. It is more difficult for a respondent in a housing case to escape into the complexities of comparative analysis of qualifications.

The communal character of housing has another important advantage. It is easier to invoke and to organize community responsibility for the implementation of collective values. The form of organization of the fair housing groups in the Boston area is of profound significance. The Greater Boston Fair Housing Association, which prepared many of the cases in the sample, was *a federation of local housing groups within neighborhoods and communities.* White leaders within communities came to feel a collective responsibility to make their communities mirror common values. We have seen that group organization to support the law is a crucial factor in producing the conditions of sucessful enforcement, that is, jurisdiction over significant cases, countervailing power, and rigorous interpretive standards. The success of group organization in the housing sphere reflected the mobilization of communal feeling. It was more difficult to evoke a feeling of community responsibility for the acts of impersonal business firms that were in the community but not of it.

It is sometimes alleged that law can be more successful in regulating activity within highly differentiated and impersonal institutional spheres. This view needs modification. When laws are intended to implement social values, they may have more leverage in more communal spheres. The personal intensity of opposition may be more than balanced by the relative ease with which the moral forces within the community can be mobilized. By the same token the relative lack of intense opposition within impersonal institutions may be balanced by the dominance of technical and instrumental attitudes toward these institutions.

On the other hand, technical, instrumental attitudes facilitate the breakdown of racial barriers even in the absence of law and moral constraint. Trained, competent Negroes have been able to take advantage of the forces of economic rationality and to attain middle-class occupational roles. The same market forces failed to make middle-class housing available to Negroes and middle-class Negroes turned to the law in their attempt to attain housing accommodations consistent with their economic status. The variable character of economic forces in the two institutional spheres produced status inconsistencies that, in turn, stimulated use of the community's legal facilities. In consequence, the housing law came to play a more focal role in mediating conflict within the community. The employment law, in contrast, was not applied to the most pressing Negro demands.

Conclusion: The question of how much discrimination can be eliminated through law remains unanswered, but the Boston experience demonstrates that the answer to that question is not "law can do nothing." The difficulties and barriers to the legal implementation of ideals are varied and complex. Without minimizing the realistic obstacles that tempered the success of the MCAD, we can say with assurance that when groups organize to create moral pressure, to transform moral pressure into binding legal demands, and to support and contribute to the enforcement process, the community can come to have moral and political leverage on established interests. The consequent change may not be sudden, dramatic, and complete, but it is none the less real.

On the other hand, the limitations of the legal approach and the deficiencies of the enforcement process have not been without consequence. Insofar as the Commission was unable to meet pressing demands, the law failed to contribute to social peace through institutionalization.

This study has suggested several conditions of successful enforcement: interpretive standards must be rigorous and must provide leverage on established interests; official ideologies must accept the existence of violations, provide a comprehensive understanding of the problems of implementation and give a realistic picture of the power of the agency; the agency must have the power to impose sanctions without threatening its own existence; the agency must obtain access to significant violations.

These conditions are linked in important ways. An agency

283

without effective social power is unlikely to be able to adopt vigorous and effective standards or to adopt policies insuring effective jurisdiction over strategic violations. An agency without access to violations is likely to fail to recognize the extent and structure of the problems that it attacks. In turn, an ideology that fails to elucidate the extent and sources of violation supports the continuation of weak policies. Thus, an initial inadequacy in the power position of an enforcement agency can be transformed into a vicious cycle of weakness. Initially precarious foundations lead to a set of compromise policies that permit an equilibrium to develop between the advocates and the enemies of institutionalization. But as the advocates of equal opportunity become increasingly aware of the static and ineffective character of the compromise, new tensions arise and more tenacious demands for change are heard.

In the case of the MCAD the initial equilibrium was long lived. For thirteen years the initial compromise was perpetuated by the cycle of weakness, but, with the passage of the housing law in 1959 the old balance was broken. The activities of civil rights groups thrust the Commission into active confrontation with more vigorous advocates and more determined opponents of equal opportunity. A few years later, with the quickening tempo of racial protest in the sixties, the Commission was forced to struggle with new and more difficult problems of social integration, problems that appeared to defy solution by the old interpretations and techniques.

284

CHAPTER X. EPILOGUE

The world was a different place before Birmingham. — [A spokeman for the Boston business community]

In recent years the established compromise has been severely strained. Since the retirement of Chairman Mahoney, the Massachusetts Commission Against Discrimination has struggled to face new political realities. It has not been an easy job, for to cope with these new realities is to successfully respond to new demands in the face of the difficult obstacles provided by the legacy of the past.

The Commission and other such agencies face a difficult dilemma. The failure of the equal-treatment concept severely challenges the ideological justification of the Commission, but at the same time its legal legitimacy and its established place in the community are firmly tied to equal treatment. Greater militancy is possible but greater militancy will not by itself solve the fundamental problem of unequal opportunity—its deep roots in the structure of the community.

Three trends have dominated the direction of the civil rights movement in recent years: Legal avenues of redress are being ignored, direct action has increased, and the demands of civil rights groups have moved toward the "fair-share" conception of equality. These trends were already apparent by the summer of 1963 when in some Northern communities demonstrations in support of racial quotas reached near riot proportions.

The course of events in Boston clearly reflects national trends. In fact, the trends were already apparent in Boston by 1962. A full year before the Birmingham demonstrations quickened the national pace of civil rights activities, the Massachusetts Committee for Jobs Unlimited, a direct action group, had begun a campaign to secure route sales positions for Negroes with bakery and liquor companies. The Massachusetts Committee had only limited success and passed from the scene rather quickly—without actually effecting a threatened boycott. In the spring of 1963 a new organization, the Boston Action Group (BAG), took up where the Massachusetts Committee had left off and organized a boycott of a bread manufacturer pending the hiring of at least twelve Negroes. The action was successful.[1]

In late June, STOP, an organization claiming to be a "people's movement," entered the scene with an attack on the construction industry and made plans to picket the construction of the Prudential Center. Meetings with the Associated General Contractors and the bricklayers' and carpenters' unions led to several agreements calling for affirmative action to increase Negro participation in the building trades. Six construction unions agreed to *search out* and hire carpenter and bricklayer apprentices.

In a manifesto published in a Negro newspaper, STOP informed the Negro community that since the "power structure of the white community" had not listened to the "voices of moderation," it was time for the Boston Negro to "stop in his tracks." They promised to use methods of "disruption and inconvenience" to assure that Negroes would come to visible positions of responsibility.

STOP called for a mass demonstrative strike to coincide with the June 26 memorial demonstration in honor of Medger Evers, slain Mississippi civil rights leader. Negroes were supposed neither to go to work nor to patronize places of business on that day in protest against economic and social injustice in the treatment of the Negro. However, the movement did not get the support of a large proportion of the Negro leadership. The NAACP, for example, supported the Evers memorial but not the STOP proposal for a one-day boycott. Although relatively few Negroes cooperated, the STOP leadership maintained that the protest was a success because industry responded positively with new offers to open positions to Negroes.

These events only illustrate the beginning of new forms of protest and new demands for affirmative action. Similar protests developed over housing and education and have continued to occur in more and more impressive dimensions.

Is the law obsolete? Will more vocal and insistent demands for substantive equality and structural change leave the law behind and throw the conflict into the streets? The considerations outlined in this study suggest that increasing reliance on mass protest is inevitable. When there is an enforcement agency with de facto deficiencies in political power and correspondingly weak policies, when unequal participation in the institutions of the community is deeply rooted, and when the legal concepts of "color-blind intent" have limited leverage, it is not surprising that an increasingly angry and aware Negro community becomes impatient with the law.

It is tempting to conclude that the emergence of impatience with the law and other symptoms of arousal in the Negro community are sure signs of the obsolescence of official civil rights agencies. However, such a conclusion is premature, since the same arousal that is sometimes expressed by sidestepping legal approaches is also sometimes expressed in insistent demands for more militant enforcement and for legal change. The new wave of civil rights activity has been both a direct and indirect challenge to the Commission. The Commission was directly and severely attacked by the leaders of the new direct action approach and the use of direct action was itself a challenge to the Commission's claims to success in its mission.

Civil rights leaders have never been completely satisfied with the MCAD, but in the early days critics went to great pains to conceal their dissatisfaction from the general public. The critics were aware that the Commission was struggling with the problems of establishment. They recognized that the presentation of a public image of successful conciliation was an important part of the process of establishing the legitimacy of the Commission and its place in the community. For example, the critical report of the blue ribbon committee of the American Jewish Congress was delivered privately to the Commission in 1953 but was never released to the public.

One of the signs of the increasing vigor of the civil rights forces has been the increasingly public character of the attack upon the Commission. It came to be felt that the Commission *was* fully established and must either take advantage of its hard-won position or answer to its critics for its failures.

The momentum of the critical movement began to accelerate in 1959 with the passage of the housing law. As we have seen, the housing law brought the Commission into regular, almost daily, confrontation with the civil rights groups because of the activity of these groups in prosecuting cases. Daily disagreements and frustrations became general feelings of dissatisfaction and came to be articulated in a body of well-defined criticisms of the Commission, its practices, its policies, and its leadership. This movement culminated in a rather quiet attempt to block the reappointment of Chairman Mahoney in the Governor's Council in 1961. The attempt was unsuccessful but Mrs. Mahoney's critics were convinced that she should not be reappointed again in 1964 and undertook a successful campaign to prevent her succession to a seventh term on the Commission.

On December 7, 1964, Mrs. Mahoney resigned. Her resignation followed a sequence of studies, reports, recommendations, charges and counter charges, thus bringing under public discussion opposing philosophies of civil rights law enforcement for the first time. The battle was clearly defined by the participants and by the newspapers as a contest between "persuasive" and "activist" approaches. Thus, Mrs. Mahoney's final resignation was a public victory for the civil rights groups and for the philosophy of "activism," a message that her successor could hardly ignore.

Malcolm Webber, Mrs. Mahoney's successor, came to the Commission in a new political climate. He has tried in several ways to adjust the policies of the Commission to the new realities of political life. A complete inventory of the policies of the new Commission and the successes and failures of these policies would require another study as long as the present one. A few significant instances of increased vigor will suffice to indicate some responsiveness of the Commission to the new demands that have been placed upon it.

1) In June of 1965 the Commission achieved legislative acceptance of a bill authorizing the Commission to award up to $1,000 damages to successful complainants.[2]

2) Shortly after taking office, Chairman Webber announced in a radio broadcast that the Commission would not hesitate to use white agents to test for discrimination in order to collect evidence in ongoing cases or to test the compliance of respondents in closed cases. In view of the uproar that has been caused in some states over the mere suspicion that a civil rights agency might be engaging in testing, this must be considered a militant step.[3]

3) On two occasions in 1965 the Commission broke its historic silence on de facto school segregation. In 1965 the NAACP had instituted a suit against the Springfield School Committee alleging that de facto segregation in Springfield was unconstitutional.[4] On April 16, 1965, the Commission filed an *amicus curiae* brief supporting the action and urging the elimination of de facto school segregation.

Later, when the opponents of de facto school segregation were involved in their successful fight for passage of a racial imbalance law designed to move students to reduce de facto segregation, the Commission unanimously endorsed passage of the law, stating that the legislation would "provide the best possible education for all children within the Commonwealth without regard to race, creed, color or national origin."[5]

4) In 1965 the Commission broke with previous policy when Commissioner John Albano released information concerning a conciliated complaint, thus responding to the urgings of the critics of the Commission that it make more effective use of publicity.[6]

5) The Commission has also sought to streamline the complaint process and to seek more effective terms of conciliation. Their success in this regard is shown by the results of the housing cases brought during 1964 when 56 percent of the complainants were offered or received housing.[7] Further, during the first quarter of 1965 the Commission's case load increased by 125 percent over the same period for the previous year.[8]

These and other changes exemplify the Commission's attempts to improve the complaint process, to recognize the weaknesses of tying enforcement to private complaints, and to recognize the significance of structural sources of the exclusion of Negroes.

The response in the community. The continuing relevance of legal avenues depends not only on strengthening the Commission Against Discrimination but also on greater recognition within the community of the structural sources of Negro exclusion and greater appreciation of the inadequacy of the concept of "color-blindness." Since the roots of the quasi-racial and color-blind approaches are very firm, it might be very difficult for the Commission to respond to and implement pressing demands for affirmative action, but, if it cannot, the law will become obsolete.

There have been some signs of changing conceptions of

290

the nature of discrimination and equal opportunity. In the first place there is growing *official* recognition of the structural dimensions of the problem. It is becoming apparent to whites and Negroes alike that the moral problem extends beyond the flagrant illegality of intentional and systematic exclusion of Negroes.

In 1963, Mayor John Collins, in a televised broadcast on the problems facing Negroes, told the community:

Some of this discrimination is active and some is passive. Some is intentional and some is doubtless circumstantial, but none is acceptable.[9]

An informed governmental attitude received institutional expression when the chairman of the Governor's Advisory Committee on Civil Rights, Malcolm Peabody, Jr., informed the business community in August 1963:

There is clear recognition that discrimination has been practiced for so long and so pervasively that a mere removal of the remaining barriers to equal opportunity would not greatly alleviate the plight in which the American Negro now finds himself . . .

Make no mistake, the law has been effective . . . The efforts of these commissions, in start were directed toward lowering racial barriers and persuading the community at large to change from a hostile to a neutral position toward employing non-whites.

However, the experiences of the past fifteen years and the current racial turmoil today show clearly that neutrality is not enough. Now we must do more. The law, though an essential first step can only prevent an employer from practicing discrimination. It cannot require him to develop a positive program to include Negroes at every level where possible, particularly when no complaint has been filed against him.[10]

In some segments of the business world the plea for affirmative action has met with a favorable response. Many businessmen seem disinclined to fight to the bitter end for the right to practice nondiscrimination passively. Recognizing the reality of structural discrimination, they are willing to take active steps to revamp the employment process itself to insure greater economic participation among nonwhites.

Many firms have responded to the urgings of the federal government and civil rights groups with realistic efforts to broaden their sources of recruitment and to tighten the control of the personnel process within the firm.

In view of the acceptance of the principle of unintentional or passive discrimination, it seems reasonable to suppose that the MCAD could retain a meaningful role in the sphere of employment discrimination by broadening its conceptions of appropriate terms of conciliation to include demands for substantive rearrangements of the personnel process. This would be especially effective if it were combined with Commission-initiated programs of enforcement within industries and occupations that have not yet experienced Negro participation. The Commission's educational function could be expanded to include the concept of "passive discrimination" and to eradicate the "suitability" definition of discrimination.

Still, businessmen are predictably reluctant to go out of their way to accept basic changes in procedures. Further, there is a general tendency to resent any outside interference with business practice, especially interference from government agencies.

Business resistance is undoubtedly strengthened to severe proportions when demands for affirmative action go beyond the capacity of the Negro community to supply qualified personnel. Such demands are inevitable when the demand for substantive equality is strong and Negro training lags behind. Further, the resistance of workers is strong when the demand for equality seems to imply replacing white workers with Negroes. Accordingly, some acrimonious collective bargaining seems unavoidable.

On the other hand, the desire to avoid such painful experiences seems capable of liberalizing the interpretation of the equal-opportunity standard. The present author and other students of discrimination have pressed for official recognition of the problems of passive discrimination for some time, but the effective catalyst that suddenly produced not only recognition but dramatic official action was the nationwide tension of the spring and summer of 1963.

In the words of an official of the Associated Industries of Massachusetts:

The world was a different place before Birmingham . . . The problem facing our society is whether we can provide upward channels or whether we are going to lose the whole thing. That is the lesson of history.

Still, the idea of color blindness dies a slow death and seems to be subject to periodic resurrection. The Commission is caught between the firm legal institutionalization of the equal-treatment standard and the equally insistent expression of demands for affirmative action. Chairman Webber has developed a phrase to reconcile the new demands placed upon the Commission with the limitations placed upon the Commission by the law. That phrase is "beyond law enforcement." As used by Commissioner Webber the phrase connotes recognition of the legal limitations placed on the Commission by its statutory authority and at the same time recognizes the need for the Commission to go beyond the law by lending moral and organizational support to projects designed to attack structural discrimination.

What can be expected of the law? Clearly the Massachusetts Commission Against Discrimination has taken steps to increase its relevance to the emerging shape of race relations. By working for more rigorous law enforcement and by going beyond law enforcement in creative ways, the Commission can continue to contribute to the integration of the community through the implementation of the ideal of equal opportunity. Yet, in a very fundamental sense, the Commission is tied to the interpretations of equal opportunity that took shape during the origins of the FEPC movement. Even if the recognition of de facto problems of segregation and discrimination grows, the older civil rights agencies may continue to operate primarily at the level of intentional discrimination. New agencies and new institutions may come to embody and implement the new interpretations and compromises that will mediate race relations in the future.

This does not mean that law will play no role; it means that the role of law will change. In the past legal attempts to alleviate racial tension have been founded on the faith that racial conflict can be mediated by the implementation of American values. It was hoped that the norm of equal treatment could solve the problem. That hope has been dealt a severe blow for substantive equality has not followed quickly from formal equality. In consequence race relations law is being transformed into a law of collective bargaining. It may be that the most pioneering change will come as the two polarized groups bargain for their share of the national wealth. In some contexts law will merely enforce the compromise. At the same time, traditional legal agencies will continue to contribute to social integration by establishing a minimum standard of equal treatment and by continuing to support organized attempts to make equal opportunity a reality.

294

NOTES   INDEX

NOTES

CHAPTER 1. INTRODUCTION: A CASE STUDY IN INSTITUTIONAL-
IZATION

[1] Peter Berger, *Invitation to Sociology* (Garden City, N.Y., 1963), ch. ii.

[2] Isidor Chein, "Notes on a Framework for the Measurement of Discrimination and Prejudice" in Marie Jahoda et al., *Research Methods in Social Relations* (New York, 1951), pp. 381-390.

[3] The factors involved in the problem are so numerous that it seems likely that there are not enough communities to provide a sample large enough to allow for all the necessary controls. The solution might lie in the direction of cross-community studies of particular types of housing so that some of the relevant factors are not allowed to vary.

[4] Between September 1961, and September 1962, and in August 1963, 105 persons were interviewed. Interviewees were not chosen on a random basis; the author sought articulate persons who had had experience in dealing with the law and people who had helped to secure or oppose passage of the law. There are several broad categories of interviewees: civil rights leaders and Negro leaders, 17; business leaders, 9; civil rights agency officials, 12; former complainants in MCAD cases, 20; former respondents in MCAD employment cases, 27; former respondents in MCAD housing cases, 20.

The sample of former respondents in Commission cases consists of representatives of all the firms who were respondents in the cases analyzed in the text who could be located and were willing to be interviewed. Twenty-seven former respondents refused to be interviewed and nineteen could not be located.

Among employers the personnel officer was interviewed in sixteen firms. If there was no full-time personnel officer, the official responsible for the personnel function was interviewed. For the housing cases sixteen informants were principal owners of the property subject to complaint. The remaining four were managing agents.

[5] For a bibliography, see Jack Greenberg, *Race Relations and American Law* (New York, 1959), pp. 421-437; and Vern Countryman, *Discrimination and the Law* (Chicago, 1965), pp. 145-152.

⁶ The recognized classic is Morroe Berger's *Equality by Statute* (New York, 1952). Berger showed that the New York State Commission Against Discrimination had established conservative and conciliatory policies but insisted that despite these policies the law was successful in buttressing the moral order and protecting minority group members. At one point (p. 168) he raises the possibility that law could be *more* effective in producing changes if its administration were directed not to settling individual cases but to systematic discovery and elimination of *patterns* of discrimination. Much of the present work is devoted to the exploration and documentation of this insight. The New York Commission has been restudied in Jay Anders Higbee, *Development and Administration of the New York State Law Against Discrimination* (Montgomery, Ala., 1967).

Other important prior studies include: Aaron Antonovsky and Lewis L. Lorwin, eds., *Discrimination and Low Incomes* (New York, 1959); Michael Bamberger and Nathan Lewin, "The Right to Equal Treatment: Administrative Enforcement of Anti-Discrimination Legislation," *Harvard Law Review* 74 (1961), 526-589; Vern Countryman, *Discrimination and the Law* (Chicago, 1965); Arthur M. Ross and Herbert Hill, *Employment Poverty, and Race* (New York, 1967); and Louis Ruchames, *Race, Jobs and Politics: The Story of FEPC* (New York, 1953). In addition to these titles the interested reader may wish to consult the many reports of the various municipal, state, and national civil rights agencies and the publications of the National Association of Intergroup Relations Officials (NAIRO), particularly their quarterly *Journal of Intergroup Relations.*

⁷ For a bibliography of the literature on this idea, see Milton M. Gordon, "Recent Trends in the Study of Minority and Race Relations," *The Annals of the American Academy of Political and Social Science* 350 (November 1963), 154-155.

⁸ There are a few sociologically sophisticated studies of certain aspects of the over-all success of antidiscrimination agencies. See especially the work of Morroe Berger (which is informative despite the lack of cooperation from the agency he studied most intensively) and the work of Harold Goldblatt and Florence Cromien, "The Effective Social Reach of the Fair Housing Practices Law of the City of New York," *Social Problems* 9 (Spring 1962), 365-370.

⁹ William G. Sumner, *Folkways* (New York, 1906).

¹⁰ *Shorter Oxford English Dictionary* (Oxford, 1933).

298

[11] Talcott Parsons and Edward A. Shils, *Towards a General Theory of Action* (Cambridge, Mass., 1951), pp. 20, 191, 194, 203.

[12] *Ibid.,* pp. 150, 174, 203.

[13] Talcott Parsons, "Problems of International Community," in James Rosenau, ed., *International Politics and Foreign Policy* (New York, 1961), pp. 120-129.

[14] *Ibid.,* p. 121. See also Talcott Parsons, "An Approach to the Sociology of Knowledge," in International Sociological Association *Transactions of the Fourth World Congress of Sociology* (1959), pp. 25-49.

[15] Parsons, "Problems of International Community," pp. 120-129.

[16] Parsons and Shils, *Towards a General Theory of Action,* pp. 20, 174-175, 191; and Parsons, "Problems of International Community," p. 122.

[17] Parsons, "An Approach to the Sociology of Knowledge."

[18] The process of socialization can be seen as one solution for the jurisdiction problem. The actor is taught to punish himself for deviance.

[19] Max Weber, *The Theory of Social and Economic Organization,* A. M. Henderson and Talcott Parsons, trans. (Glencoe, Ill., 1947), pp. 363-373.

[20] Roberto Michels, *Political Parties,* Eden and Cedar Paul, trans. (Glencoe, Ill., 1949).

[21] Philip Selznick, *TVA and the Grass Roots* (Berkeley, 1953).

[22] Seymour Lipset, *Agrarian Socialism* (Berkeley, 1950), pp. 255-275.

[23] Thomas F. Pettigrew and Ernest Q. Campbell, *Christians in Racial Crisis* (Washington, D.C., 1959).

[24] Burton Clark, "Organizational Adaptation and Precarious Values: A Case Study," *American Sociological Review* 21 (1956), 327-336.

[25] Marver Bernstein, *Regulating Business by Independent Commission* (Princeton, 1955); U. S. Senate Judiciary Committee, 2nd session, 86th Congress, *Report on the Federal Regulatory Agencies,* prepared by James Landis (Washington, D.C., 1960); Bernard Schwartz, *The Professor and the Commissions* (New York, 1959). See also Carl Auerbach et al., *The Legal Process* (San Francisco, 1961), ch. xv.

[26] Avery Leiserson, *Administrative Regulation* (Chicago, 1942).

[27] *Ibid.,* p. 268.

[28] *Ibid.,* p. 269.

[29] Alvin W. Gouldner, "Metaphysical Pathos and the Theory of Bureaucracy," *American Political Science Review* 49 (1955), 496-507.

[30] Peter Blau, *Dynamics of Bureaucracy* (Chicago, 1955), p. 184.

[31] *Ibid.,* pp. 193-290. For another study of a succession of goals, see David Sills, *The Volunteers* (Glencoe, Ill., 1957).

[32] Luigi Laurenti, *Property Values and Race* (Berkeley, 1960).

[33] Gerhard Saenger and Emily Gilbert, "Customer Reaction to the Integration of Negro Sales Personnel," *International Journal of Opinion and Attitude Research* 4 (1960), 57-76.

CHAPTER II. DISCRIMINATION AND THE NEGRO COMMUNITY

[1] Chicago did not become 10 percent Negro until the end of World War II. See St. Clair Drake and Horace Cayton, *Black Metropolis* (New York, 1945).

[2] John Daniels, *In Freedom's Birthplace* (Boston, 1914), pp. 1, 7.

[3] Commonwealth v. Aves, 18 Pickering 209.

[4] Daniels, *In Freedom's Birthplace,* p. 57. For a general discussion of Garrison and the abolition movement in Massachusetts, see Dwight Dumond, *Anti-Slavery* (Ann Arbor, 1961), pp. 114-115, 166-174.

[5] Malcolm Ross, *All Manner of Men* (New York, 1948), p. 186.

[6] Daniels, *In Freedom's Birthplace,* p. 84.

[7] See Roberts v. Boston, 5 Cushing 198, and Plessy v. Ferguson, 163 U. S. 537.

[8] See Daniels, *In Freedom's Birthplace,* pp. 25-27, and Ross, *All Manner of Men,* p. 185.

[9] See Commonwealth v. Sylvester, 13 Allen 247. The act was amended in 1884, 1885, and 1887. See Daniels, *In Freedom's Birthplace,* pp. 94-95.

[10] *Ibid.,* p. 321.

[11] These figures and all other figures in this section are taken from the U. S. Census of Population for 1940, 1950, and 1960 unless otherwise noted.

[12] This statement does not refer to the electrical equipment industry.

[13] See, for example, the "Report on the Governors' Conference on Civil Rights" in the Massachusetts Commission Against Discrimination, *Annual Report* (Boston, 1958), p. 29. At least three officials have used this phrase in conversation with the author.

[14] Comparisons between the nonwhite population and the total

population are roughly comparable to comparisons between Negroes and whites because most of the total population is white and most of the nonwhite population is Negro. It should also be pointed out that 1960 census runs behind the trend on the number of school years completed. The data reported is for the population twenty-five years old and over. Hence current rates of high school completion are not reflected in the data.

[15] National Urban League, *Proceedings, Eighth Urban Renewal Institute,* Boston, Massachusetts, April 25-26, 1962, p. 5.

[16] U. S. Department of Commerce, *Census of Housing,* 1960, vol., I part 4.

[17] J. Westbrook McPherson, *The Situation of Non-White Families in Boston's Urban Renewal Program* (Urban League of Greater Boston, 1962), p. 3.

[18] Commonwealth of Massachusetts, Brief for Petitioner, Commission Against Discrimination v. A.J. Colangelo et al., Supreme Judicial Court for the Commonwealth, January sitting, 1962, Appendix B (prepared by Helen Kistin).

[19] *Ibid.,* table 7.

[20] *Ibid.,* table 8.

[21] *Ibid.,* computed from table 7.

[22] *Ibid.*

[23] Karl E. Taeuber and Alma F. Taeuber, *Negroes in Cities,* (Chicago, 1965), p. 39.

CHAPTER III: DISCRIMINATION: VALUES, NORMS, AND SOCIAL STRUCTURE

[1] Bernard Rosenberg and Penney Chapin, "Management and Minority Groups," in Aaron Antonovsky and Lewis L. Lorwin, eds., *Discrimination and Low Incomes* (New York, 1959).

[2] Gunnar Myrdal, *An American Dilemma* (New York, 1944).

[3] For some examples and summaries of this approach, see Herbert Blumer, "Recent Research on Racial Relations, United States of America," *UNESCO International Social Science Bulletin* 10 (1959), 403-447; Warren Breed, "Group Structure and Resistance to Discrimination in the Deep South," *Social Problems* 10 (1962), 84-94; J. D. Lohman and D. C. Reitzes, "Note on Race Relations in Mass Society," *American Journal of Sociology* 58 (1952), 241-246; D. C. Reitzes, "Institutional Structure and Race Relations," *Phylon* 20 (Spring 1959), 48-66; George Simpson and Milton Yinger, *Racial and Cultural Minorities* (New York, 1965), pp. 81-109; George

Simpson and Milton Yinger, "The Sociology of Race and Ethnic Relations," in Robert Merton et al., *Sociology Today* (New York, 1959).

[4] Lohman and Reitzes, "Note on Race Relations in Mass Society," p. 241.

[5] Carleton Putnam, *Race and Reason* (Washington, D.C., 1961).

[6] Massachusetts Commission Against Discrimination, *Annual Report* (Boston, 1958), pp. 12-13.

[7] Gladys Lang, "Discrimination in the Hiring Hall," in Antonovsky and Lorwin, eds., Discrimination and Low Incomes, pp. 195-248.

[8] Eight other businessmen were unable or unwilling to respond to the hypothetical nature of this question.

[9] Confidential interview with a MCAD commissioner.

[10] Charles Hurd, ed., *A Treasury of Great American Speeches* (New York, 1959).

[11] See Louis Lomax, *The Negro Revolt* (New York, 1962), especially ch. vii.

[12] See Theodore Malm, "Recruiting Patterns and the Functioning of Labor Markets," *Industrial and Labor Relations Review* 7 (1954), pp. 508-525.

[13] Orvis Collins, "Ethnic Behavior in Industry: Sponsorship and Rejection in a New England Factory," *American Journal of Sociology* 52 (1946), 293-298.

[14] Lang, "Discrimination in the Hiring Hall," See also Sally Becker and Harry Harris, "Progress Toward Integration: Four Case Studies," in Antonovsky and Lorwin, eds., *Discrimination and Low Incomes,* pp. 281-304.

[15] Allison Davis and John Dollard, *Children of Bondage* (Washington, D.C., 1940); Abram Kardiner and Lionel Ovesey, *The Mark of Oppression* (New York, 1951); Bernard C. Rosen, "Race, Ethnicity and Achievement," *American Sociological Review* 24 (1959), 47-60.

[16] Jack Greenberg, "An NAACP Lawyer Answers Some Question," *The New York Times Magazine,* August 18, 1963, p. 86.

CHAPTER IV. THE STATUTES

[1] Herbert Garfinkel, *When Negroes March* (Glencoe, Ill., 1959), p. 18.

[2] Louis Ruchames, *Race, Jobs and Politics: The Story of FEPC* (New York, 1953), pp. 13-16. See also the Garfinkel book for a full account of the March on Washington movement and Louis Kesselman, *The Social Politics of FEPC* (Chapel Hill, N.C., 1948), pp. 93-97.

3 Ruchames, *Race, Jobs and Politics*, p. 131.

4 John Duffy, *State Organization for Fair Employment Practices* (Berkeley, 1942), pp. 26-27.

5 Interview with Chairman Mahoney.

6 *Boston Globe,* February 6, 1946, p. 1.

7 *Boston Herald,* June 20, 1945, p. 1.

8 *Ibid.*

9 *Boston Herald,* June 21, 27, 28, 1945, p. 1.

10 Henry Silverman, "How We Won in Massachusetts," *New Republic,* July 8, 1946, pp. 10-11.

11 *Boston Herald,* February 7, 1946, p. 1

12 This is the Massachusetts counterpart of the National Association of Manufacturers.

13 The passage of the bill was throughly reported in the Boston daily papers in February, March, April, and May 1946.

14 *Boston Herald,* March 8, 1946, p. 22.

15 *Boston Herald,* May 7, 1946, p. 1.

16 *Boston Herald,* May 9, 1946, p. 1.

17 *Ibid.*

18 *Ibid.*

19 *Ibid.*

20 *Boston Herald,* May 15, 1946, p. 1.

21 *Boston Herald,* May 15, 1946, p. 1; June 21, 1945, p. 1.

22 For example: "Let these minority groups wait another hundred years."

23 *Boston Herald,* May 15, 1946, p. 1.

24 This witness would have liked to oppose.

25 This account is based on interviews with representatives of both the American Jewish Congress and the Massachusetts Home Rental Association.

26 Interview with an official of the Massachusetts Home Rental Association.

27 *Apartment Management* 26 (May 1960), 7-13.

28 *Christian Science Monitor,* January 20, 1959, p. 2; February 12, 1959, p. 1.

29 *Christian Science Monitor,* February 25, 1959, p. 2.

30 *Boston Globe,* February 6, 1946, p. 17.

31 *Boston Herald,* May 22, 1946, p. 7. A legislator is being quoted.

32 Commission Against Discrimination v. A. J. Colangelo, 6 *Race Relations Law Reporter,* 349.

33 Commonwealth of Massachusetts, Acts of 1920, chapter 376.

[34] There is perhaps a third type, exemplified by Alaska, Oregon, and Wisconsin where other government departments, for example, the Bureau of Labor, administers the civil rights law.

[35] Michael A. Bamberger and Nathan Lewin, "The Right to Equal Treatment: Administrative Enforcement of Anti-Discrimination Legislation," *Harvard Law Review* 74 (1961), 562.

[36] The difference between race and color is not clear. The commissioners do not know what difference there might be.

[37] Massachusetts Commission Against Discrimination, *Rulings Interpretive of the Fair Employment Practice Law* (Boston, 1961), p. 4.

[38] Bamberger and Lewin, "The Right to Equal Treatment," p. 560.

[39] Commonwealth of Massachusetts, General Laws, chapter 151 B, section 4.

[40] Massachusetts Commission Against Discrimination, *Rulings,* p. 2. Capitalization is original.

[41] Commonwealth of Massachusetts, General Laws, chapter 151 B, section 3, article 5.

[42] *Ibid.,* article 8.

[43] *Ibid.,* article 9.

[44] Bamberger and Lewin. "The Right to Equal Treatment," p. 535.

[45] The conciliative procedures called for by the various antidiscrimination statutes are modeled to some extent on the techniques of the National Labor Relations Board and reflect the success of the National Labor Relations Acts of 1935 in creating machinery for arbitrating social conflict in the context of administrative law. Bamberger and Levin, p. 527. See also R. A. Smith and Leroy Merrifield, *Case and Materials in Labor Relations Law* (Indianapolis, 1960), pp. 72-76; Jack Greenberg, *Race Relations and American Law* (New York, 1959), pp. 195, 197.

[46] Greenberg, *Race Relations and American Law,* p. 196.

[47] Bamberger and Lewin, "The Right to Equal Treatment," p. 535.

[48] Anti-Defamation League of B'nai B'rith, *Comparative Analysis of State Fair Employment Practices Law* (New York, 1959), p. 14.

[49] Commonwealth of Massachusetts, General Laws, chapter 151 B, sections 4 and 5.

[50] Commonwealth of Massachusetts, Acts and Resolves, 1948, chapter 51.

[51] *Ibid.,* 1950, sections 1 and 2.

[52] *Ibid.,* section 3.

[53] 5 *Race Relations Law Reporter,* 253. Chapter 181 of the legislature put teeth in this ruling by specifically providing for suspension

or revocation of the license of a real estate broker or salesman who fails to comply with an order of the MCAD.

⁵⁴ Commonwealth of Massachusetts, Acts and Resolves, 1956, chapter 334.

⁵⁵ *Ibid.,* 1949, chapter 726.

⁵⁶ *Ibid.,* section 2.

⁵⁷ *Ibid.,* 1957, chapter 426.

⁵⁸ *Ibid.,* 1959, chapter 239.

⁵⁹ *Ibid.,* section 1, article 12.

⁶⁰ *Ibid.,* 1963, chapter 197.

⁶¹ U.S. Housing and Home Finance Agency, *State Statutes and Local Ordinances and Resolutions Prohibiting Discrimination in Housing and Urban Renewal Operations* (Washington, D.C., 1961).

⁶² Commonwealth of Massachusetts, Acts and Resolves, 1961, chapter 128.

⁶³ *Ibid.,* 1960, chapter 163.

⁶⁴ *Ibid.,* 1961 chapter 570.

CHAPTER V. THE POLICIES AND PRACTICES OF THE COMMISSION

¹ Interview with Chairman Mahoney.

² Louis Ruchames, *Race, Job and Politics: The Story of FEPC* (New York, 1963); Malcolm Ross, *All Manner of Men* (New York, 1948). Also reports of U.S. Fair Employment Practices Committee.

³ Torstein Eckhoff, "Sociology of Law in Scandinavia," *Scandinavian Studies in Law* (1960), pp. 31-58.

⁴ Interview with Mr. Walter Nolan, executive secretary of the Commission.

⁵ Also president of the Retail Trade Board of Boston.

⁶ Massachusetts Commission Against Discrimination, *Annual Report* (Boston, 1952, 1953, 1954, 1956, 1958, 1959.

⁷ *Ibid.,* 1959, p. 17.

⁸ *Ibid.,* 1958, p. 15.

⁹ Philip Selznick, *TVA and the Grass Roots* (Berkeley, 1953), p. 13.

¹⁰ *Ibid,* p. 15.

¹¹ Massachusetts Commission Against Discrimination, *Annual Report* (Boston, 1952).

¹² See pp. 246-253.

¹³ Massachusetts Commission Against Discrimination, *Annual Report* (Boston, 1958), pp. 13-14; *Annual Report* (Boston, 1959), p. 11.

¹⁴ *Boston Herald,* December 8, 1960.

[15] Morroe Berger, *Equality by Statute* (New York, 1952), pp. 132-154.

[16] Blue Ribbon Report of the Jewish Community Council and the American Jewish Congress (Boston, September 1953), mimeographed.

[17] Massachusetts Commission Against Discrimination, *Annual Report* (Boston, 1960), pp. 17-18.

[18] Four such hearings were held within thirty months of the passage of the housing law. This is twice as many hearings as were held in employment cases in seventeen years.

[19] Massachusetts Commission Against Discrimination, *Annual Report* (Boston, 1962), pp. 35-36.

[20] Massachusetts Commission Against Discrimination, *Annual Report* (Boston, 1959), p. 3.

[21] Peter Blau, *Dynamics of Bureaucracy* (Chicago, 1955). The author once asked the Commission's statistician to estimate the number of employment cases brought by Negroes in a recent year. The estimate was three times larger than the correct figure.

[22] See, for example, the Chairman's speech to the Trinity College alumnae, reported in the *Boston Globe,* February 12, 1963.

[23] Massachusetts Commission Against Discrimination, *Annual Report* (Boston, 1951), p. 9.

CHAPTER VI. THE COMPLAINT PROCESS: I. SOURCES, TARGETS, AND TYPES OF COMPLAINTS

[1] Harold Goldblatt and Florence Cromien have shown that complaints brought under the New York fair housing ordinance are predominately middle class, "The Effective Social Reach of the Fair Housing Practices Law of the city of New York," *Social Problems* 9 (1962), 365-370.

[2] This figure is based on the 1960 U.S. Census and consists of the number of persons in professional, managerial, clerical, and sales occupations over the total number of persons for whom an occupation was reported.

[3] Data as to the quantity and type of Negro employment were available from the case records in most instances. The figures were supplemented and checked by personal interviews with respondents. In some cases the amount of Negro employment must be estimated. This is especially true in the case of large firms that do not keep racial records. Estimates were made by informants, not by the author. Estimates were verified by plant tours, visits to company cafeterias, and talks with Negro employees.

[4] For a similar finding in Connecticut, see the report by Henry

Stetler, Commission on Civil Rights, *Minority Group Integration by Labor and Management* (Hartford, 1953).

[5] Those communities are Boston, Cambridge, Somerville, Newton, Watertown, Belmont, Arlington, Medford, Malden, Everett, Chelsea, Revere, and Winthrop. Population figures are used rather than labor force figures because the labor force figures are not available for communities within the SMSA. The differences are not substantial. The use of labor force figures would probably not result in the reclassification of any cases.

[6] The use of this threefold standard classification seems more accurate in view of the ecology of job location. Use of a single standard of 3 percent does not materially strengthen or weaken the associations reported here.

CHAPTER VII. THE COMPLAINT PROCESS: II. INTERPRETING THE LAW

[1] Interview with a Commission member.

[2] New York Supreme Court, June 27, 1956, 1 *Race Relations Law Reporter,* 685.

[3] *Ibid.* Italics added.

[4] Thompson v. Erie Railroad, 2 *Race Relations Law Reporter,* 237.

[5] 2 *Race Relations Law Reporter,* 244.

[6] Arthur Goodheart, "Determining the Ratio Decidendi of a Case," *Yale Law Journal* 40 (1930), 161-183.

[7] This was the airline stewardess case.

CHAPTER VIII. THE COMPLAINT PROCESS: III. THE OUTCOMES OF COMPLAINTS

[1] This was one of the largest rental offices in Boston.

[2] The promise was purchased at the price of a counter-promise to close the case with a finding of no probable cause.

[3] In the few cases that reach a public hearing, the Commission treats respondents less delicately. Thus, in the Colangelo case, the respondent was ordered to include a notice of open occupancy in all advertising, to issue written instructions to all employees and agents, to inform the Commission of all openings, and to pay the respondent various types of compensatory damages. See Massachusetts Commission Against Discrimination, *Annual Report* (Boston, 1961), pp. 22-23.

[4] Massachusetts Commission Against Discrimination, *Annual Report* (Boston, 1952), pp. 9-10.

[5] It is interesting to note that the new purchaser of this building converted to Negro occupancy, raised rents, and made a large profit.

[6] There is evidence of a growing recognition of the inefficiency of the private law approach. See Jack Greenberg, *Race Relations and American Law* (New York, 1959), p. 196; John Hope II, "Equal Employment Opportunity: Changing Problems, Changing Techniques," *Journal of Intergroup Relations* 4 (1963), 29-36; William Becker, "After FEPC — What?" *Journal of Intergroup Relations* 3 (1962), 137-148.

CHAPTER IX. AN INTERPRETIVE OVERVIEW: 1946-1962

[1] For an analysis of the role of prejudice, see Gordon Allport, *The Nature of Prejudice* (Cambridge, Mass., 1954).

[2] See, for example, Lewis Killian and Charles Grigg, *Racial Crisis in America: Leadership in Conflict* (Englewood Cliffs, N.J., 1964).

[3] Emory Bogardus, *Immigration and Race Attitudes* (Boston, 1928).

CHAPTER X. EPILOGUE

[1] *Boston Sun,* April 17, 1963, p. 1.

[2] Commonwealth of Massachusetts, Acts of 1965, chapter 569.

[3] *Boston Globe,* January 20, 1965.

[4] School Committee of Springfield v. Abraham Barksdale, Jr., 348 F2d 281.

[5] Massachusetts Commission Against Discrimination, press release, June 16, 1965.

[6] Massachusetts Commission Against Discrimination, press release, undated [1965].

[7] Massachusetts Commission Against Discrimination, *Annual Report* (Boston, 1964), p. 24.

[8] Massachusetts Commission Against Discrimination, press release, April 19, 1965.

[9] *Boston Globe,* June 21, 1963, p. 7.

[10] Malcolm Peabody, Jr., "Government-Industry United for Civil Rights Program," *Industry,* August 1963, pp. 11-12.

INDEX

Albano, John, 290
Allport, Gordon, v, 308n
American Federation of Labor, 127
American Jewish Congress, Committee on Law and Social Action, 94; and employment law, 79, 81, 82; and housing law, 92, 93-94; representation on housing council, 136. *See also* Blue Ribbon Committee
American Legion, 82
Antidiscrimination law in Massachusetts: constitutionality of, 97-98; provisions of, 101-119, 289-290; rules of, 221-234
Antonovsky, Aaron, 298n, 301n, 302n
Application forms: policing of, 140-141, 143, 146, 264
Arnold, Thurman, 21
Associated Industries of Massachusetts, 83-85, 89, 124-125, 293
Auerbach, Carl, 299n

Bamberger, Michael, 298n, 304n
Becker, Sally, 302n
Becker, William, 308n
Berger, Morroe, 134, 298n, 305n
Berger, Peter, 297n
Bernstein, Marver, 21, 299n
Blau, Peter, 23-24, 300n
Blue Ribbon Committee of the Jewish Community Council and the American Jewish Congress, 134, 288
Blumer, Herbert, 301n
Bogardus, Emory, 308n
Boston Action Group (BAG), 286-287
Boston Chamber of Commerce, 84-85
Bradford, Robert F., 81
Breed, Warren, 301n
Brown, W.W., 35

Campbell, Ernest Q., 21, 299n
Case study: significance of, 3-6, 297n
Cayton, Horace, 32, 300n
Cella, Alexander J., 93
Channing, William Ellery, 35
Chapin, Penney, 56, 301n
Chein, Isidor, 297n
Civil rights groups: attacks on MCAD, 285-289; and complaints to MCAD, 152ff, 254-255; and passage of law, 93-94, 98-101; role of, 274-276, 282-283. *See also* under headings for specific groups
Clark, Burton, 21, 299n
Classic era of antidiscrimination law, v, 30-31, 137, 258-259
Colangelo, A.J., 98. *See also* Massachusetts v. Colangelo
Color blindness, 31, 66-67, 74, 264, 287, 290-294
"Color tax," 52-53, 55
Collins, John, 291
Collins, Orvis, 302n
Commission Against Discrimination v. A.J. Colangelo et al., 301n, 302n. *See also* Massachusetts v. Colangelo
Commonwealth v. Aves, 300n
Commonwealth v. Sylvester, 300n
Committee for a Massachusetts FEPC, 81, 84-89, 92
Complaints, initiation by MCAD: failure to, 126, 134; legal power, 108, 111, 118; statistics on, 142-143; consequences of MCAD reluctance, 178, 198, 274
Complaints to MCAD: bases for, 178-197; conciliation of, 235-295; consequences of, 245-253, 290; comparison of housing and employment, 159, 206, 221, 244; credibility of, 186-197; incidence vs. rates, 157-159; individual vs. group,

Sumner, Charles, 35
Sumner, William Graham, 8-9, 298n

Taeuber, Alma F., 301n
Taeuber, Karl E., 301n
Taylor, Charles H., 85
Testing in civil rights cases: change in policy, 289; and credibility of complaints, 179-180, 185, 189, 229-231; and equal-treatment standard, 212-220, 274-275; of promises, 240-241
Thompson v. Erie Railroad, 200-202, 307n
Tobin, Maurice J., 81
Turner, Henry, 83
Truman, Harry S, 77

Urban League: and affirmative action, 60, 73; and community councils, 136; and complaints to MCAD, 152;

and Massachusetts law, 82; national level, 76

Values: achievement of ideal goals, 24; and discrimination in Boston, 55, 56, 58, 259-261; institutionalization of, 9-10, 98-101; and legislative campaigns, 80-81

Washington, Booker T., 65
Webber, Malcolm, 289, 293
Weber, Max, 19-20, 299n
Whittier, John Greenleaf, 35
Willis, Frederick B., 86

Yinger, Milton, 301n, 302n
Young, Whitney, 73
Young Women's Christian Association, 82

PUBLICATIONS OF THE
JOINT CENTER FOR URBAN STUDIES

The Joint Center for Urban Studies, a cooperative venture of the Massachusetts Institute of Technology and Harvard University, was founded in 1959 to organize and encourage research on urban and regional problems. Participants have included scholars from the fields of anthropology, architecture, business, city planning, economics, education, engineering, history, law, philosophy, political science, and sociology.

The findings and conclusions of this book are, as with all Joint Center publications, solely the responsibility of the author.

PUBLISHED BY HARVARD UNIVERSITY PRESS

The Intellectual versus the City: From Thomas Jefferson to Frank Lloyd Wright, by Morton and Lucia White, 1962

Streetcar Suburbs: The Process of Growth in Boston, 1870-1900, by Sam B. Warner, Jr., 1962

City Politics, by Edward C. Banfield and James Q. Wilson, 1963

Law and Land: Anglo-American Planning Practice, edited by Charles M. Haar, 1964

Location and Land Use: Toward a General Theory of Land Rent, by William Alonso, 1964

Poverty and Progress: Social Mobility in a Nineteenth Century City, by Stephan Thernstrom, 1964

Boston: The Job Ahead, by Martin Meyerson and Edward C. Banfield, 1966

The Myth and Reality of Our Urban Problems, by Raymond Vernon, 1966

Muslim Cities in the Later Middle Ages, by Ira Marvin Lapidus, 1967

The Fragmented Metropolis: Los Angeles, 1850-1930, by Robert M. Fogelson, 1967

Law and Equal Opportunity: A Study of the Massachusetts Commission Against Discrimination, by Leon H. Mayhew, 1968

PUBLISHED BY THE M.I.T. PRESS

The Image of the City, by Kevin Lynch, 1960

Housing and Economic Progress: A Study of the Housing Experiences of Boston's Middle-Income Families, by Lloyd Rodwin, 1961

Beyond the Melting Pot: The Negroes, Puerto Ricans, Jews, Italians, and Irish of New York City, by Nathan Glazer and Daniel Patrick Moynihan, 1963

The Historian and the City, edited by Oscar Handlin and John Burchard, 1963

The Federal Bulldozer: A Critical Analysis of Urban Renewal, 1949-1962, by Martin Anderson, 1964

The Future of Old Neighborhoods: Rebuilding for a Changing Population, by Bernard J. Frieden, 1964

Man's Struggle for Shelter in an Urbanizing World, by Charles Abrams, 1964

The View from the Road, by Donald Appleyard, Kevin Lynch, and John R. Myer, 1964

The Public Library and the City, edited by Ralph W. Conant, 1965

Regional Development Policy: A Case Study of Venezuela, by John Friedmann, 1966

Urban Renewal: The Record and the Controversy, edited by James Q. Wilson, 1966

Transport Technology for Developing Regions, by Richard M. Soberman, 1966

The Joint Center also publishes monographs and reports.